SEVEN SEAS ENTERTAINMENT PRESENTS

DUNGEON BUILDER:
THE DEMON KING'S LABYRINTH IS A MODERN CITY!

story by RUI TSUKIYO   art by HIDEAKI YOSHIKAWA   VOLUME 1

TRANSLATION
Elina Ishikawa-Curran

ADAPTATION
Julia Kinsman

LETTERING AND RETOUCH
Roland Amago & Bambi Eloriaga-Amago

COVER DESIGN
KC Fabellon

PROOFREADING
Marykate Jasper
Tom Speelman

EDITOR
Shanti Whitesides

PREPRESS TECHNICIAN
Rhiannon Rasmussen-Silverstein

PRODUCTION MANAGER
Lissa Pattillo

MANAGING EDITOR
Julie Davis

ASSOCIATE PUBLISHER
Adam Arnold

PUBLISHER
Jason DeAngelis

MAOU-SAMA NO MACHIZUKURI! SAIKYOU NO DUNGEON WA KINDAI TOSHI VOL. 1
© 2018 Hideaki Yoshikawa
© Rui Tsukiyo/SB Creative Corp.
First published in Japan in 2018 by OVERLAP Inc., Ltd., Tokyo.
English translation rights arranged with OVERLAP Inc., Ltd., Tokyo.

Seven Seas press and purchase enquiries can be sent to Marketing Manager Lianne Sentar at press@gomanga.com. Information regarding the distribution and purchase of digital editions is available from Digital Manager CK Russell at digital@gomanga.com.

Seven Seas and the Seven Seas logo are trademarks of Seven Seas Entertainm

ISBN: 978-1-64505-12

Printed in Canada

First Printing: January

10 9 8 7 6 5 4 3

FOLLOW US ONLINE: www.sevenseasentertainment.com

READING DIRECTIONS

This book reads from *right to left*, Japanese style. If this is your first time reading manga, you start reading from the top right panel on each page and take it from there. If you get lost, just follow the numbered diagram here. It may seem backwards at first, but you'll get the hang of it! Have fun!!

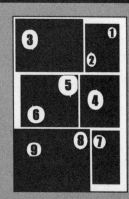

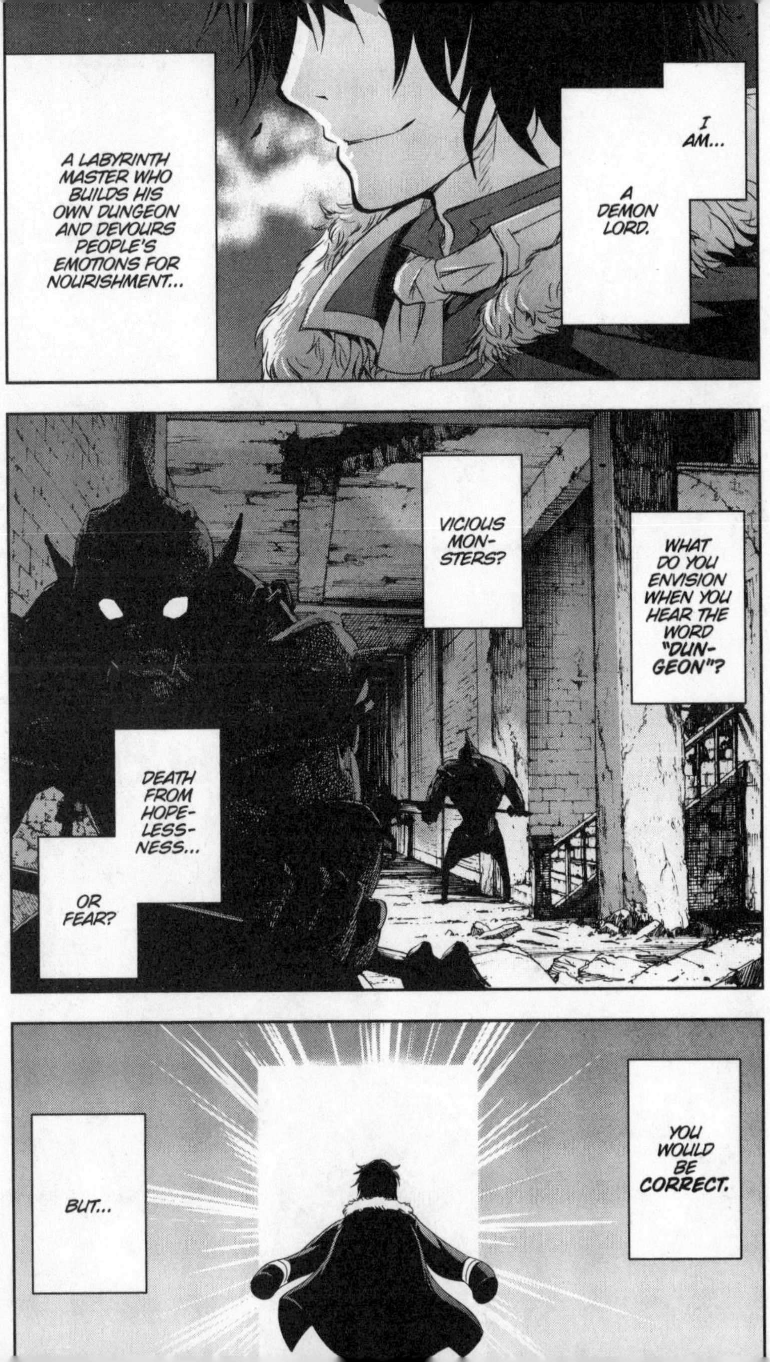
I AM...
A DEMON LORD.
A LABYRINTH MASTER WHO BUILDS HIS OWN DUNGEON AND DEVOURS PEOPLE'S EMOTIONS FOR NOURISHMENT...
WHAT DO YOU ENVISION WHEN YOU HEAR THE WORD "DUNGEON"?
VICIOUS MONSTERS?
DEATH FROM HOPELESSNESS...
OR FEAR?
YOU WOULD BE CORRECT.
BUT...

BEAM

THE DUNGEON I HAVE CONSTRUCTED...

IS A CITY.

Chapter 1:
The Power of Creation

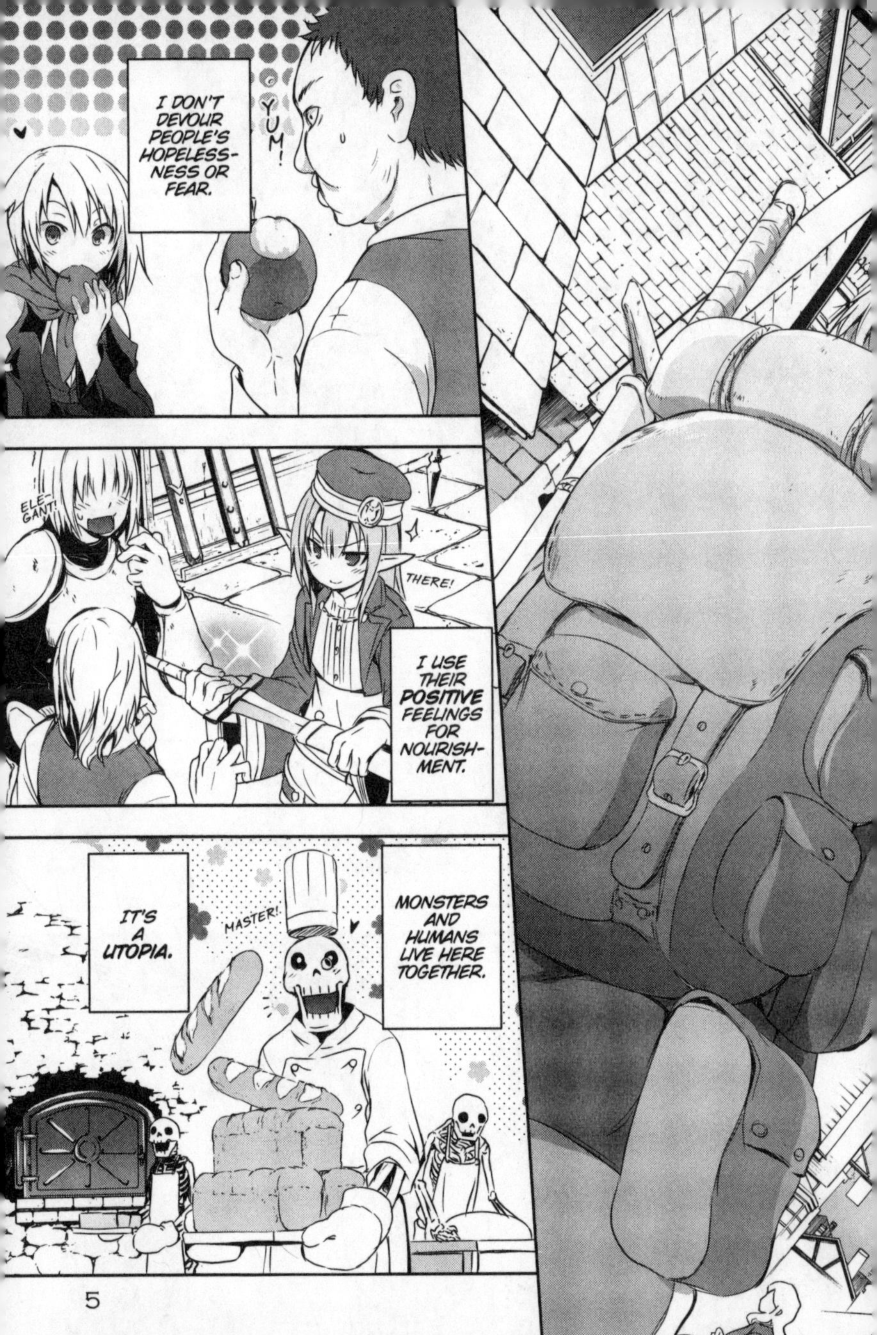

I DON'T DEVOUR PEOPLE'S HOPELESSNESS OR FEAR.
YUM!
I USE THEIR POSITIVE FEELINGS FOR NOURISHMENT.
THERE!
ELEGANT!
MONSTERS AND HUMANS LIVE HERE TOGETHER.
MASTER!
IT'S A UTOPIA.

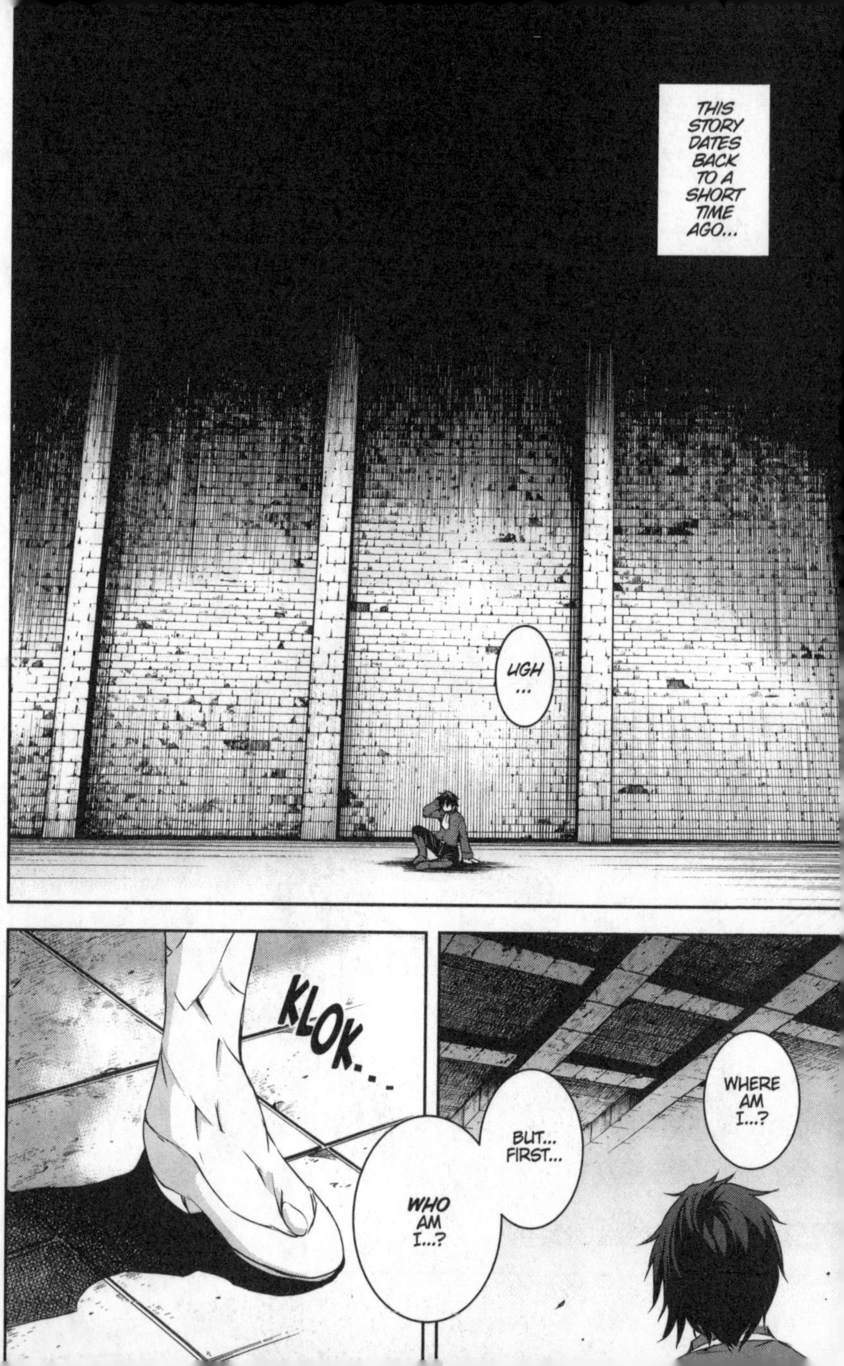
THIS STORY DATES BACK TO A SHORT TIME AGO...
UGH...
WHERE AM I...?
BUT... FIRST...
WHO AM I...?
KLOK...

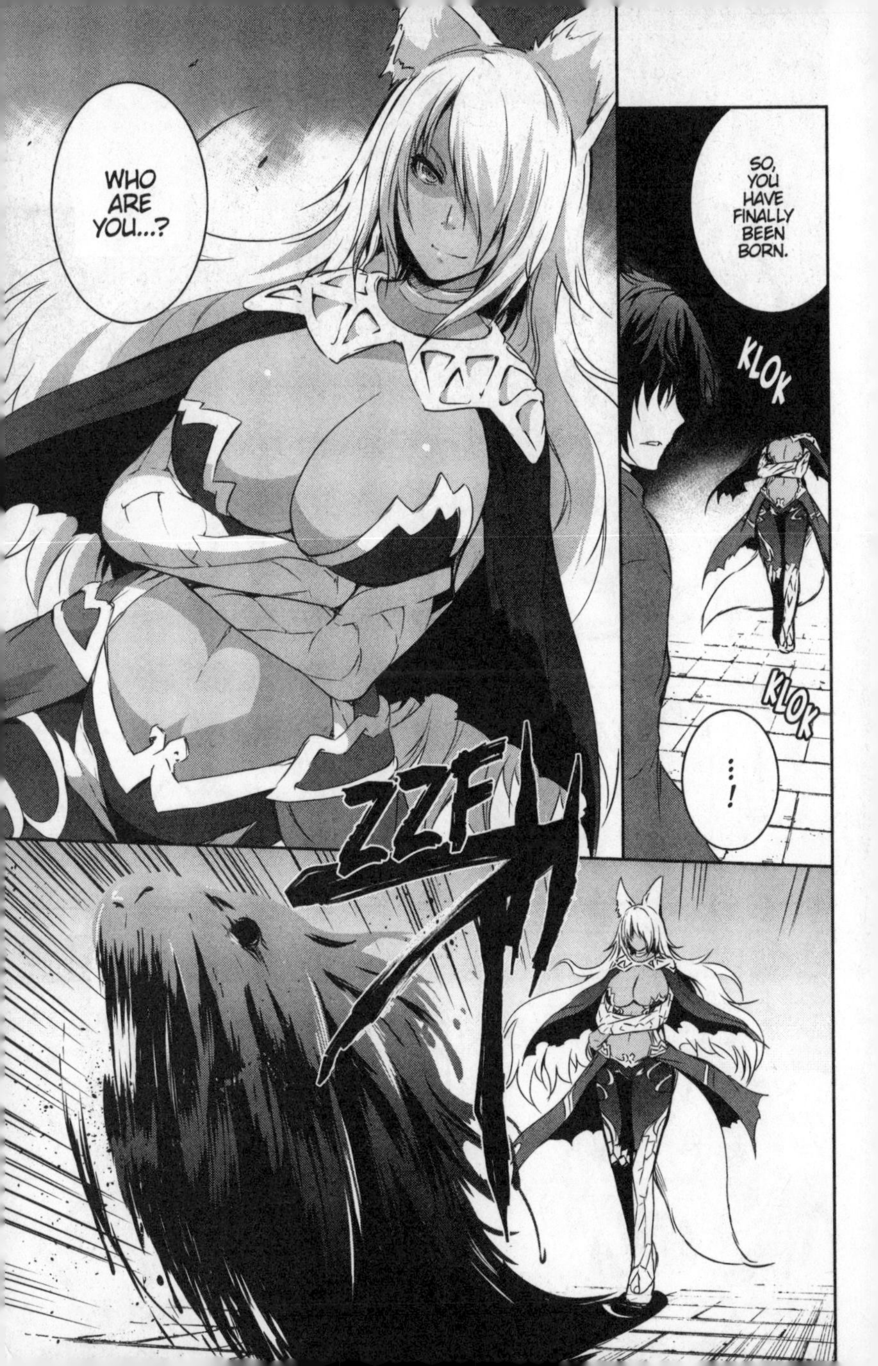
SO, YOU HAVE FINALLY BEEN BORN.
KLOK
KLOK
...!
WHO ARE YOU...?
ZZF

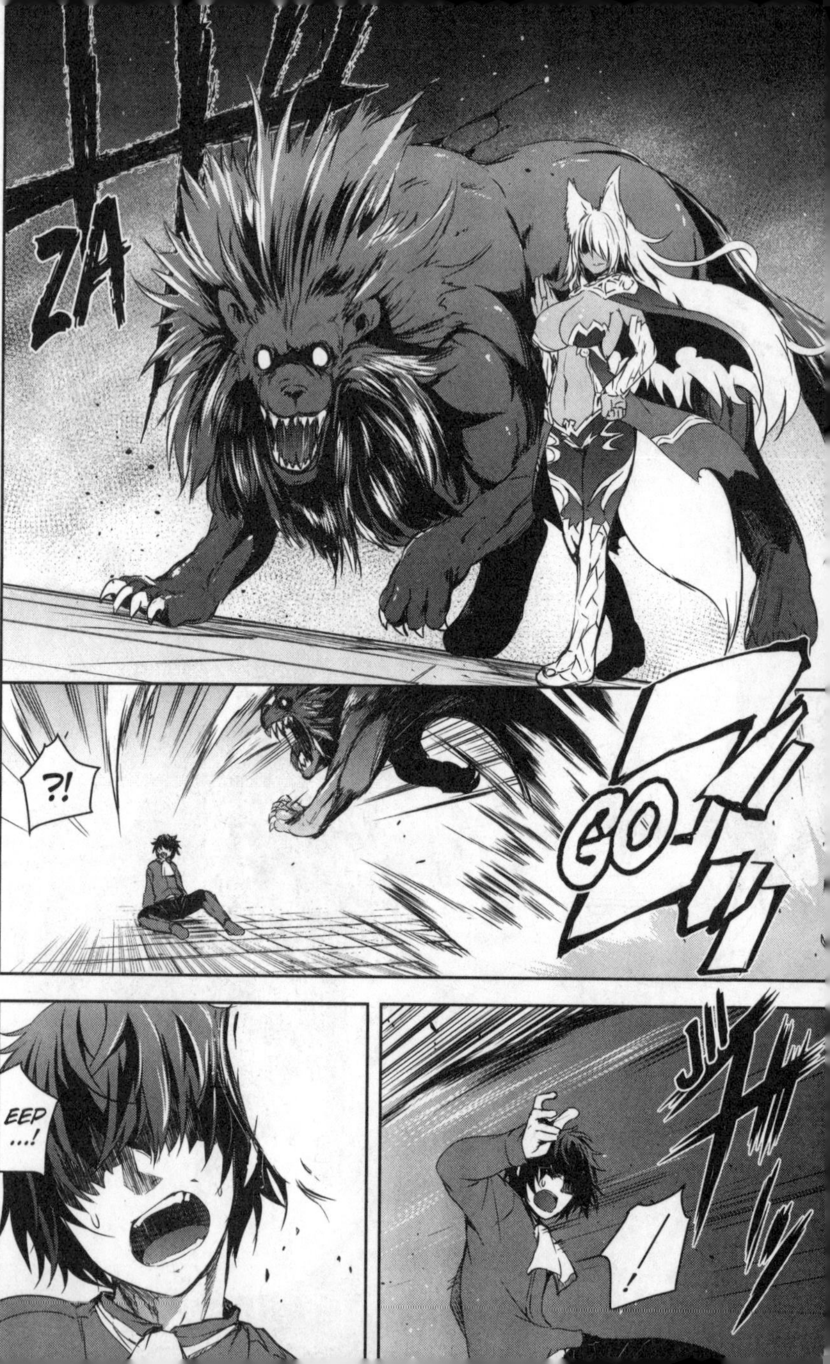
ZA
GO-
?!
JI
!
EEP ...!

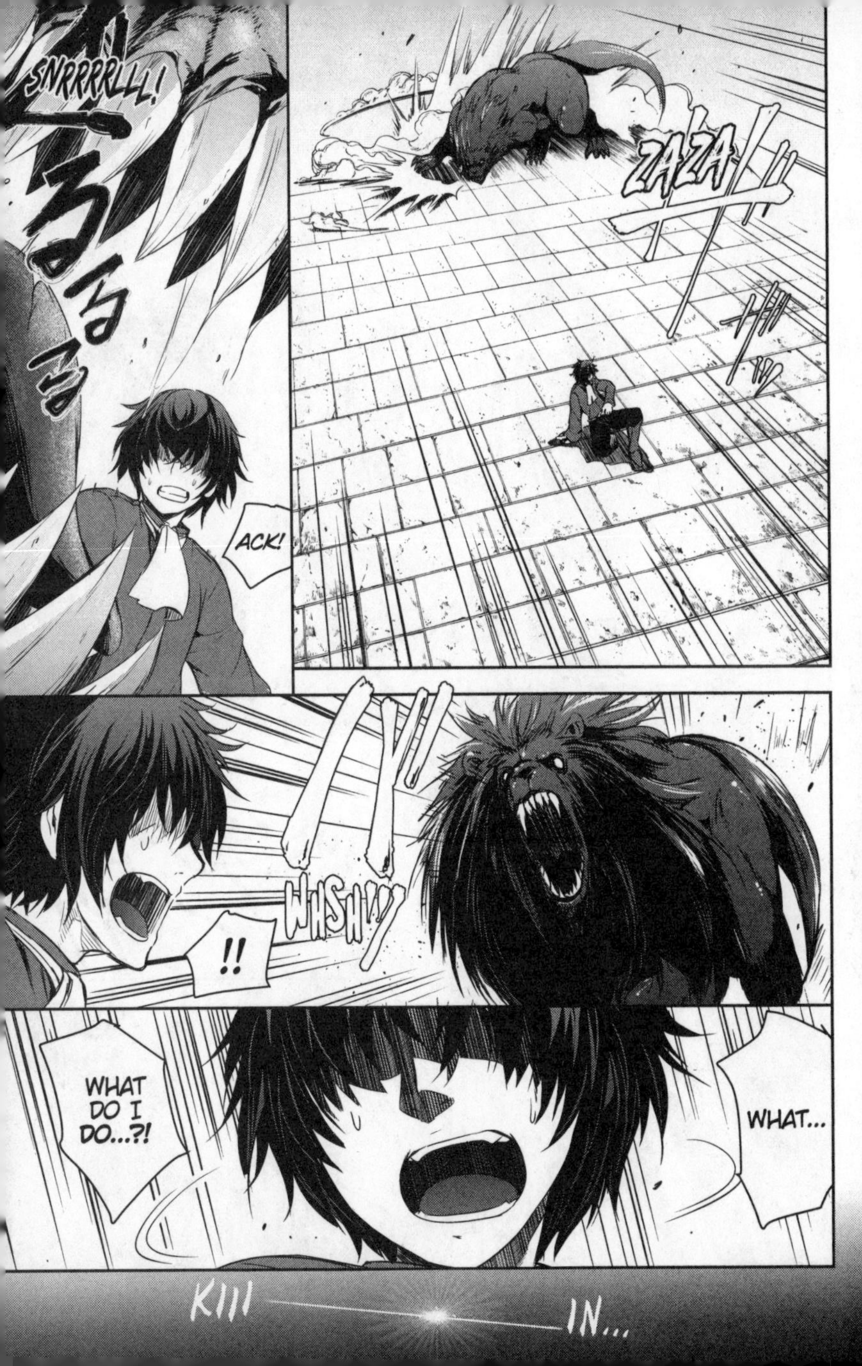
ZAZA!!
SNRRRRLLL!
ACK!
WHSH!!
!!
WHAT...
WHAT DO I DO...?!
KIII
IN...

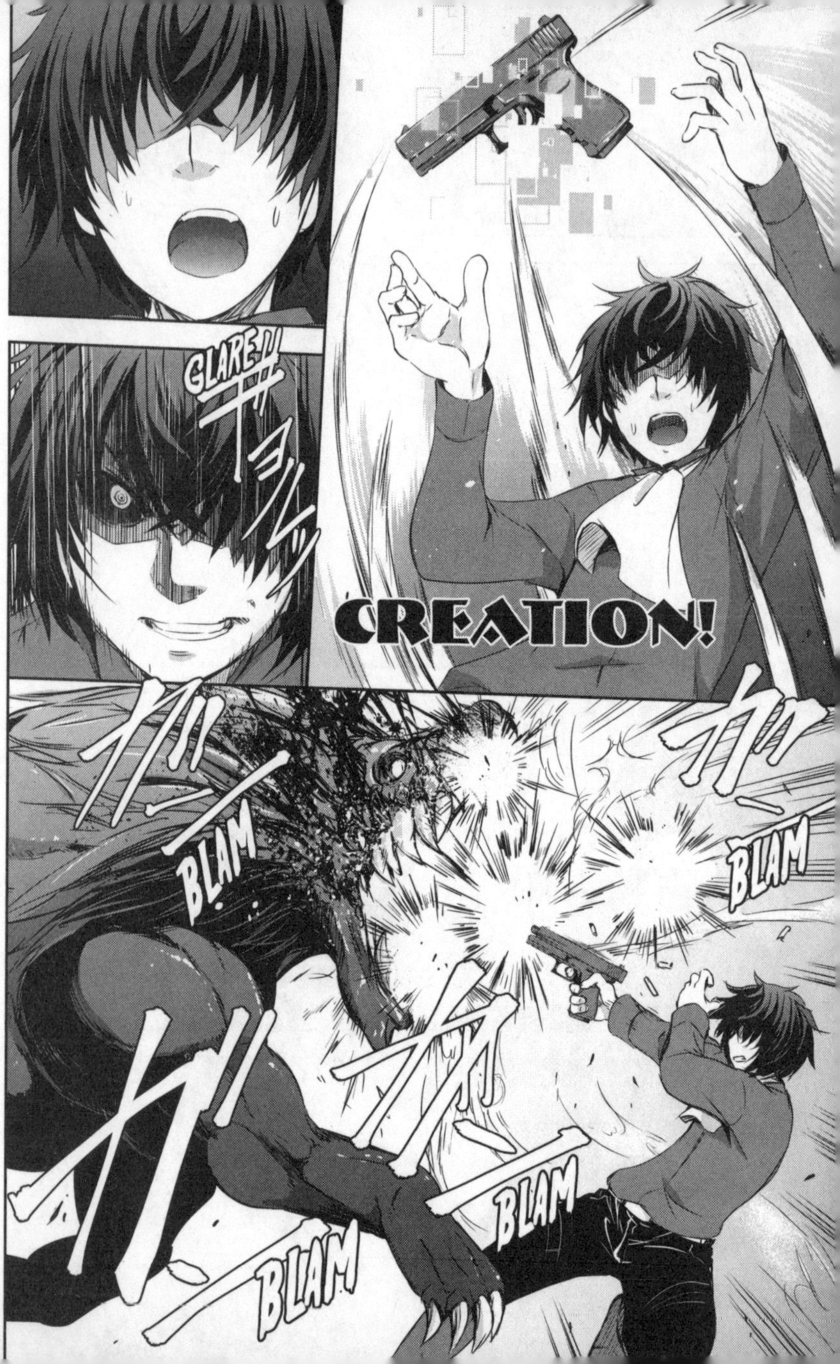
CREATION!
GLARE!!
BLAM
BLAM
BLAM
BLAM

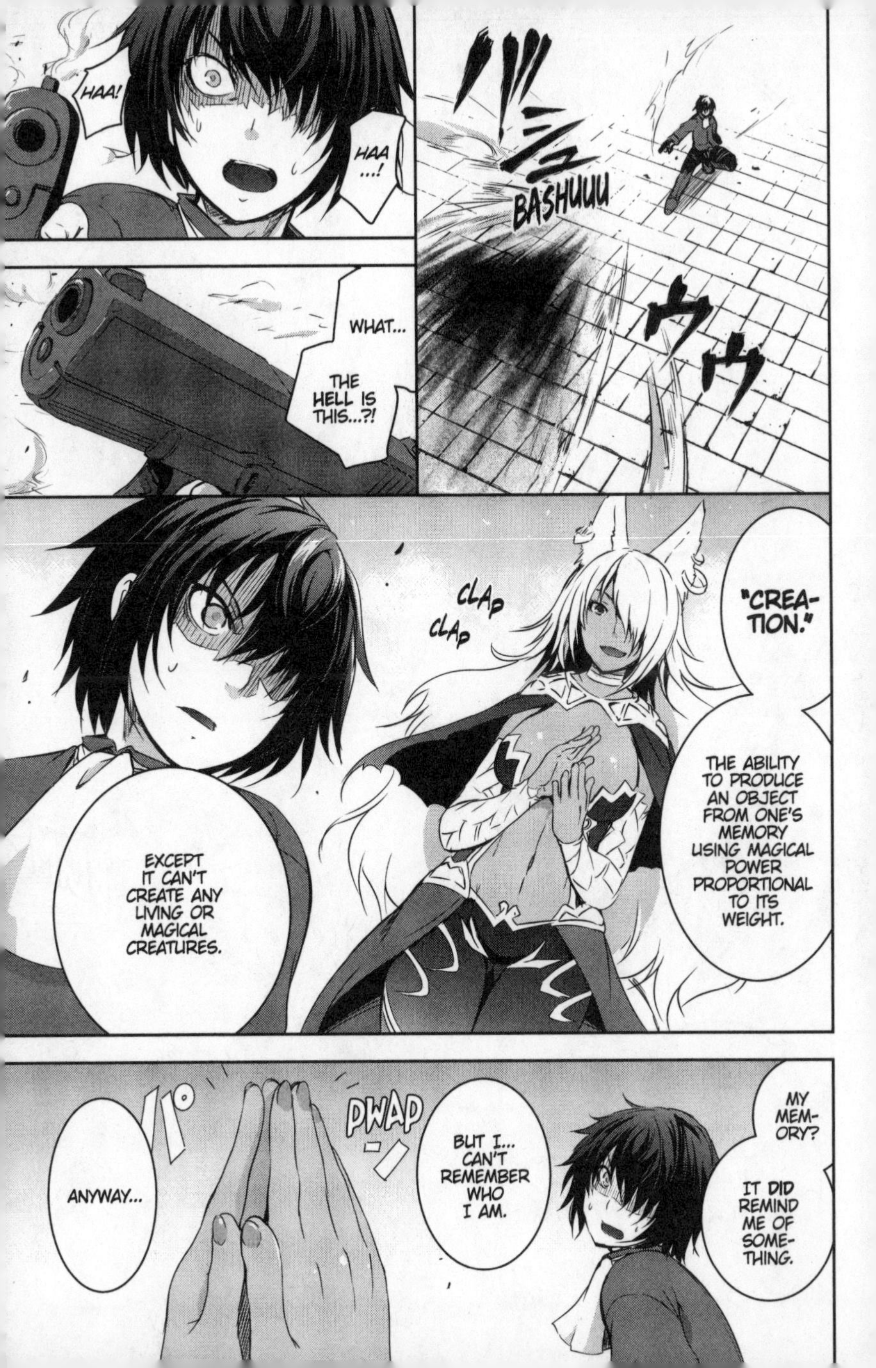
バシュ
BASHUUU
ウウ
HAA!
HAA ...!
WHAT...
THE HELL IS THIS...?!
"CREATION."
THE ABILITY TO PRODUCE AN OBJECT FROM ONE'S MEMORY USING MAGICAL POWER PROPORTIONAL TO ITS WEIGHT.
CLAP CLAP
EXCEPT IT CAN'T CREATE ANY LIVING OR MAGICAL CREATURES.
MY MEM-ORY?
IT DID REMIND ME OF SOME-THING.
BUT I... CAN'T REMEMBER WHO I AM.
PWAP
パ
ANYWAY...

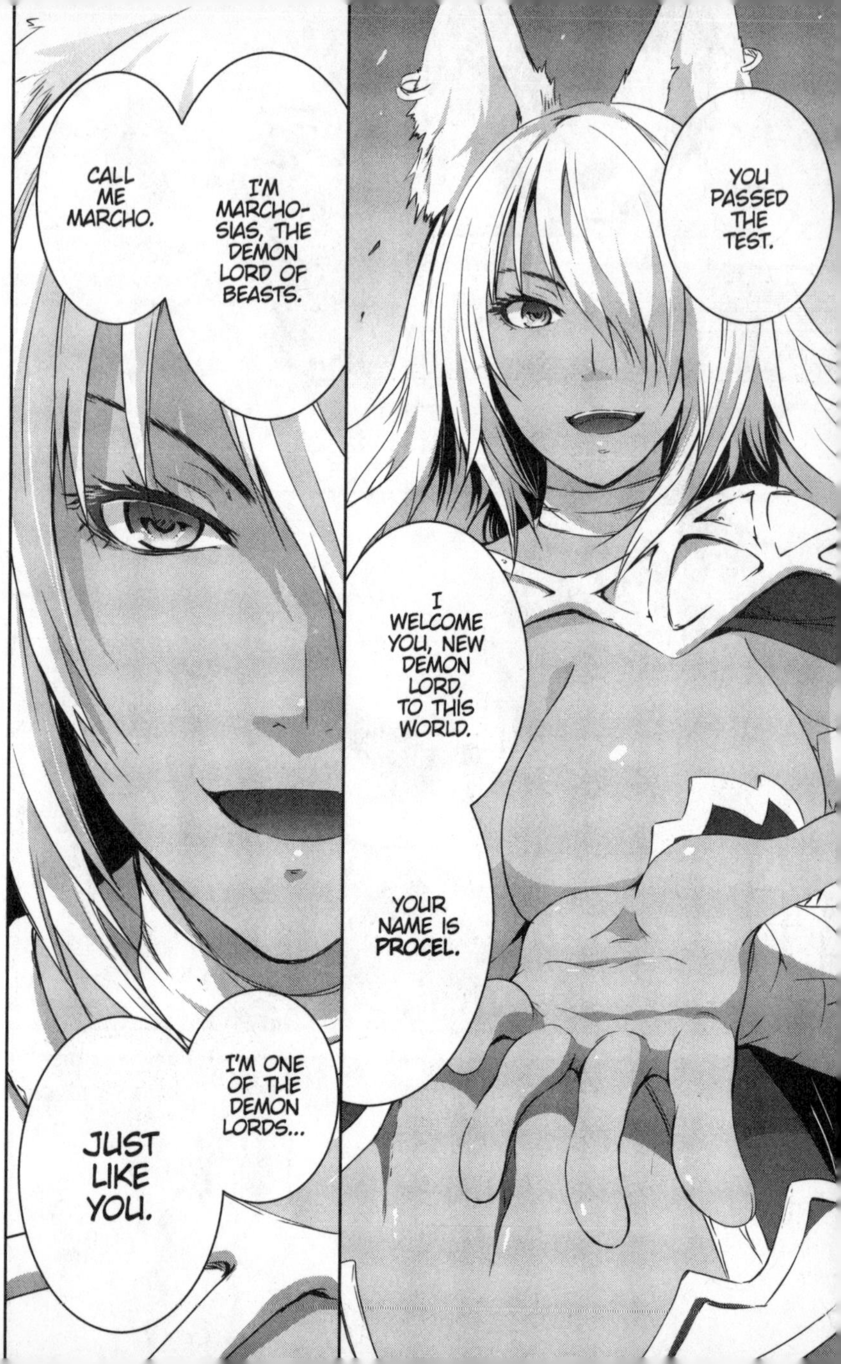
YOU PASSED THE TEST.
I WELCOME YOU, NEW DEMON LORD, TO THIS WORLD.
YOUR NAME IS PROCEL.
I'M MARCHOSIAS, THE DEMON LORD OF BEASTS.
CALL ME MARCHO.
I'M ONE OF THE DEMON LORDS...
JUST LIKE YOU.

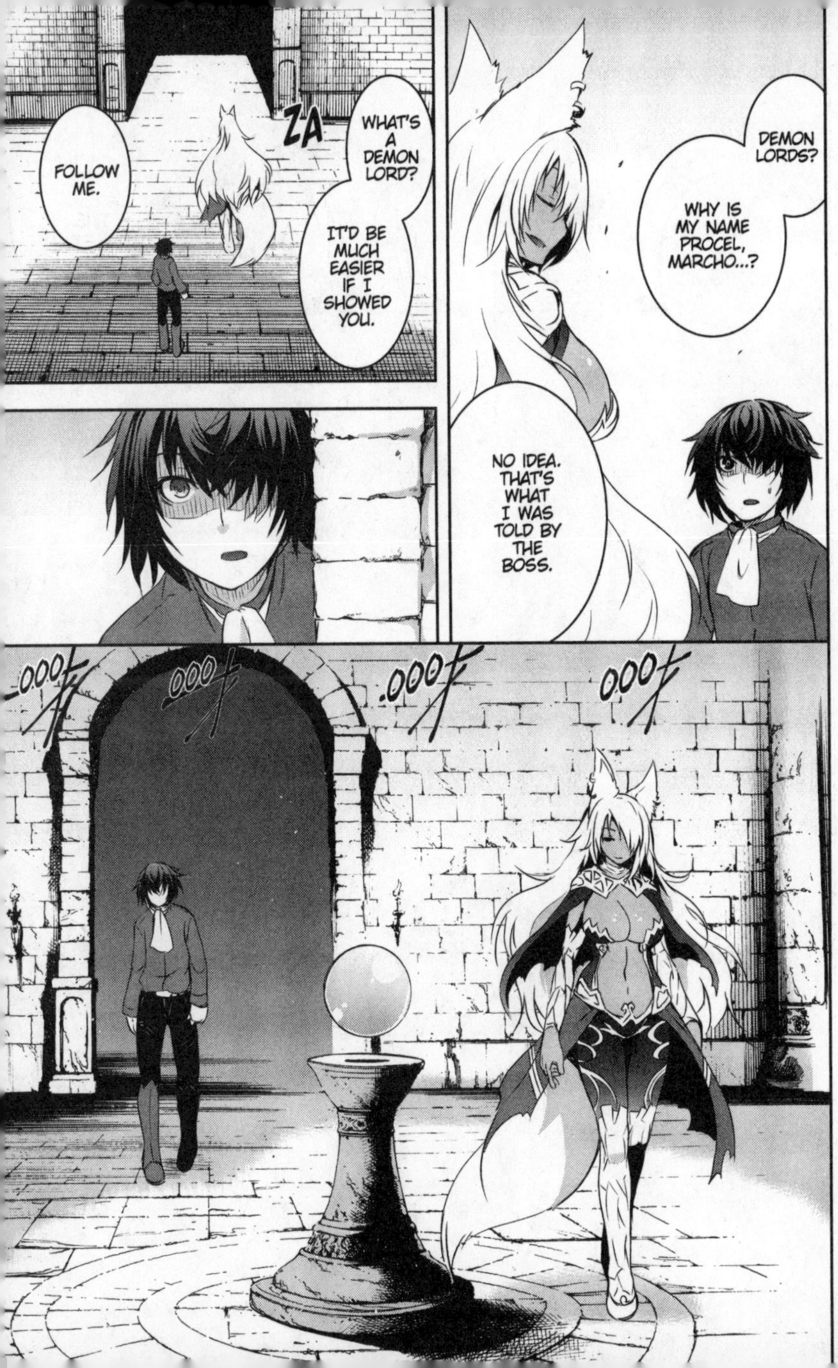
DEMON LORDS?
WHY IS MY NAME PROCEL, MARCHO...?
NO IDEA. THAT'S WHAT I WAS TOLD BY THE BOSS.
WHAT'S A DEMON LORD?
IT'D BE MUCH EASIER IF I SHOWED YOU.
ZA
FOLLOW ME.

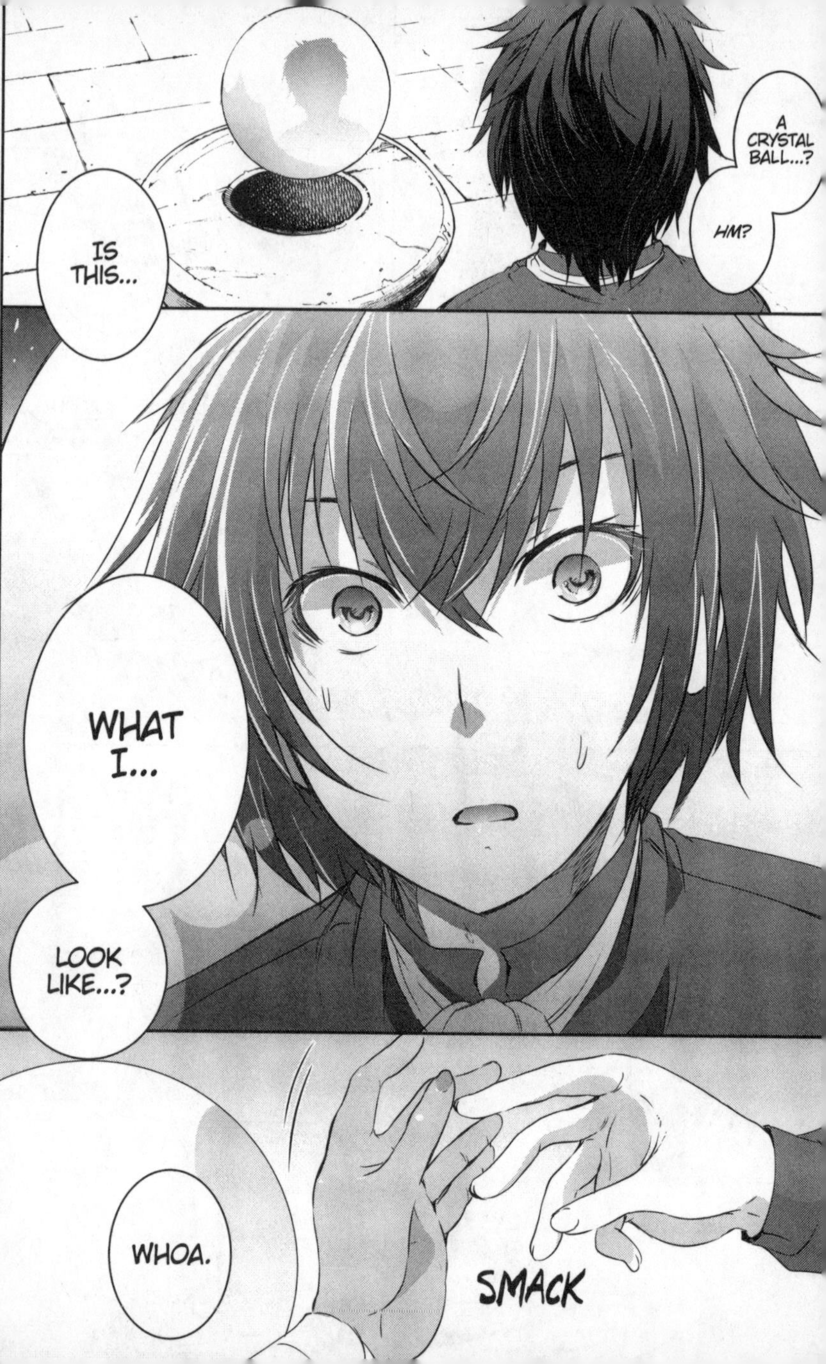
A CRYSTAL BALL...?
HM?
IS THIS...
WHAT I...
LOOK LIKE...?
SMACK
WHOA.

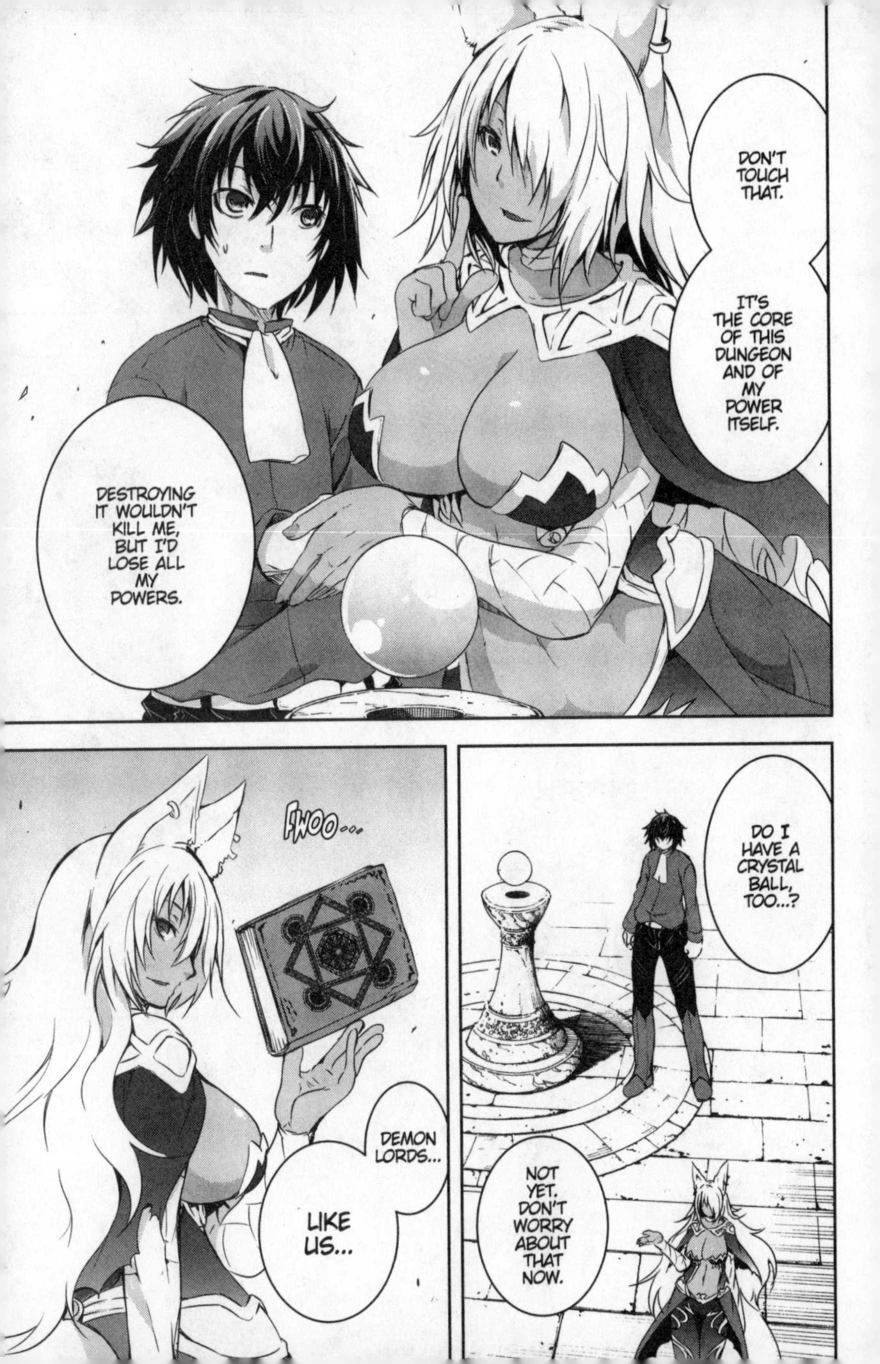
DON'T TOUCH THAT.
IT'S THE CORE OF THIS DUNGEON AND OF MY POWER ITSELF.
DESTROYING IT WOULDN'T KILL ME, BUT I'D LOSE ALL MY POWERS.
DO I HAVE A CRYSTAL BALL, TOO...?
NOT YET. DON'T WORRY ABOUT THAT NOW.
FWOO...
DEMON LORDS...
LIKE US...

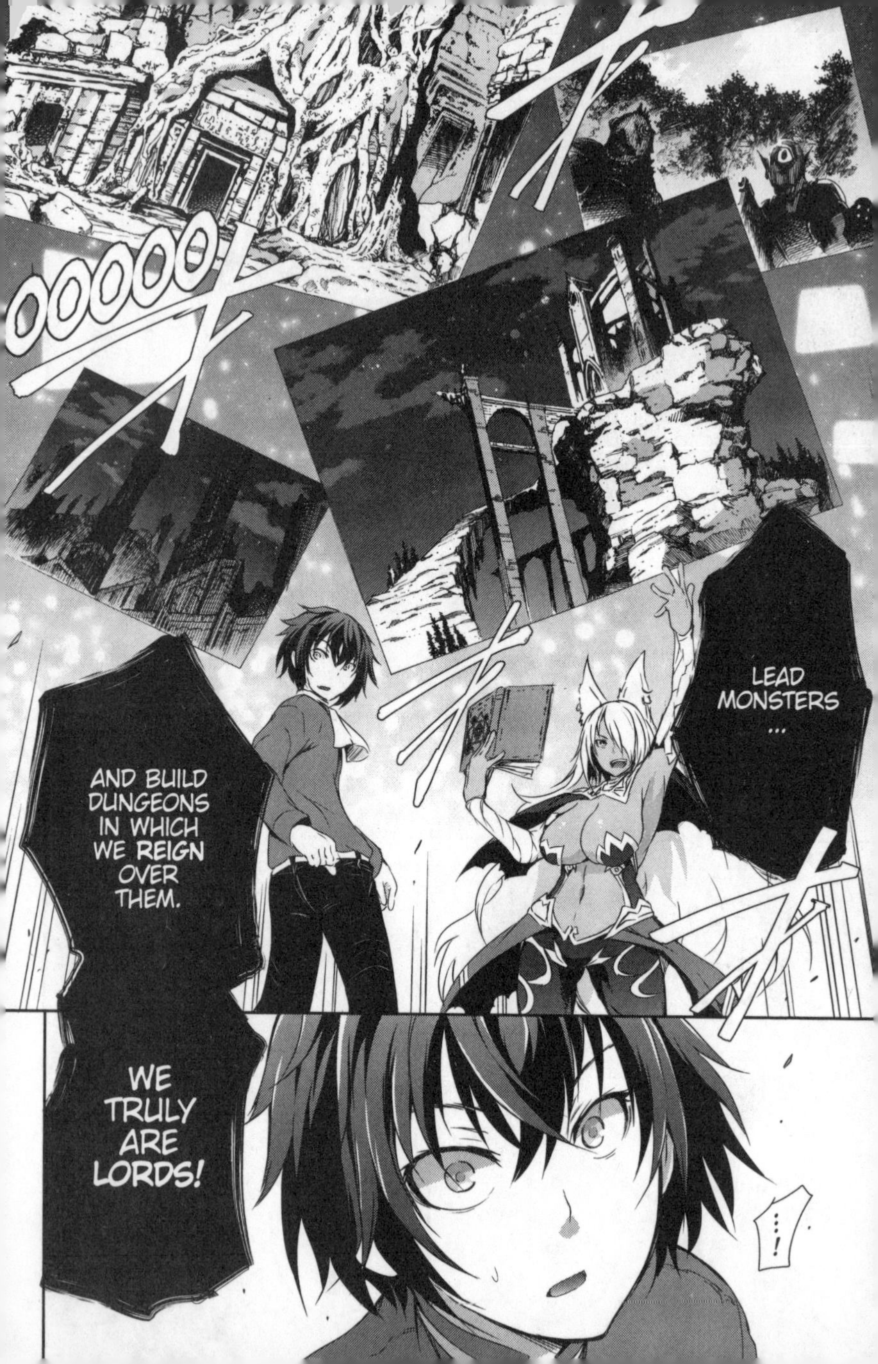
OOOOOX
LEAD MONSTERS ...
AND BUILD DUNGEONS IN WHICH WE REIGN OVER THEM.
WE TRULY ARE LORDS!
...!

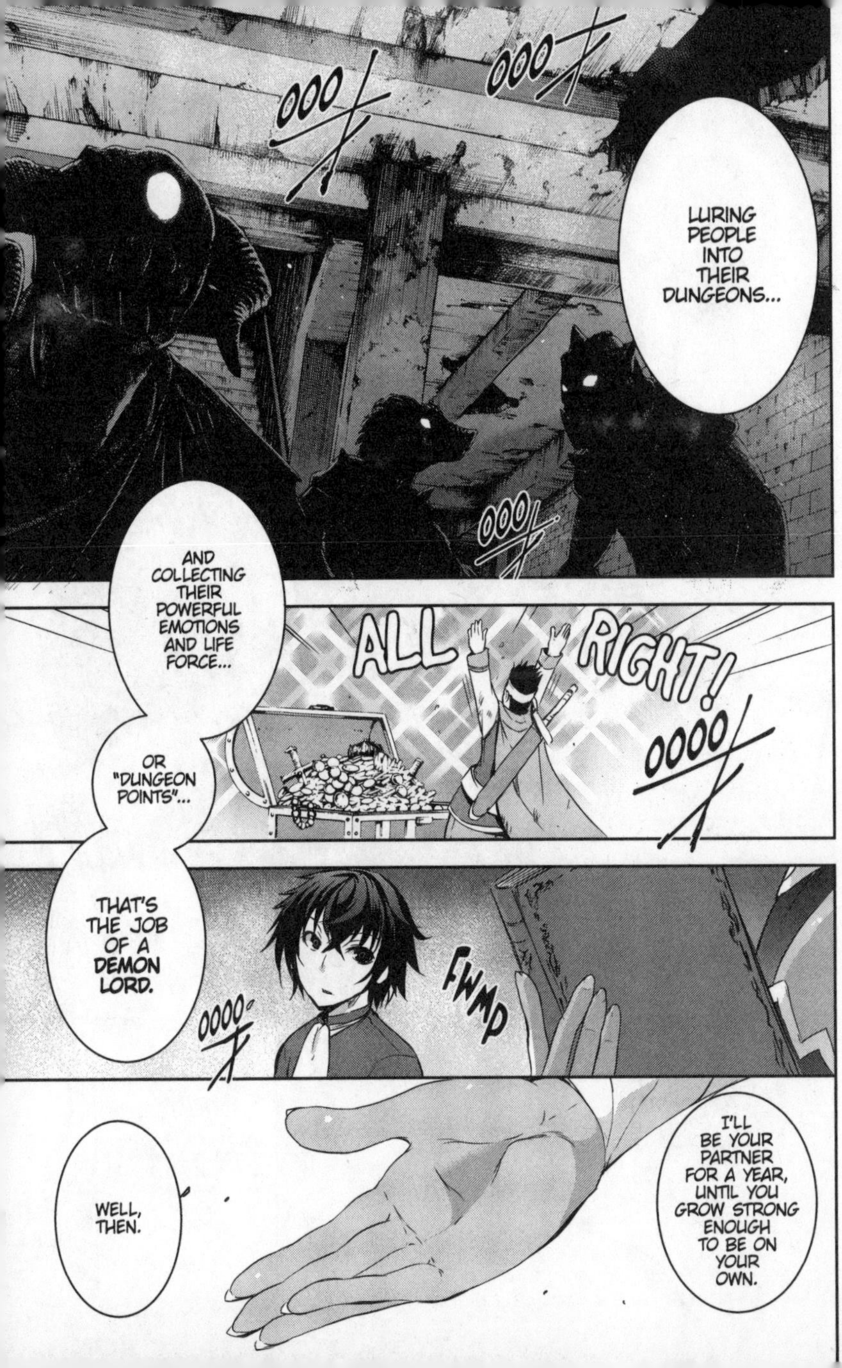
OOO
OOO
LURING PEOPLE INTO THEIR DUNGEONS...
OOO
AND COLLECTING THEIR POWERFUL EMOTIONS AND LIFE FORCE...
OOOO
ALL RIGHT!
OR "DUNGEON POINTS"...
FWMP
THAT'S THE JOB OF A DEMON LORD.
OOOO
I'LL BE YOUR PARTNER FOR A YEAR, UNTIL YOU GROW STRONG ENOUGH TO BE ON YOUR OWN.
WELL, THEN.

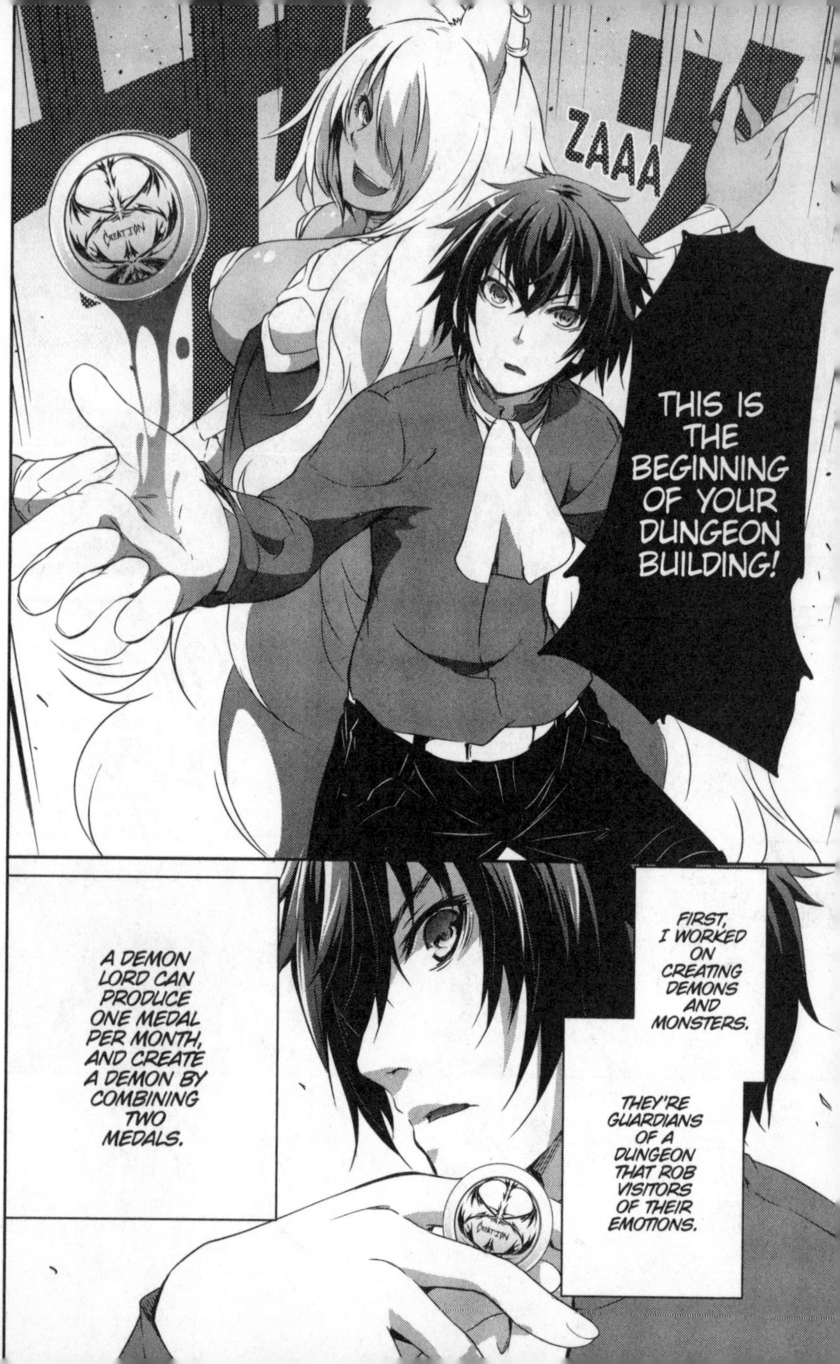
ZAAA
THIS IS THE BEGINNING OF YOUR DUNGEON BUILDING!
CREATION
FIRST, I WORKED ON CREATING DEMONS AND MONSTERS.
THEY'RE GUARDIANS OF A DUNGEON THAT ROB VISITORS OF THEIR EMOTIONS.
A DEMON LORD CAN PRODUCE ONE MEDAL PER MONTH, AND CREATE A DEMON BY COMBINING TWO MEDALS.
CREATION

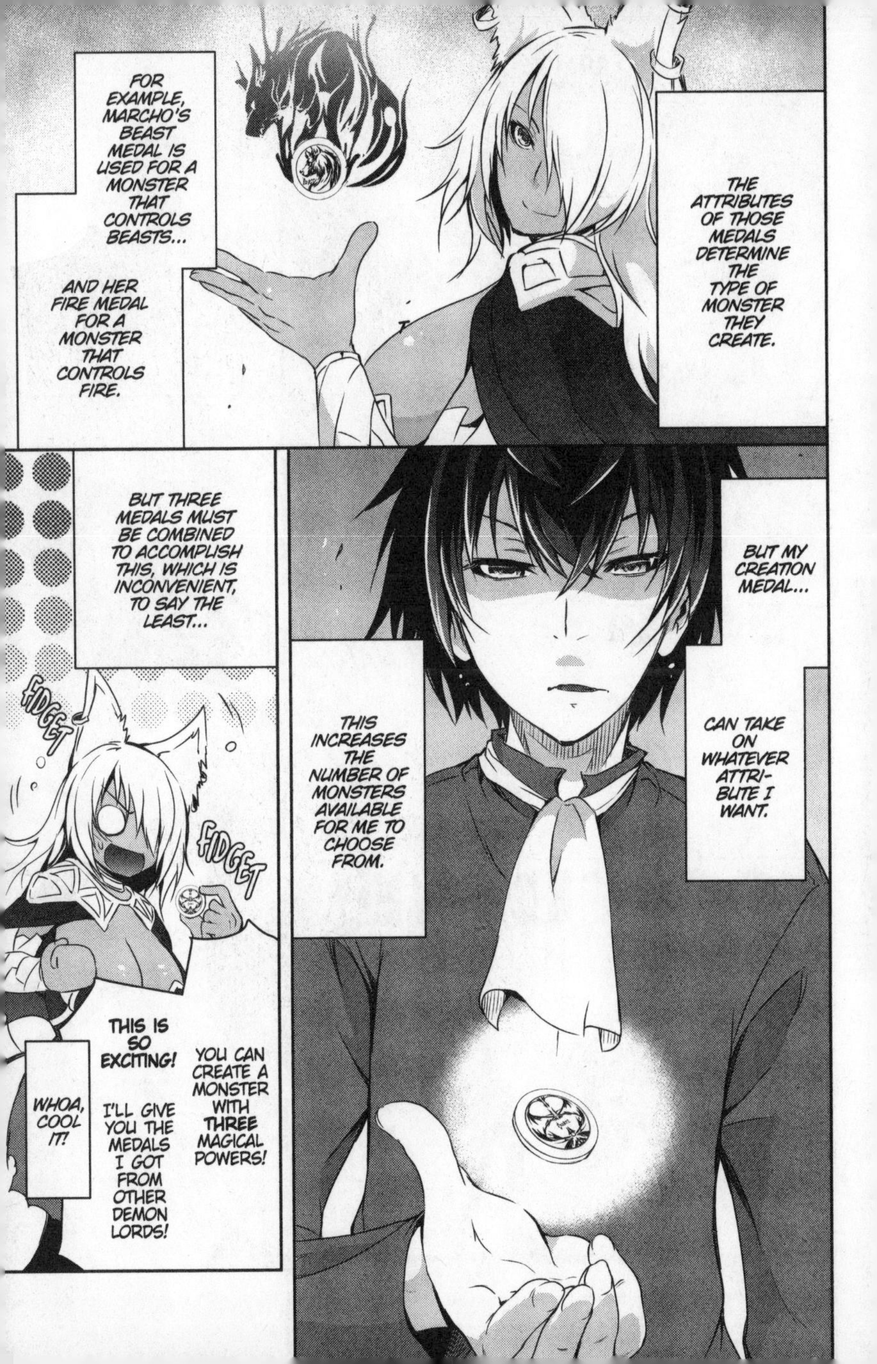
THE ATTRIBUTES OF THOSE MEDALS DETERMINE THE TYPE OF MONSTER THEY CREATE.
FOR EXAMPLE, MARCHO'S BEAST MEDAL IS USED FOR A MONSTER THAT CONTROLS BEASTS...
AND HER FIRE MEDAL FOR A MONSTER THAT CONTROLS FIRE.
BUT MY CREATION MEDAL...
CAN TAKE ON WHATEVER ATTRI-BUTE I WANT.
THIS INCREASES THE NUMBER OF MONSTERS AVAILABLE FOR ME TO CHOOSE FROM.
BUT THREE MEDALS MUST BE COMBINED TO ACCOMPLISH THIS, WHICH IS INCONVENIENT, TO SAY THE LEAST...
FIDGET
FIDGET
YOU CAN CREATE A MONSTER WITH THREE MAGICAL POWERS!
THIS IS SO EXCITING!
I'LL GIVE YOU THE MEDALS I GOT FROM OTHER DEMON LORDS!
WHOA, COOL IT!

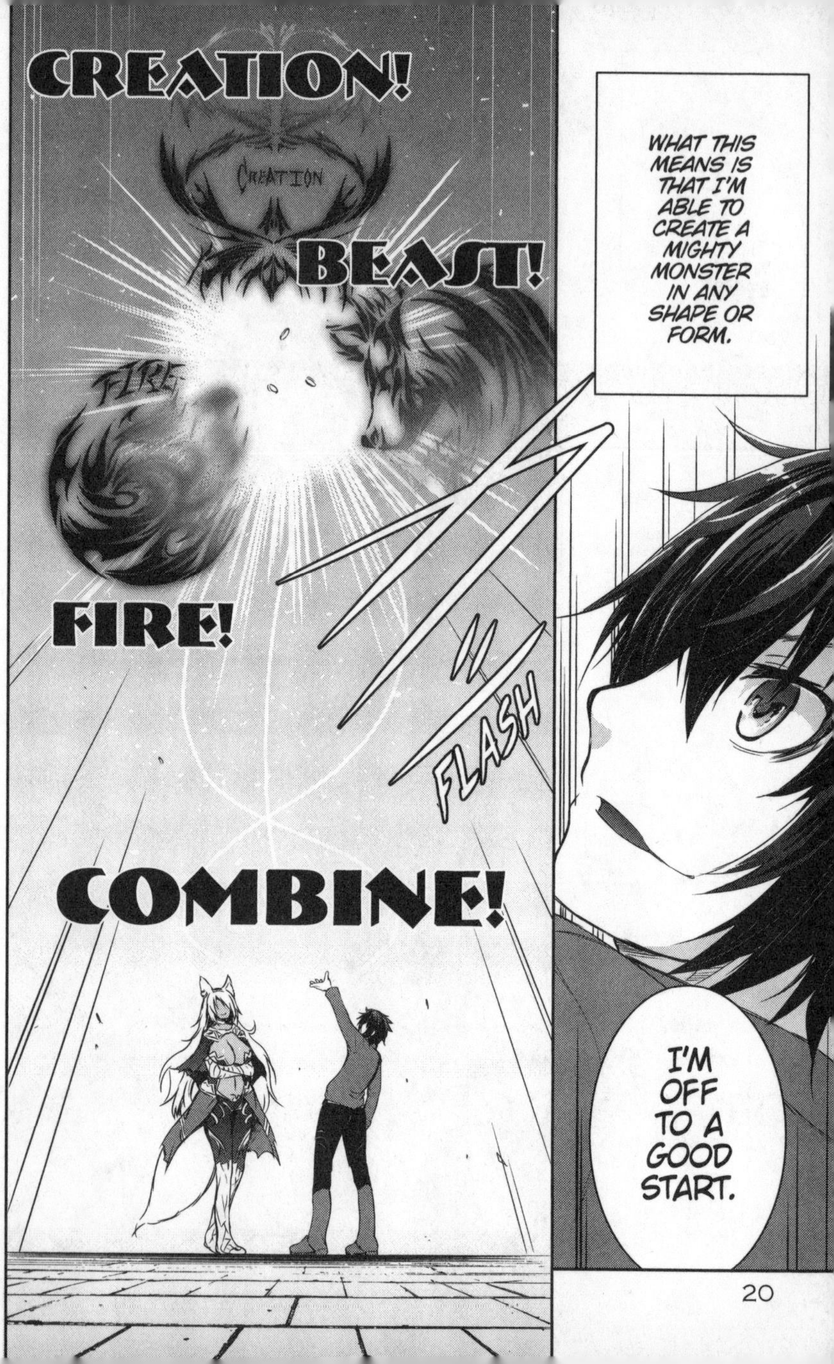
WHAT THIS MEANS IS THAT I'M ABLE TO CREATE A MIGHTY MONSTER IN ANY SHAPE OR FORM.
I'M OFF TO A GOOD START.
CREATION!
CREATION
BEAST!
FIRE
FIRE!
FLASH
COMBINE!

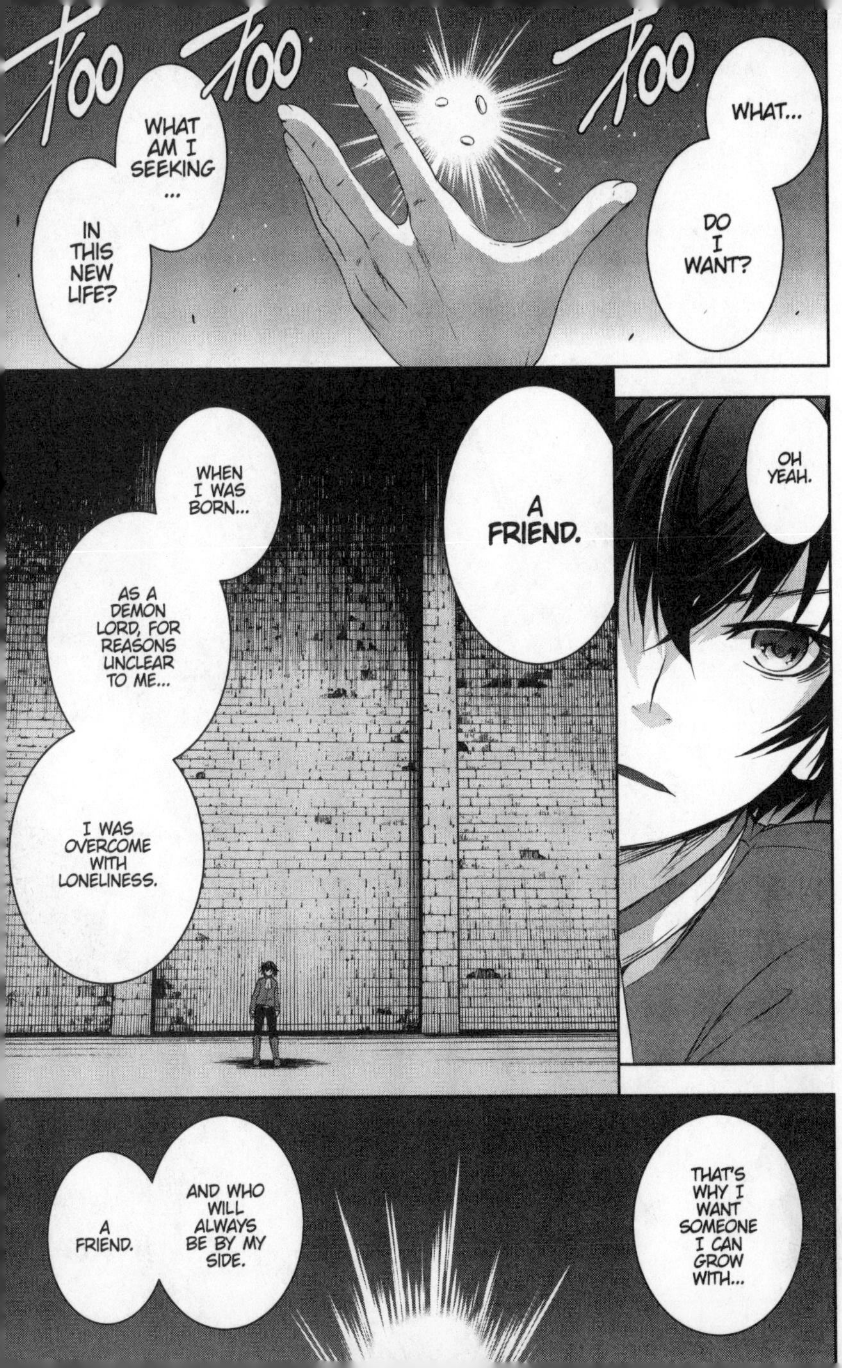
FOO
FOO
FOO
WHAT... DO I WANT?
WHAT AM I SEEKING... IN THIS NEW LIFE?
OH YEAH.
A FRIEND.
WHEN I WAS BORN...
AS A DEMON LORD, FOR REASONS UNCLEAR TO ME...
I WAS OVERCOME WITH LONELINESS.
THAT'S WHY I WANT SOMEONE I CAN GROW WITH...
AND WHO WILL ALWAYS BE BY MY SIDE.
A FRIEND.

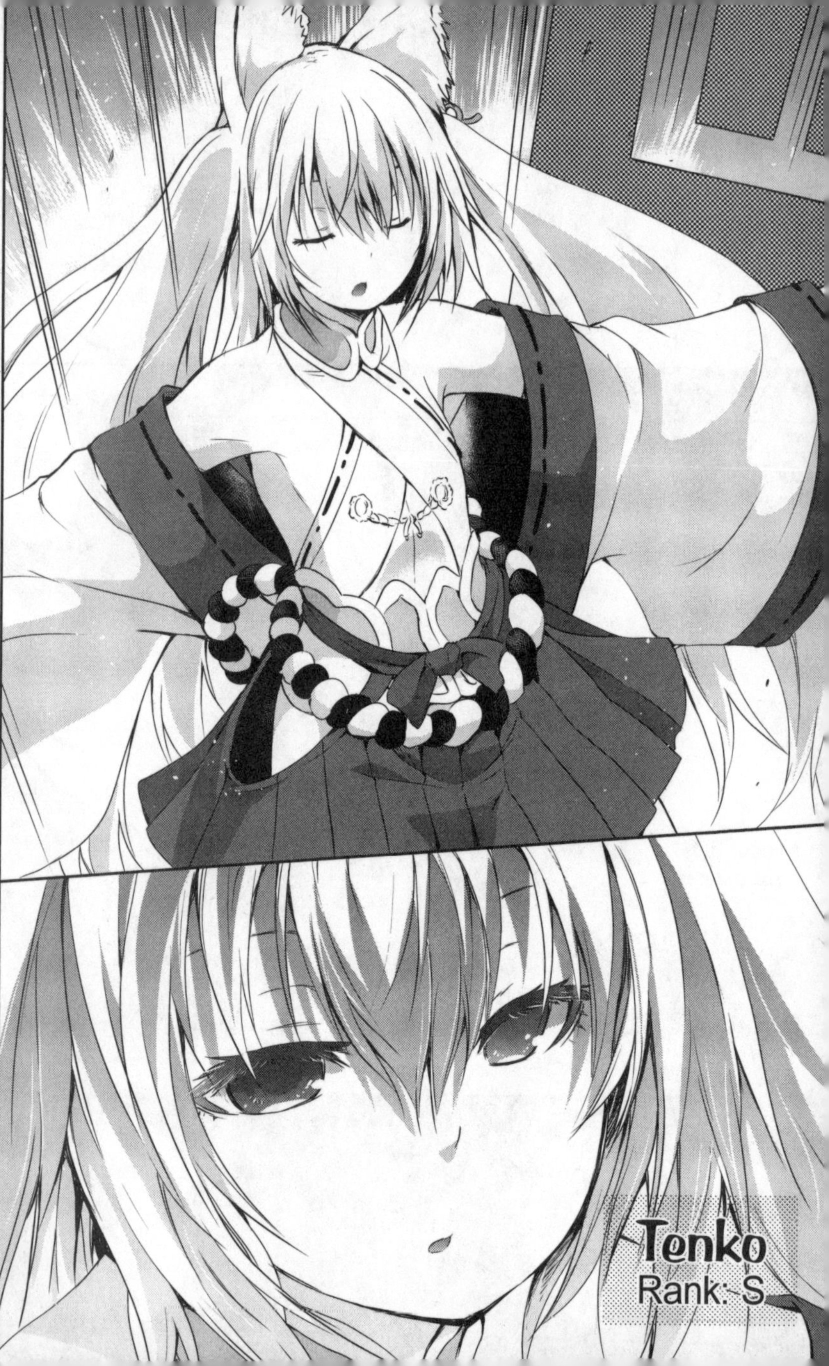
Tenko
Rank: S

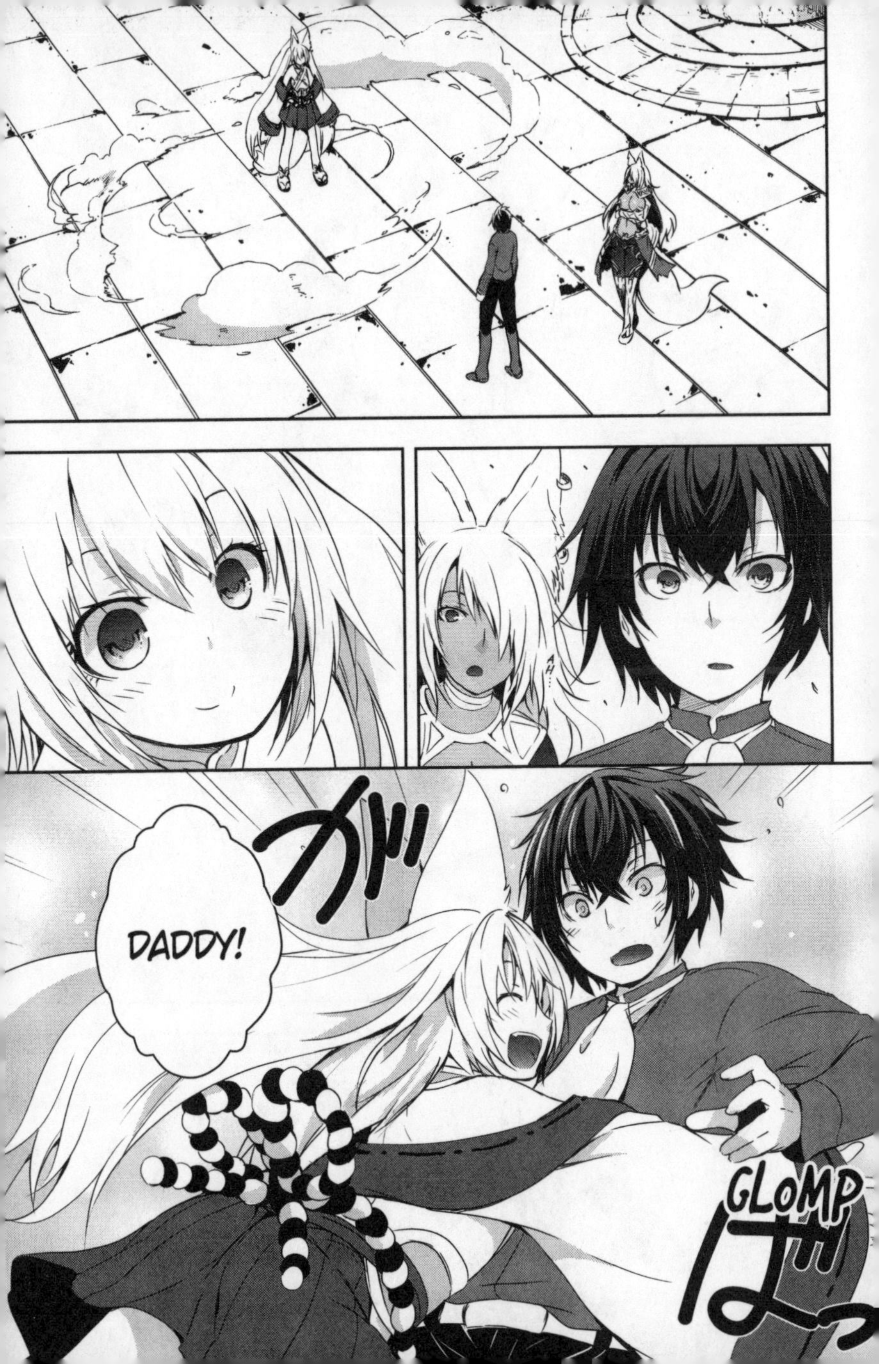
AH...
DADDY!
GLOMP

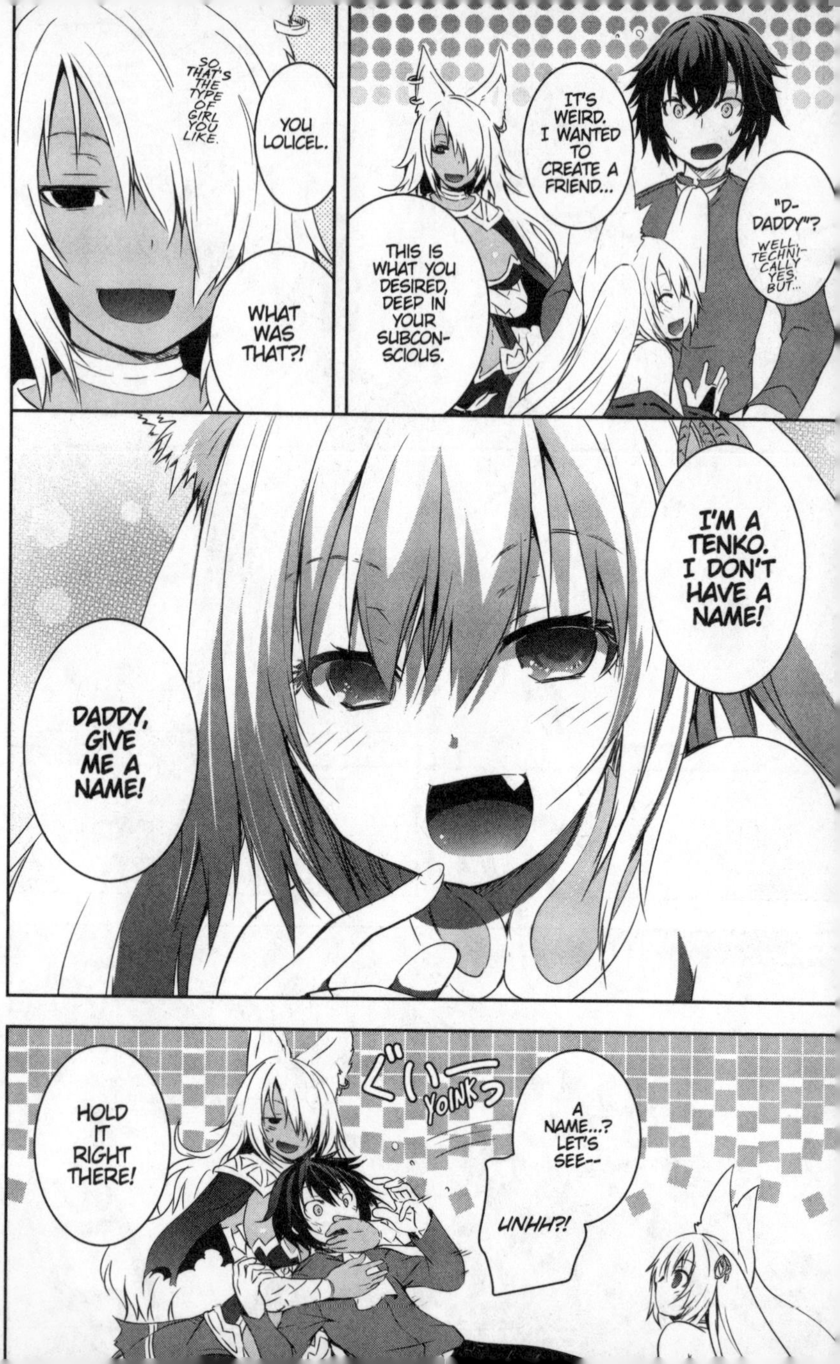
"D-DADDY"?
WELL, TECHNICALLY YES, BUT...
IT'S WEIRD. I WANTED TO CREATE A FRIEND...
THIS IS WHAT YOU DESIRED, DEEP IN YOUR SUBCONSCIOUS.
YOU LOLICEL.
SO THAT'S THE TYPE OF GIRL YOU LIKE.
WHAT WAS THAT?!
I'M A TENKO. I DON'T HAVE A NAME!
DADDY, GIVE ME A NAME!
A NAME...? LET'S SEE--
UNHH?!
ぐいーっ
YOINK
HOLD IT RIGHT THERE!

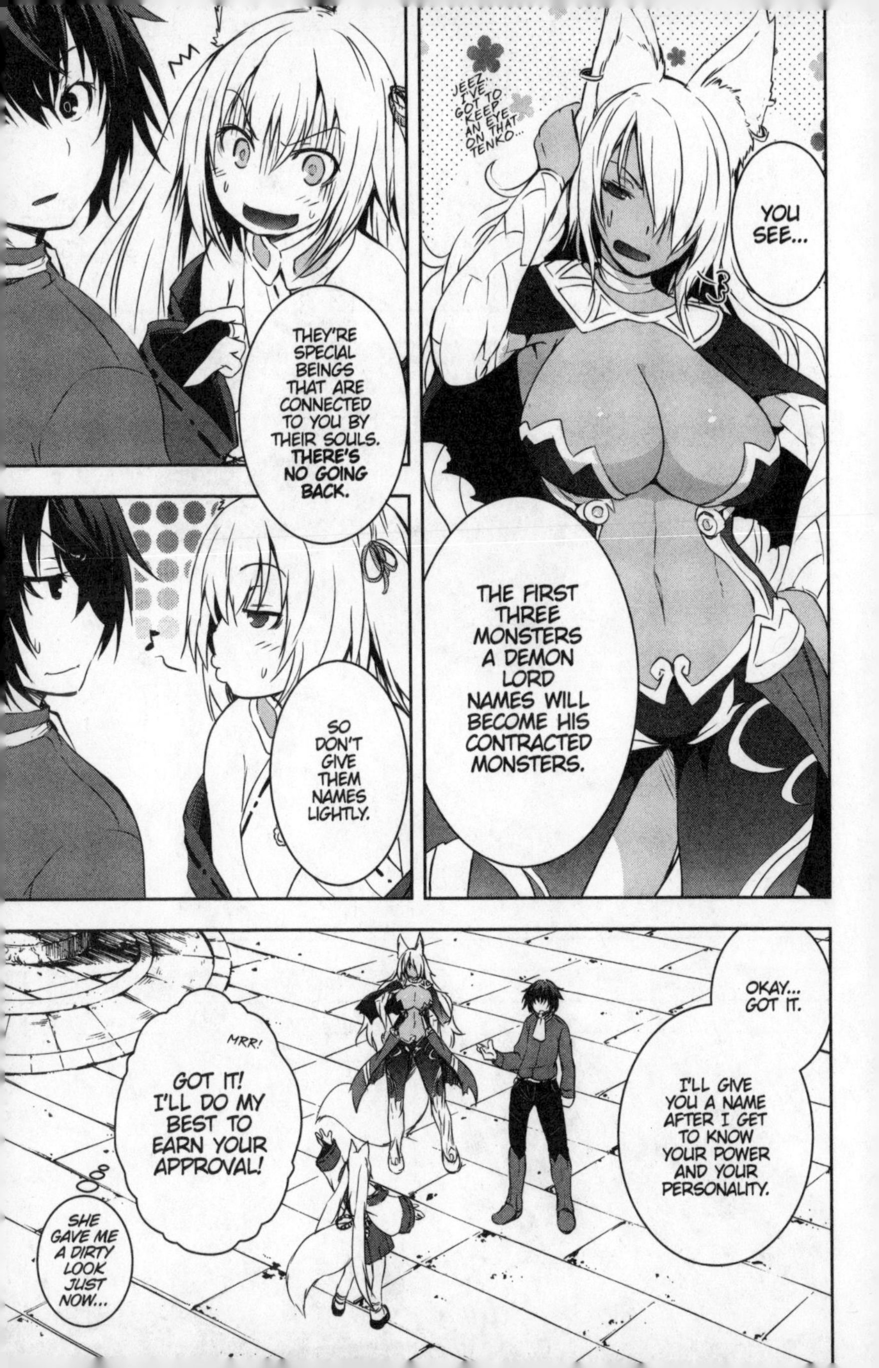
JEEZ. I'VE GOT TO KEEP AN EYE ON THAT TENKO...
YOU SEE...
THE FIRST THREE MONSTERS A DEMON LORD NAMES WILL BECOME HIS CONTRACTED MONSTERS.
THEY'RE SPECIAL BEINGS THAT ARE CONNECTED TO YOU BY THEIR SOULS. THERE'S NO GOING BACK.
SO DON'T GIVE THEM NAMES LIGHTLY.
OKAY... GOT IT.
I'LL GIVE YOU A NAME AFTER I GET TO KNOW YOUR POWER AND YOUR PERSONALITY.
MRR!
GOT IT! I'LL DO MY BEST TO EARN YOUR APPROVAL!
SHE GAVE ME A DIRTY LOOK JUST NOW...

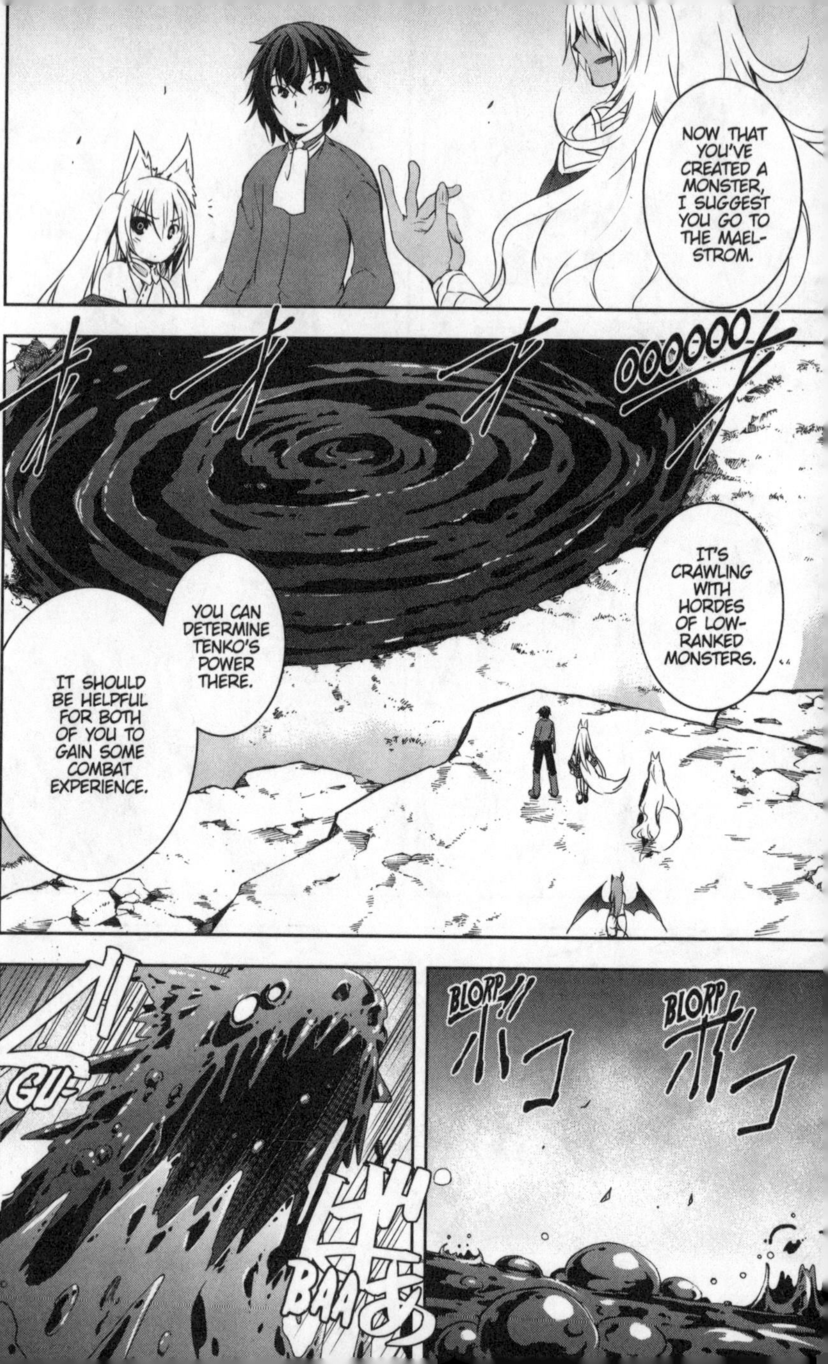
NOW THAT YOU'VE CREATED A MONSTER, I SUGGEST YOU GO TO THE MAEL-STROM.
OOOOOO
IT'S CRAWLING WITH HORDES OF LOW-RANKED MONSTERS.
YOU CAN DETERMINE TENKO'S POWER THERE.
IT SHOULD BE HELPFUL FOR BOTH OF YOU TO GAIN SOME COMBAT EXPERIENCE.
BLORP
BLORP
GU-
BAA

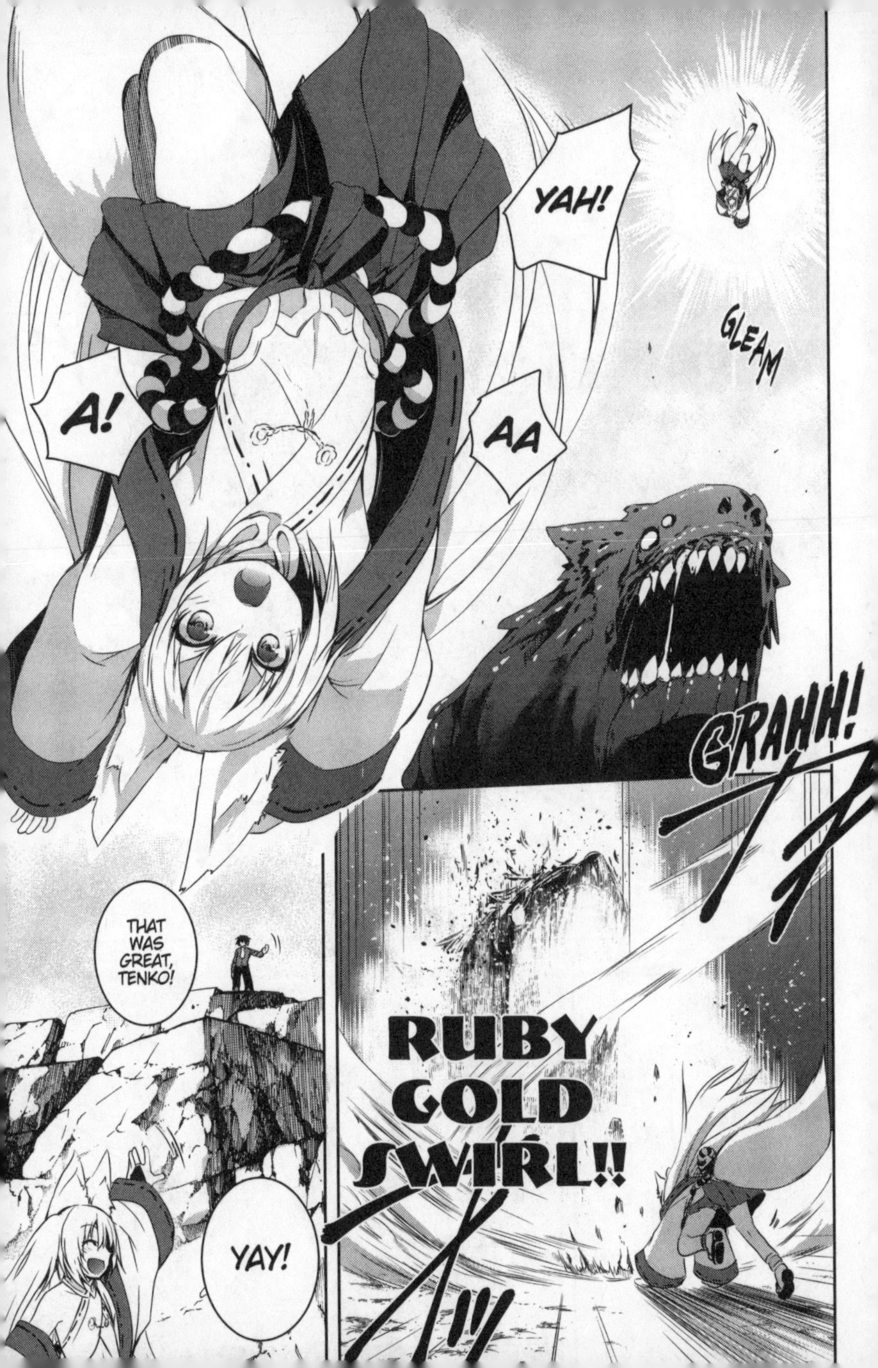
YAH!
GLEAM
AA
A!
GRAHH!
RUBY GOLD SWIRL!!
THAT WAS GREAT, TENKO!
YAY!

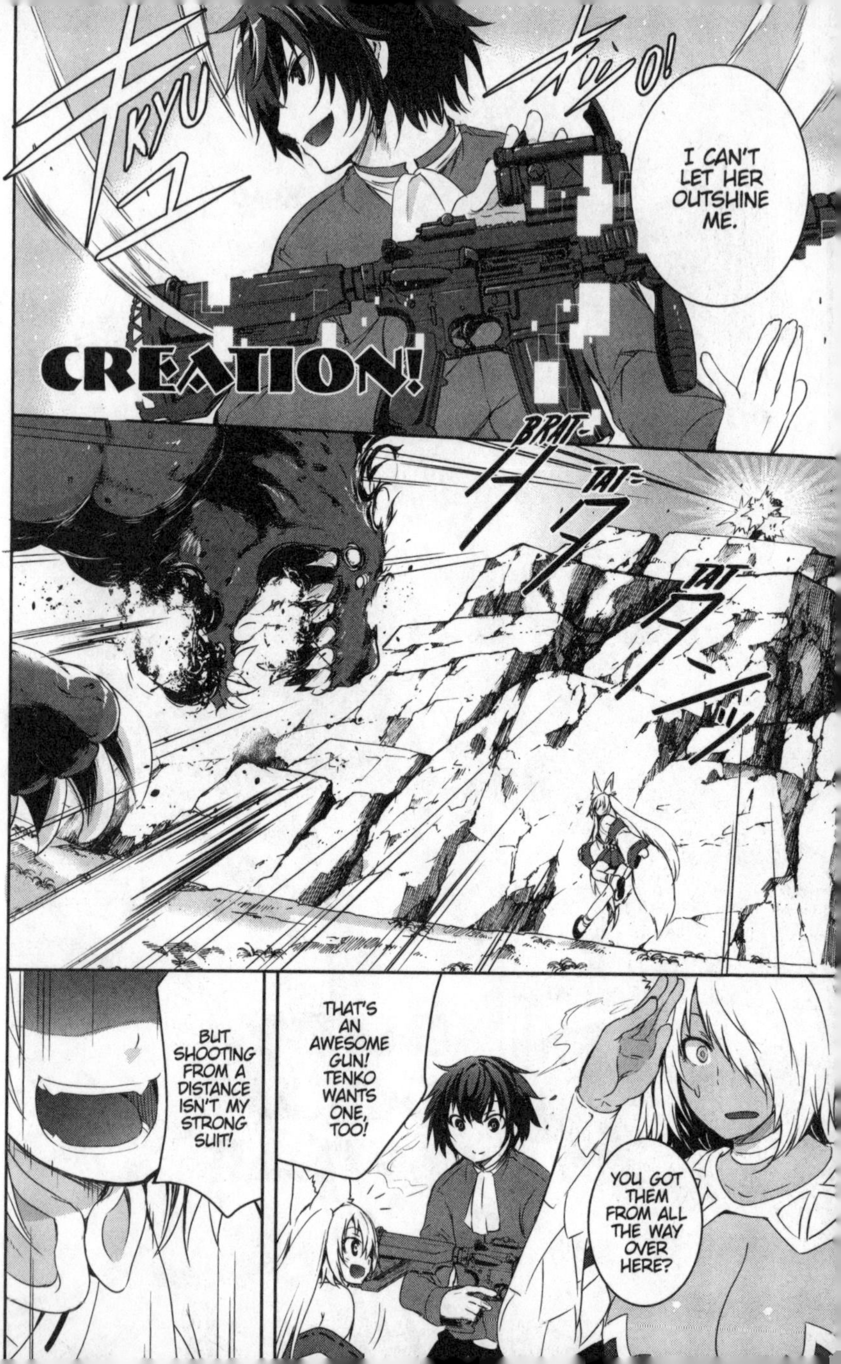
I CAN'T LET HER OUTSHINE ME.
O!
KYU
CREATION!
BRAT-
TAT-
TAT
YOU GOT THEM FROM ALL THE WAY OVER HERE?
THAT'S AN AWESOME GUN! TENKO WANTS ONE, TOO!
BUT SHOOTING FROM A DISTANCE ISN'T MY STRONG SUIT!

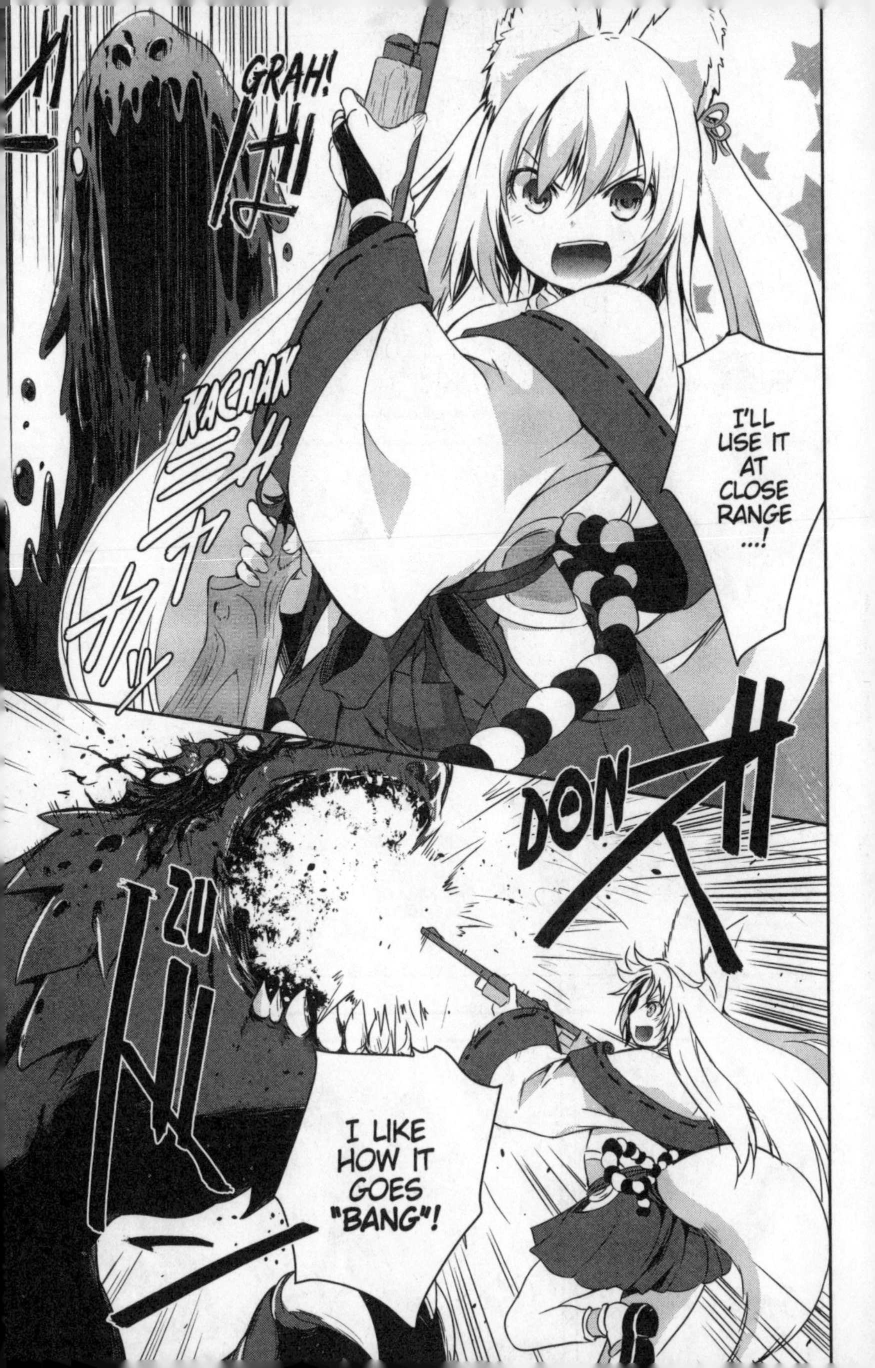
GRAH!
I'LL USE IT AT CLOSE RANGE ...!
KACHAK
DON
I LIKE HOW IT GOES "BANG"!
ZU

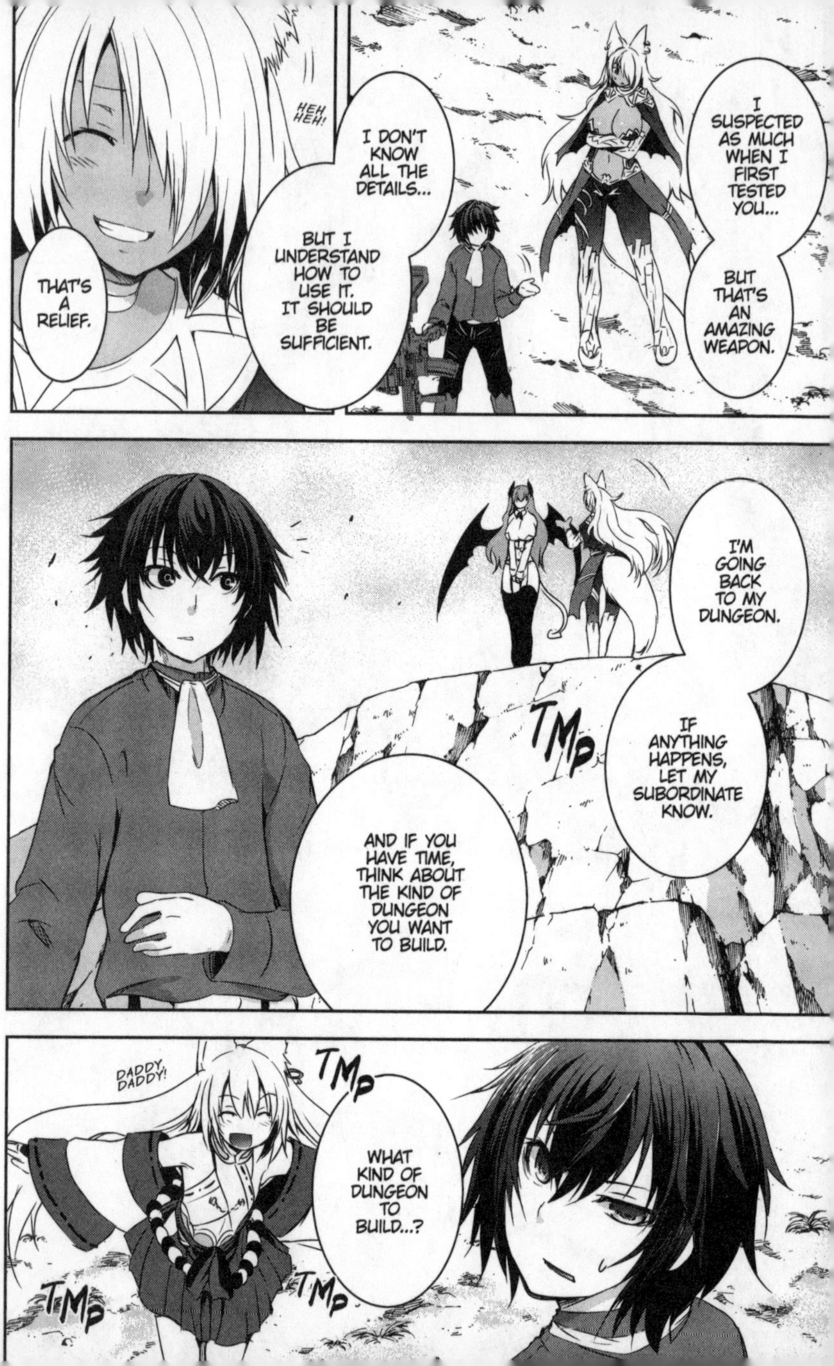
I SUSPECTED AS MUCH WHEN I FIRST TESTED YOU...
BUT THAT'S AN AMAZING WEAPON.
I DON'T KNOW ALL THE DETAILS...
BUT I UNDERSTAND HOW TO USE IT. IT SHOULD BE SUFFICIENT.
HEH HEH!
THAT'S A RELIEF.
I'M GOING BACK TO MY DUNGEON.
IF ANYTHING HAPPENS, LET MY SUBORDINATE KNOW.
TMP
AND IF YOU HAVE TIME, THINK ABOUT THE KIND OF DUNGEON YOU WANT TO BUILD.
TMP
DADDY, DADDY!
WHAT KIND OF DUNGEON TO BUILD...?
TMP
TMP

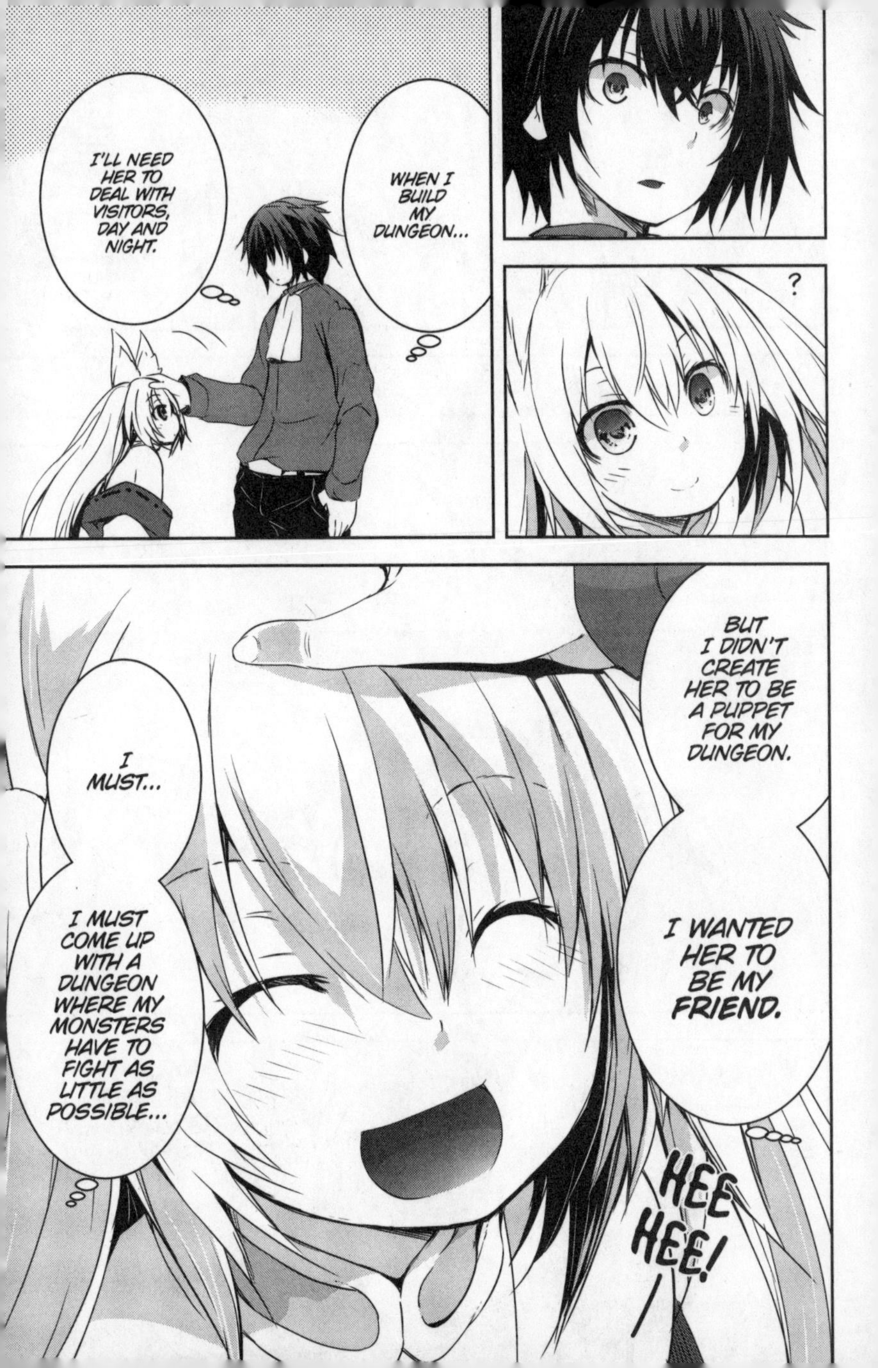
?
WHEN I BUILD MY DUNGEON...
I'LL NEED HER TO DEAL WITH VISITORS, DAY AND NIGHT.
BUT I DIDN'T CREATE HER TO BE A PUPPET FOR MY DUNGEON.
I WANTED HER TO BE MY FRIEND.
HEE HEE!
I MUST...
I MUST COME UP WITH A DUNGEON WHERE MY MONSTERS HAVE TO FIGHT AS LITTLE AS POSSIBLE...

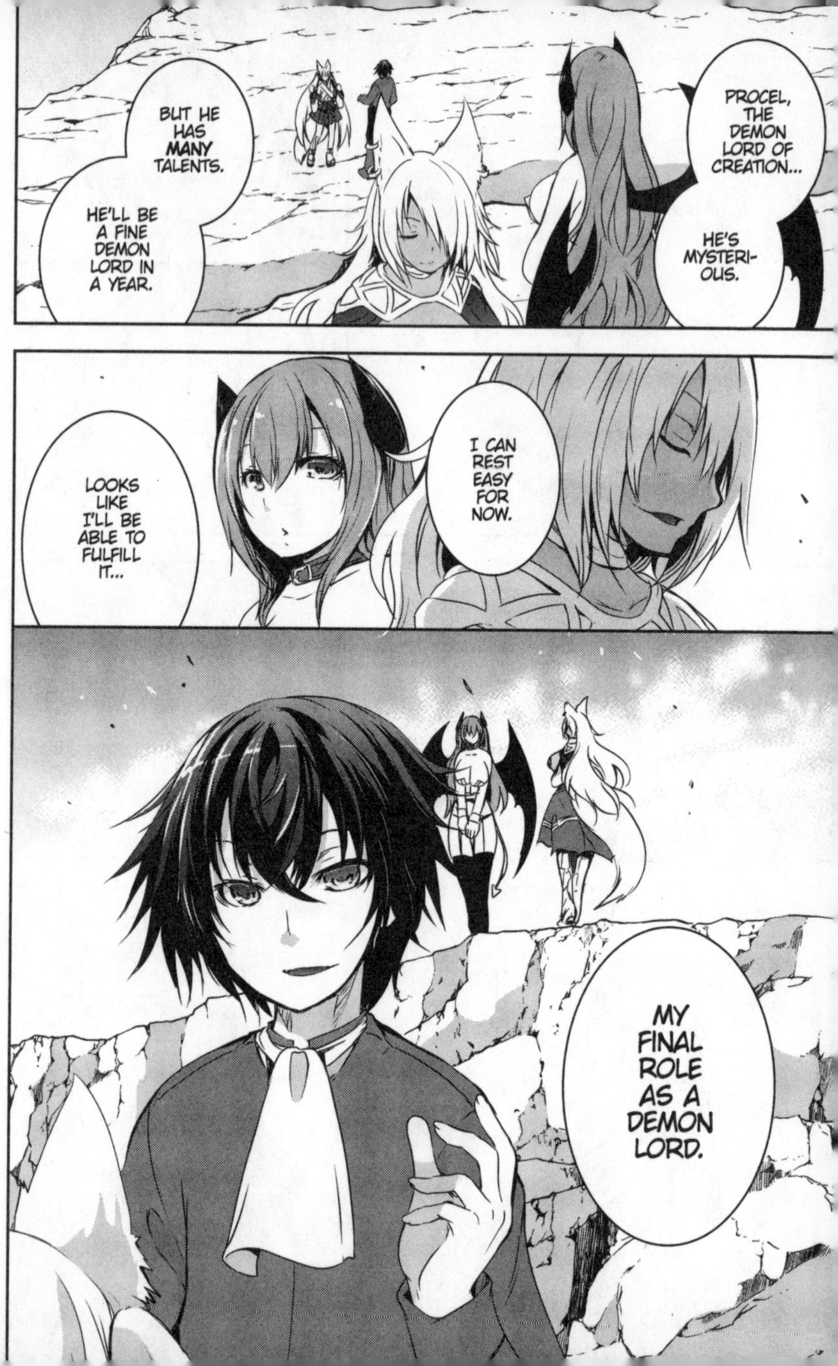
PROCEL, THE DEMON LORD OF CREATION...
HE'S MYSTERI-OUS.
BUT HE HAS MANY TALENTS.
HE'LL BE A FINE DEMON LORD IN A YEAR.
I CAN REST EASY FOR NOW.
LOOKS LIKE I'LL BE ABLE TO FULFILL IT...
MY FINAL ROLE AS A DEMON LORD.

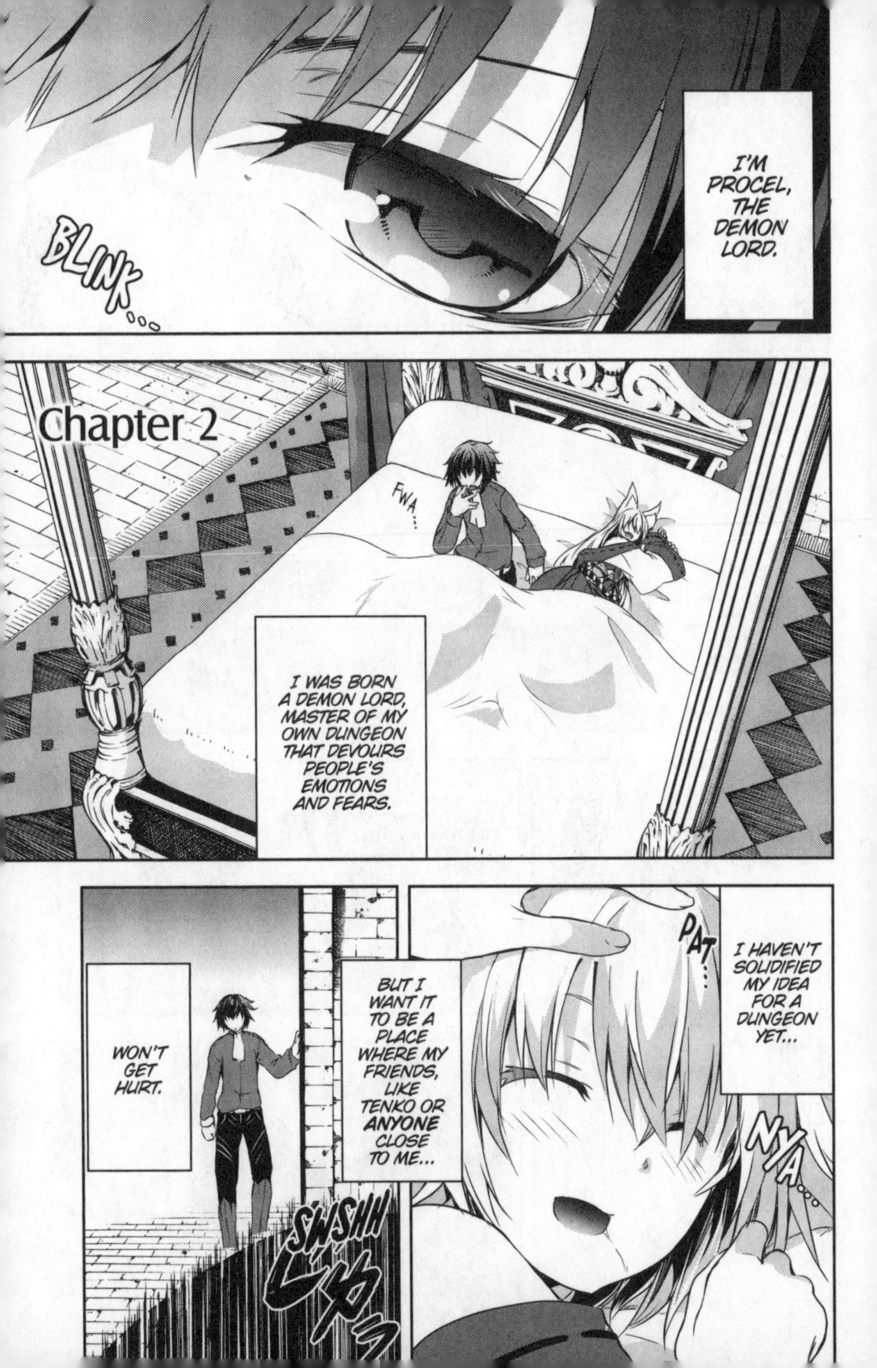
I'M PROCEL, THE DEMON LORD.
BLINK...
Chapter 2
FWA...
I WAS BORN A DEMON LORD, MASTER OF MY OWN DUNGEON THAT DEVOURS PEOPLE'S EMOTIONS AND FEARS.
I HAVEN'T SOLIDIFIED MY IDEA FOR A DUNGEON YET...
PAT...
NYA...
BUT I WANT IT TO BE A PLACE WHERE MY FRIENDS, LIKE TENKO OR ANYONE CLOSE TO ME...
WON'T GET HURT.
SWSHH

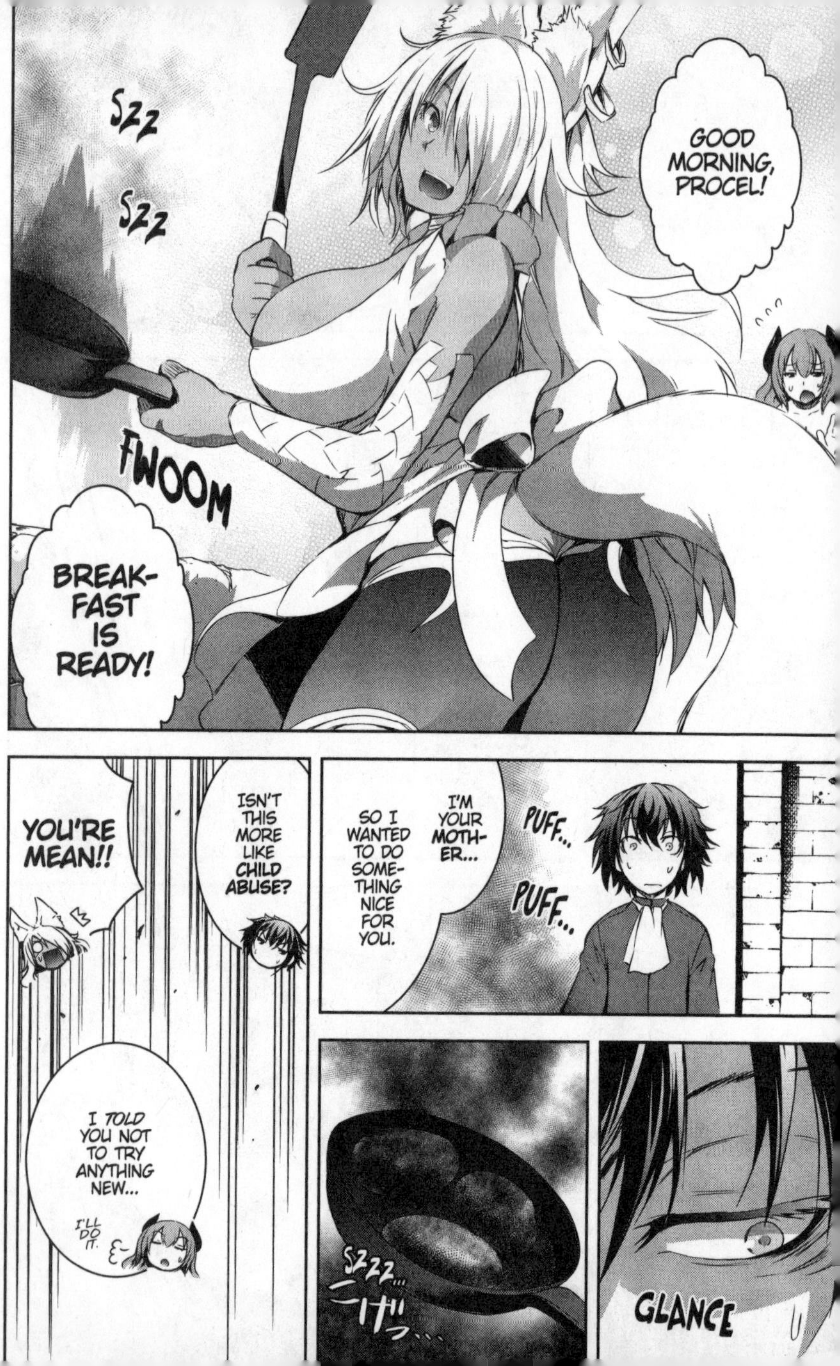
GOOD MORNING, PROCEL!
SZZ
SZZ
FWOOM
BREAK-FAST IS READY!
PUFF...
PUFF...
I'M YOUR MOTH-ER...
SO I WANTED TO DO SOME-THING NICE FOR YOU.
GLANCE
SZZZ...
ISN'T THIS MORE LIKE CHILD ABUSE?
YOU'RE MEAN!!
I TOLD YOU NOT TO TRY ANYTHING NEW...
I'LL DO IT.

Chapter 2: **Tenko's Little Sister**

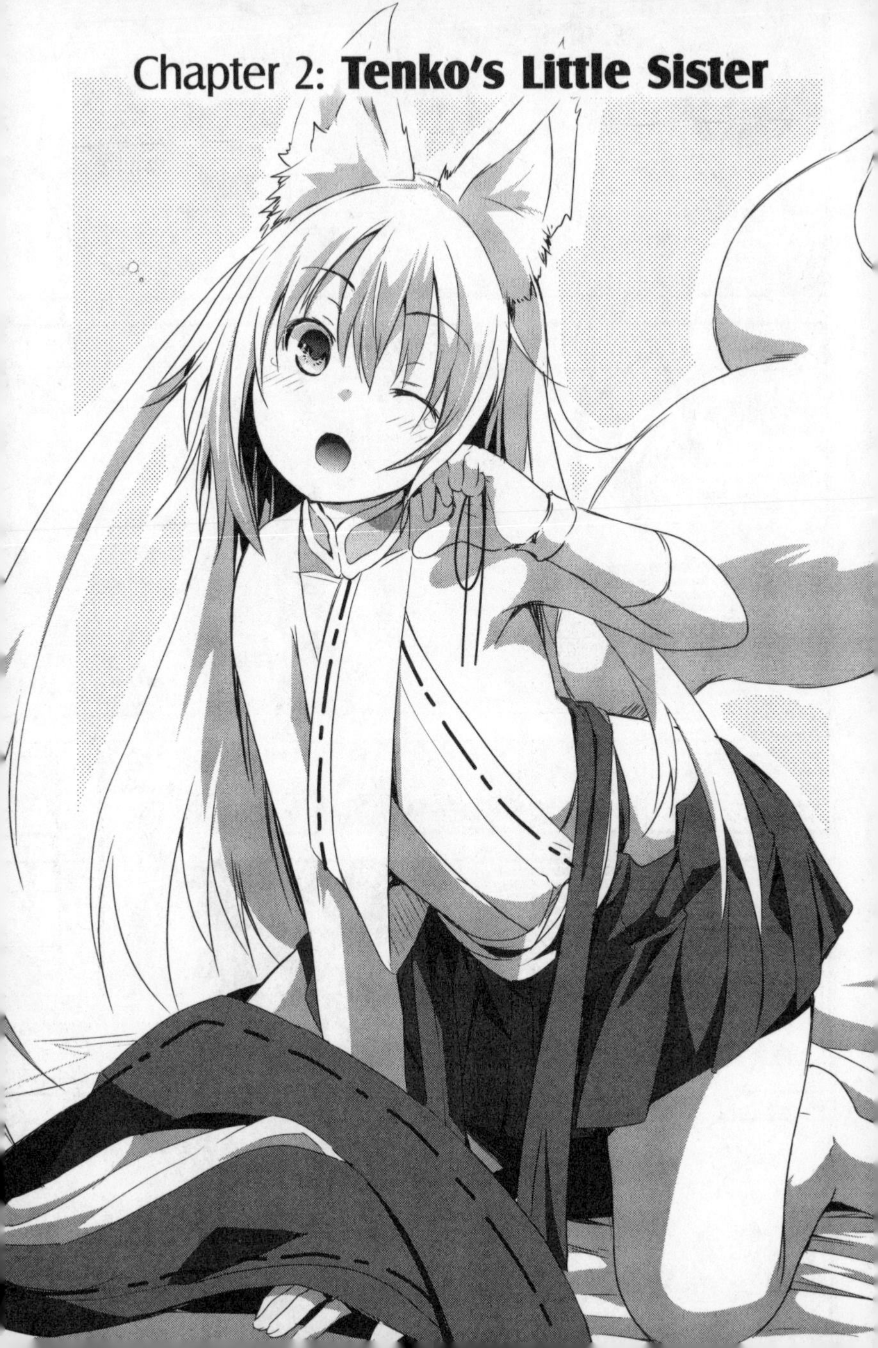

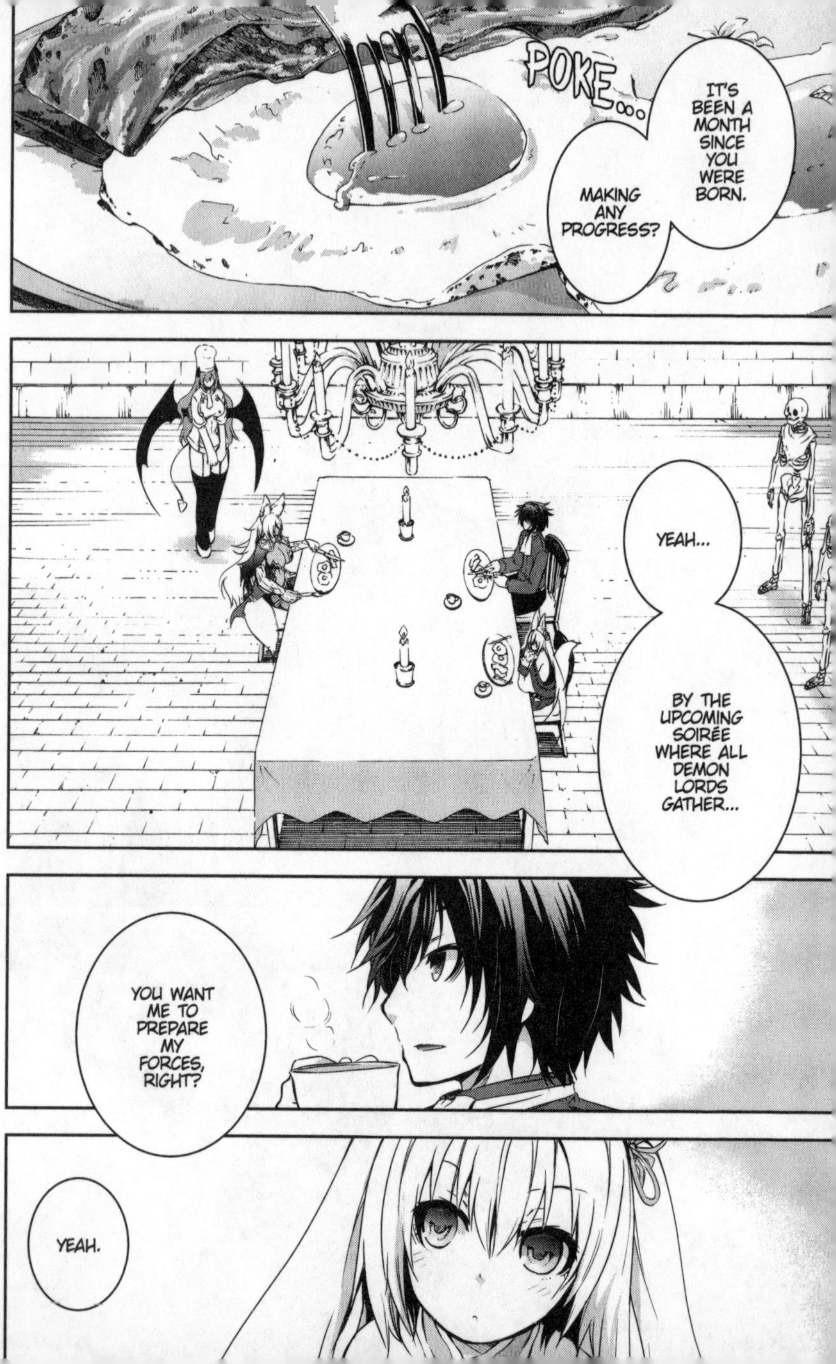
IT'S BEEN A MONTH SINCE YOU WERE BORN.
POKE...
MAKING ANY PROGRESS?
YEAH...
BY THE UPCOMING SOIRÉE WHERE ALL DEMON LORDS GATHER...
YOU WANT ME TO PREPARE MY FORCES, RIGHT?
YEAH.

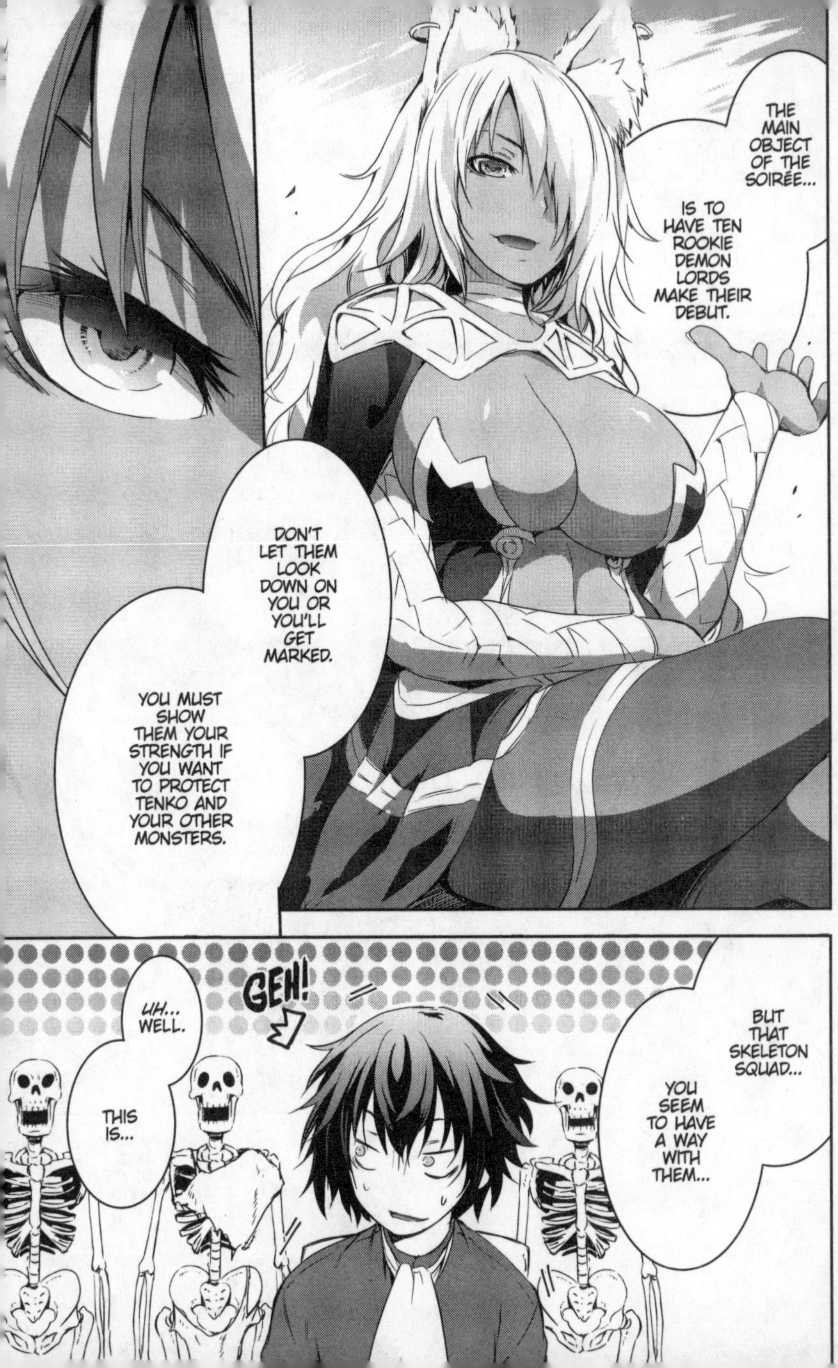
THE MAIN OBJECT OF THE SOIRÉE...
IS TO HAVE TEN ROOKIE DEMON LORDS MAKE THEIR DEBUT.
DON'T LET THEM LOOK DOWN ON YOU OR YOU'LL GET MARKED.
YOU MUST SHOW THEM YOUR STRENGTH IF YOU WANT TO PROTECT TENKO AND YOUR OTHER MONSTERS.
BUT THAT SKELETON SQUAD...
YOU SEEM TO HAVE A WAY WITH THEM...
GEH!
UH... WELL.
THIS IS...

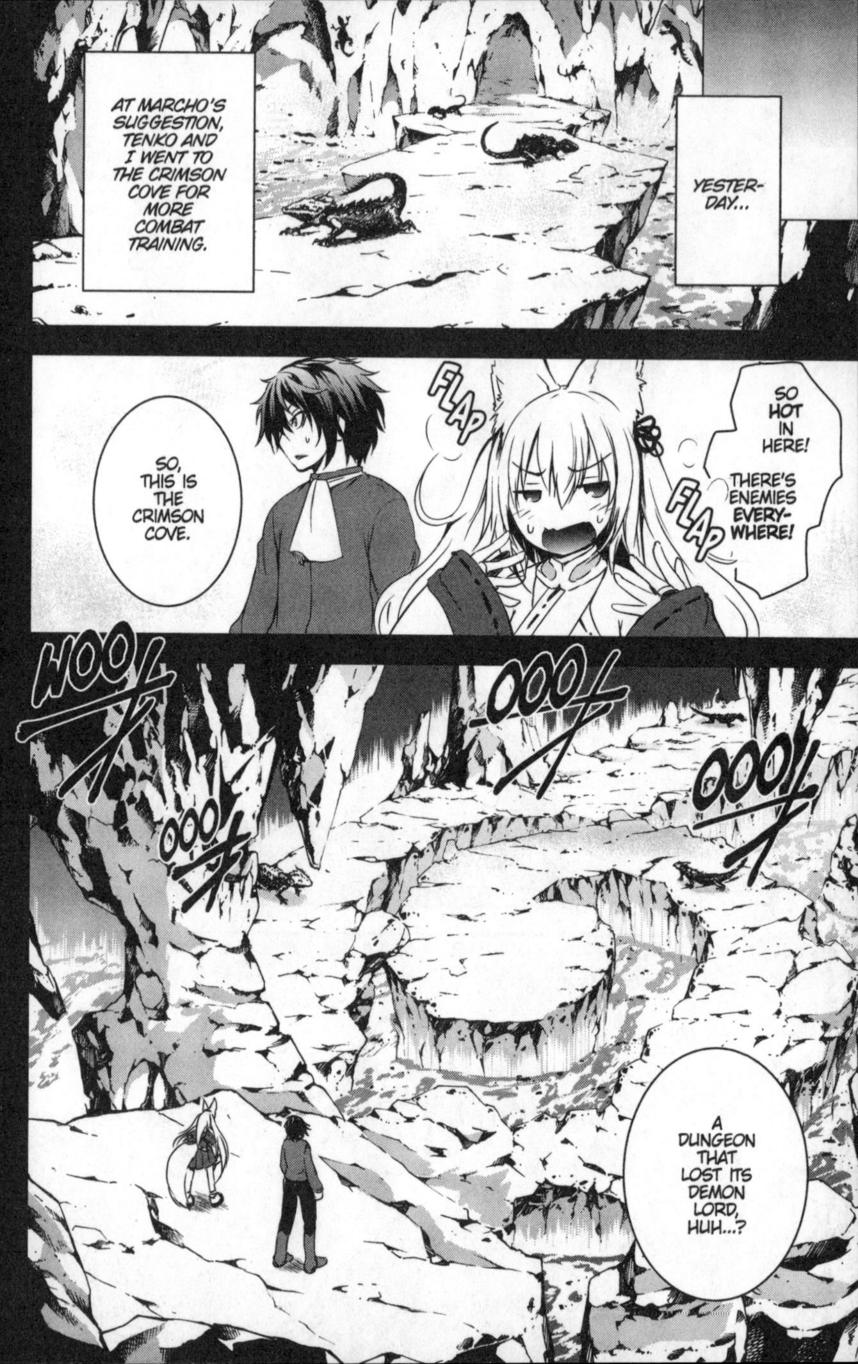
YESTER-DAY...
AT MARCHO'S SUGGESTION, TENKO AND I WENT TO THE CRIMSON COVE FOR MORE COMBAT TRAINING.
SO HOT IN HERE!
THERE'S ENEMIES EVERY-WHERE!
FLAP
FLAP
SO, THIS IS THE CRIMSON COVE.
-OOO
OOO
WOO
OOO
A DUNGEON THAT LOST ITS DEMON LORD, HUH...?

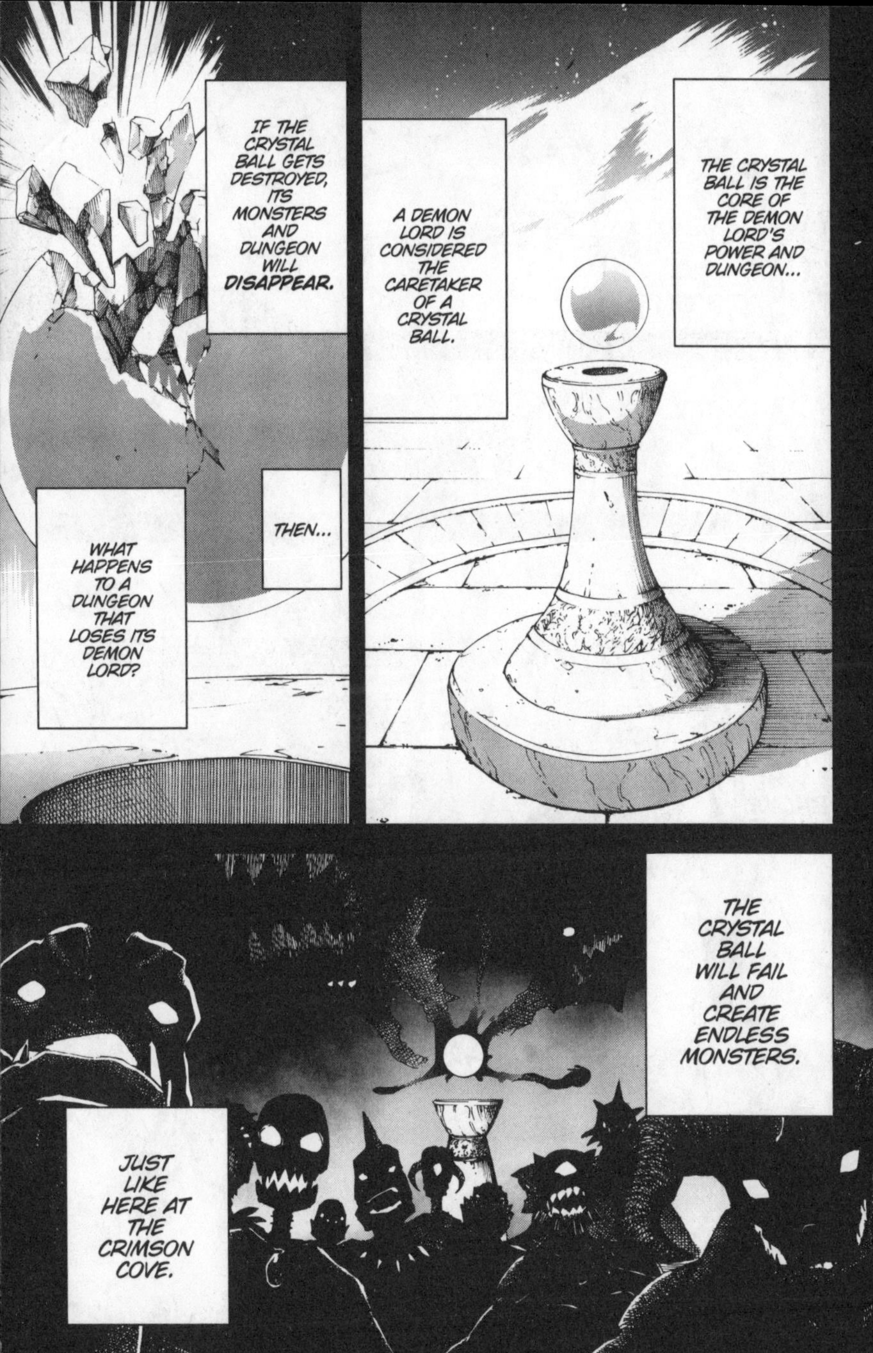
THE CRYSTAL BALL IS THE CORE OF THE DEMON LORD'S POWER AND DUNGEON...
A DEMON LORD IS CONSIDERED THE CARETAKER OF A CRYSTAL BALL.
IF THE CRYSTAL BALL GETS DESTROYED, ITS MONSTERS AND DUNGEON WILL DISAPPEAR.
THEN...
WHAT HAPPENS TO A DUNGEON THAT LOSES ITS DEMON LORD?
THE CRYSTAL BALL WILL FAIL AND CREATE ENDLESS MONSTERS.
JUST LIKE HERE AT THE CRIMSON COVE.

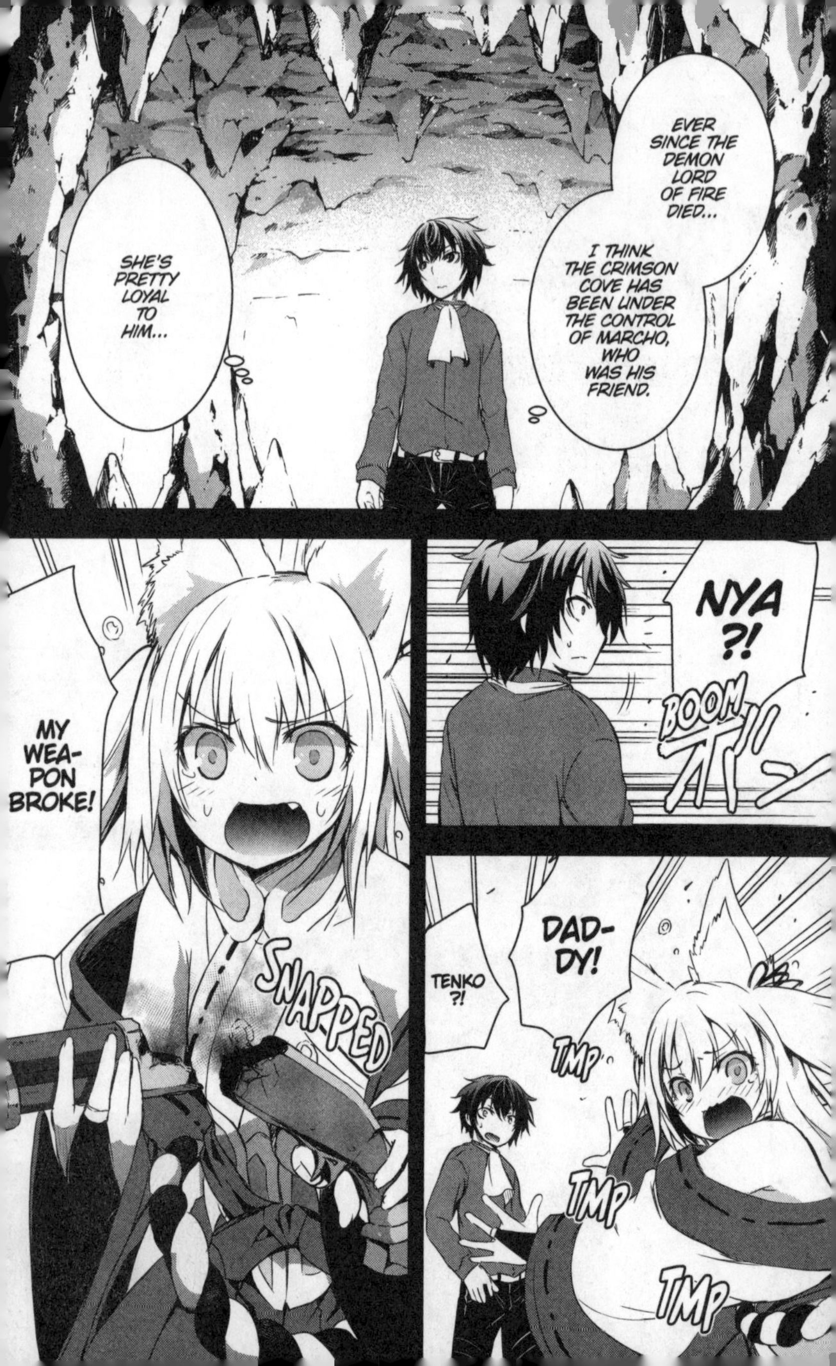
EVER SINCE THE DEMON LORD OF FIRE DIED...
I THINK THE CRIMSON COVE HAS BEEN UNDER THE CONTROL OF MARCHO, WHO WAS HIS FRIEND.
SHE'S PRETTY LOYAL TO HIM...
NYA ?!
BOOM
DAD-DY!
TENKO ?!
TMP
TMP
TMP
MY WEA-PON BROKE!
SNAPPED

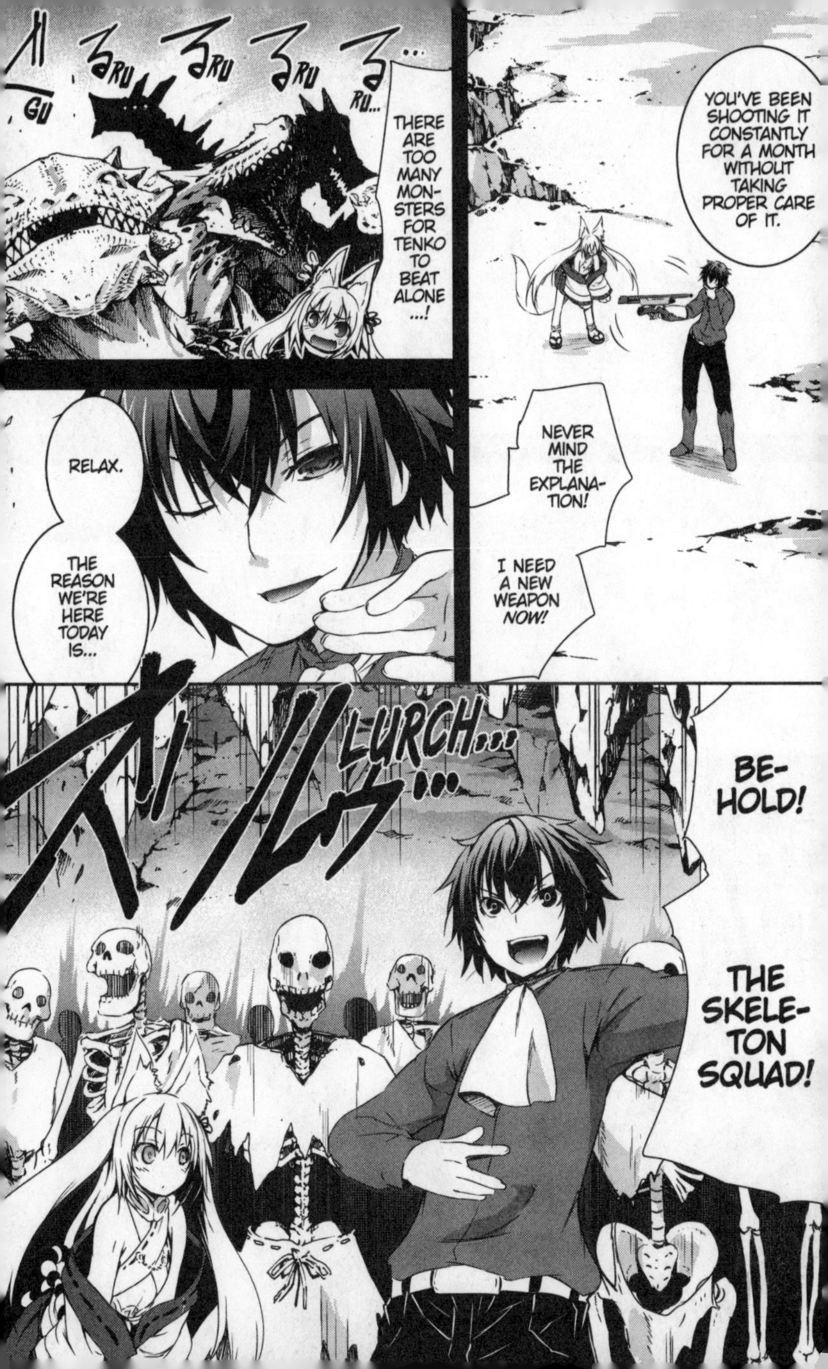
YOU'VE BEEN SHOOTING IT CONSTANTLY FOR A MONTH WITHOUT TAKING PROPER CARE OF IT.
NEVER MIND THE EXPLANATION!
I NEED A NEW WEAPON NOW!
GU
RU RU RU RU...
THERE ARE TOO MANY MON-STERS FOR TENKO TO BEAT ALONE ...!
RELAX.
THE REASON WE'RE HERE TODAY IS...
BE-HOLD!
THE SKELE-TON SQUAD!
LURCH...

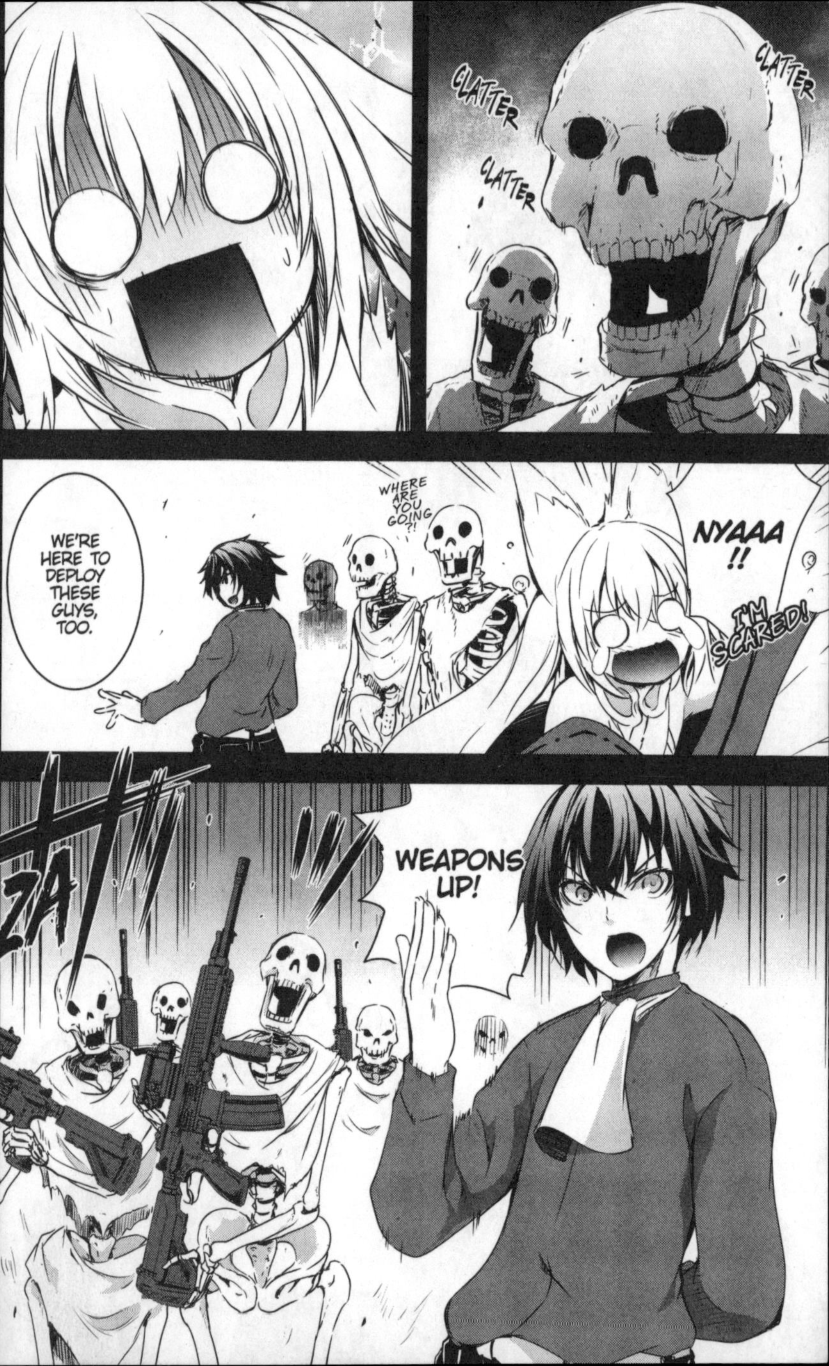
CLATTER
CLATTER
CLATTER
NYAAA!!
I'M SCARED!
WHERE ARE YOU GOING?!
WE'RE HERE TO DEPLOY THESE GUYS, TOO.
WEAPONS UP!
ZA

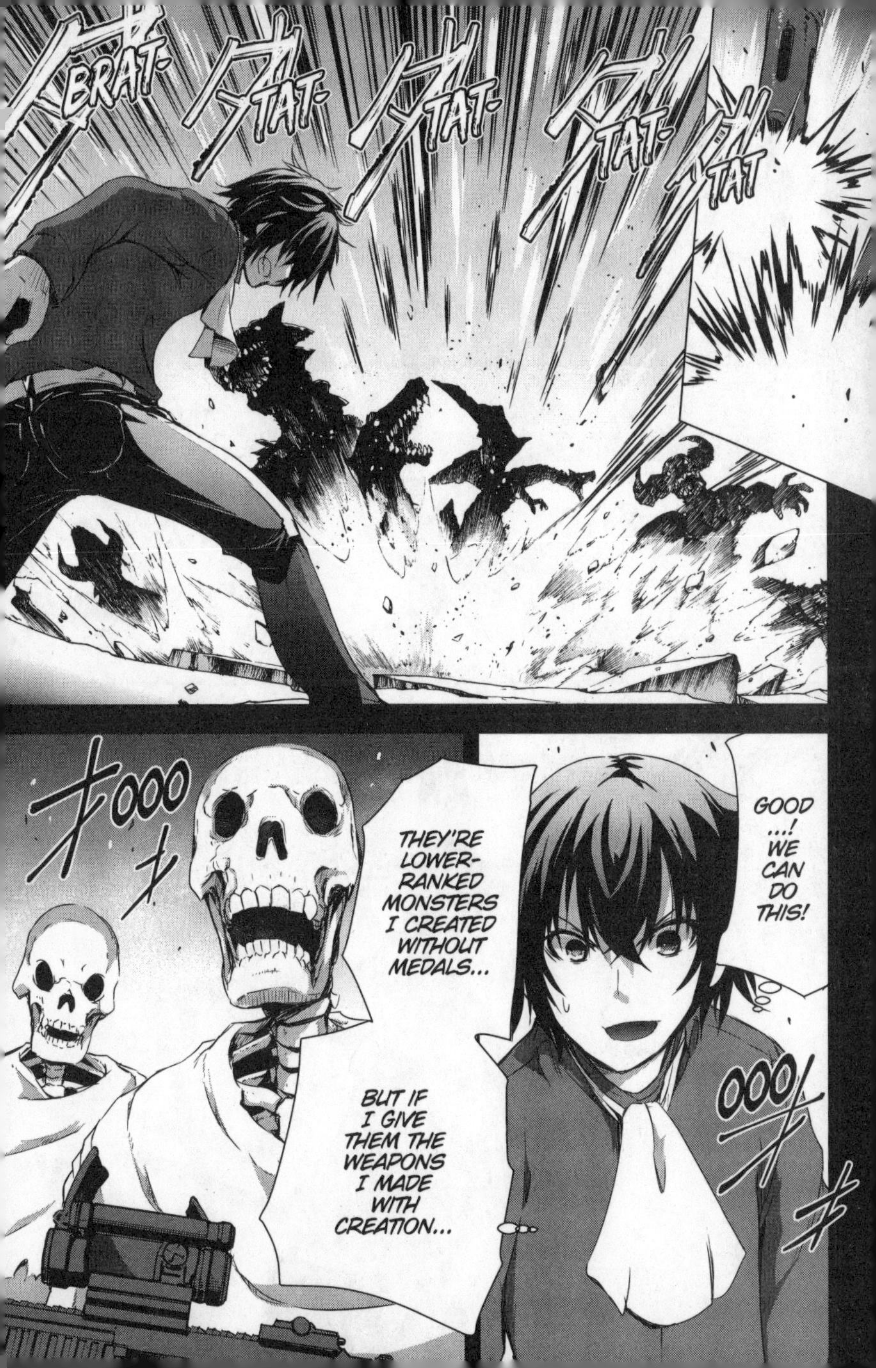
BRAT- TAT- TAT- TAT- TAT
GOOD ...! WE CAN DO THIS!
OOO
OOO
THEY'RE LOWER-RANKED MONSTERS I CREATED WITHOUT MEDALS...
BUT IF I GIVE THEM THE WEAPONS I MADE WITH CREATION...

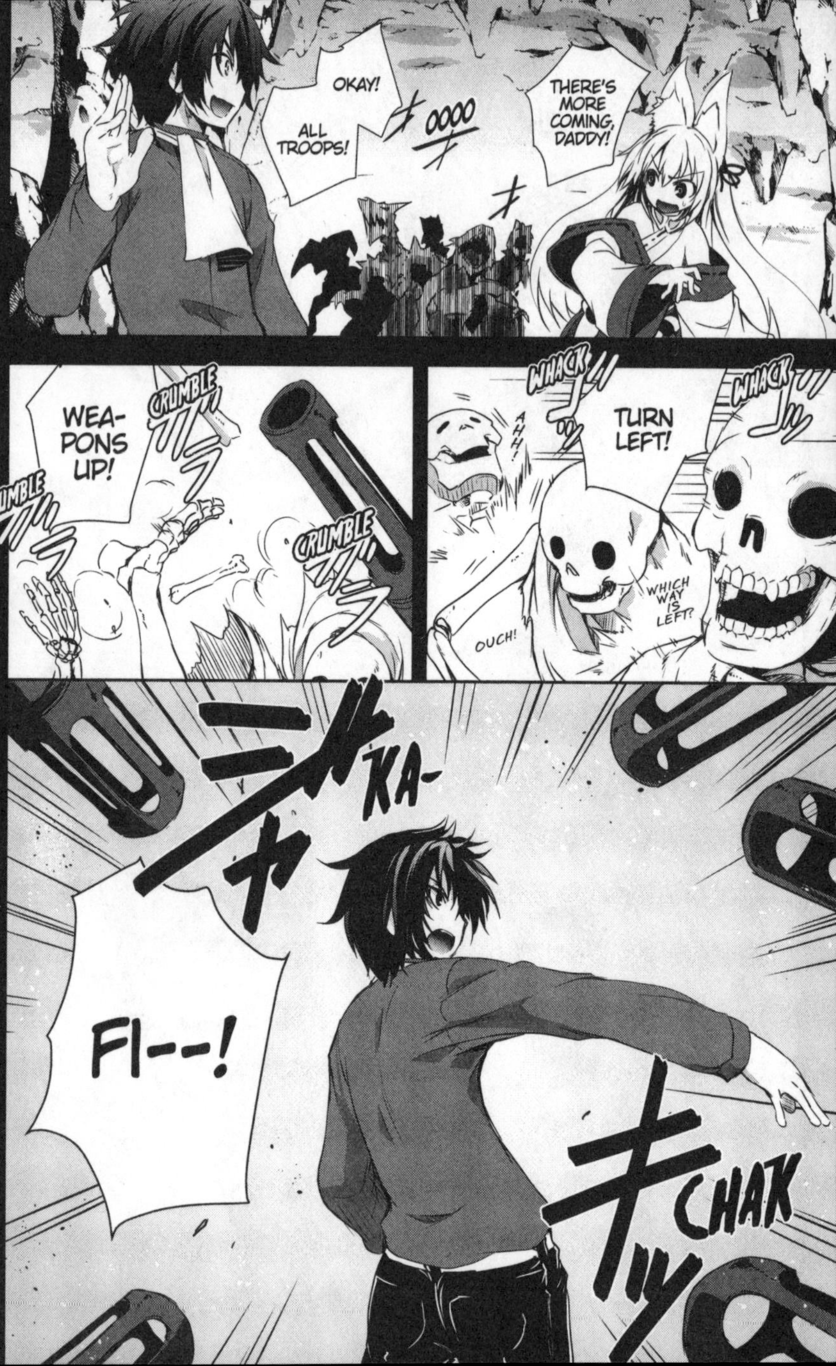
THERE'S MORE COMING, DADDY!
OKAY!
ALL TROOPS!
OOOO
WHACK
AHH!
TURN LEFT!
WHACK
WHICH WAY IS LEFT?
OUCH!
WEA-PONS UP!
CRUMBLE
CRUMBLE
CRUMBLE
KA-
FI--!
CHAK

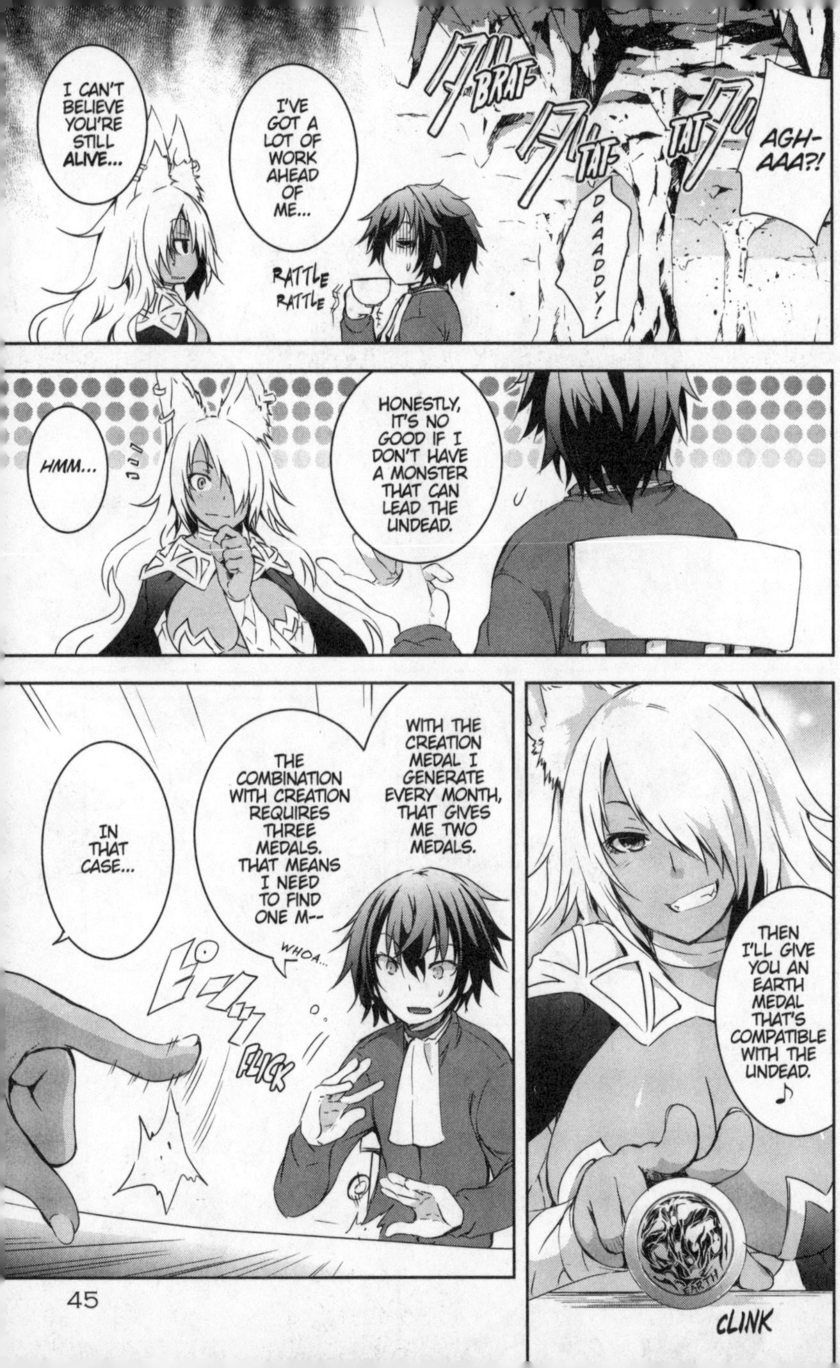
AGH-AAA?!
TAT
DAAAADDY!
TAT
BRAT
I'VE GOT A LOT OF WORK AHEAD OF ME...
RATTLE RATTLE
I CAN'T BELIEVE YOU'RE STILL ALIVE...
HONESTLY, IT'S NO GOOD IF I DON'T HAVE A MONSTER THAT CAN LEAD THE UNDEAD.
HMM...
THEN I'LL GIVE YOU AN EARTH MEDAL THAT'S COMPATIBLE WITH THE UNDEAD. ♪
EARTH
CLINK
WITH THE CREATION MEDAL I GENERATE EVERY MONTH, THAT GIVES ME TWO MEDALS.
THE COMBINATION WITH CREATION REQUIRES THREE MEDALS. THAT MEANS I NEED TO FIND ONE M--
IN THAT CASE...
WHOA...
FLICK

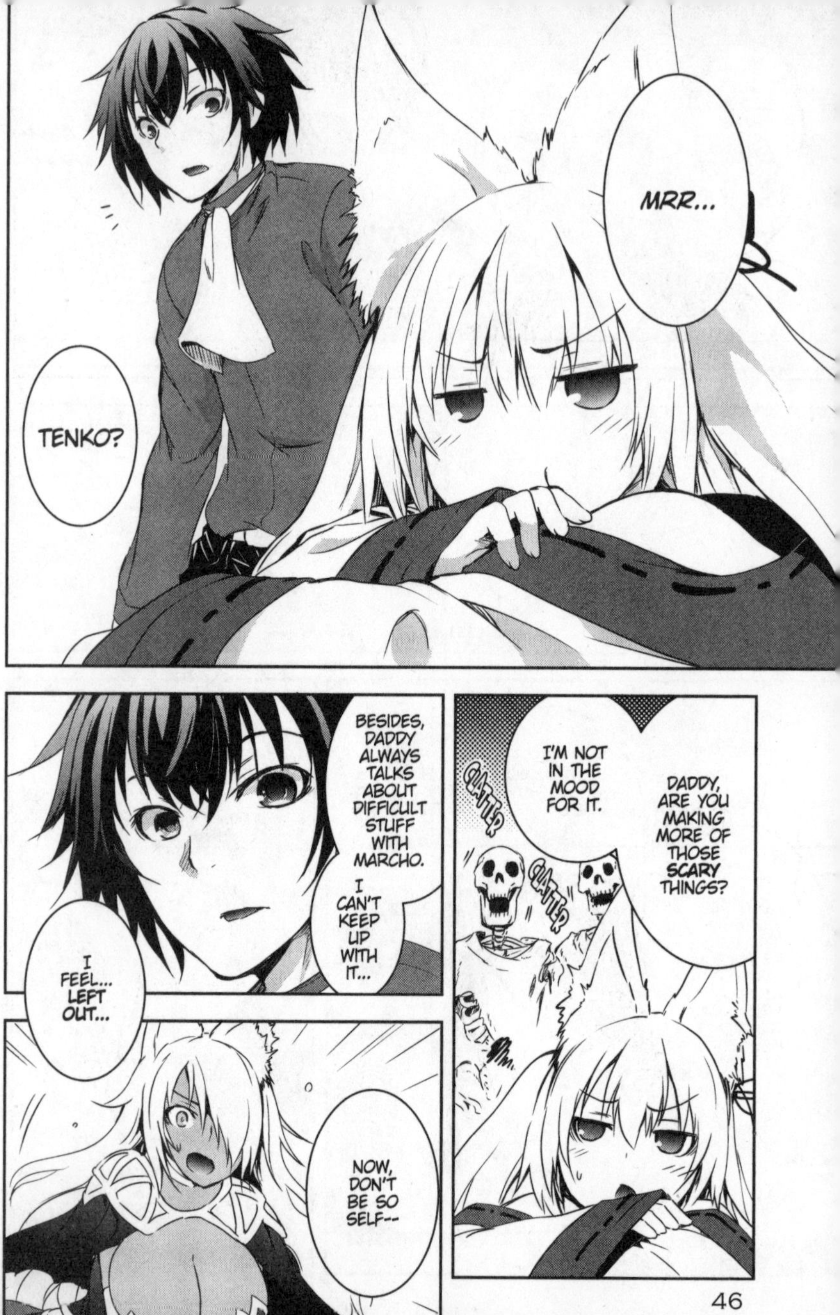
MRR...
TENKO?
DADDY, ARE YOU MAKING MORE OF THOSE SCARY THINGS?
I'M NOT IN THE MOOD FOR IT.
CLATTER
CLATTER
BESIDES, DADDY ALWAYS TALKS ABOUT DIFFICULT STUFF WITH MARCHO.
I CAN'T KEEP UP WITH IT...
I FEEL... LEFT OUT...
NOW, DON'T BE SO SELF--

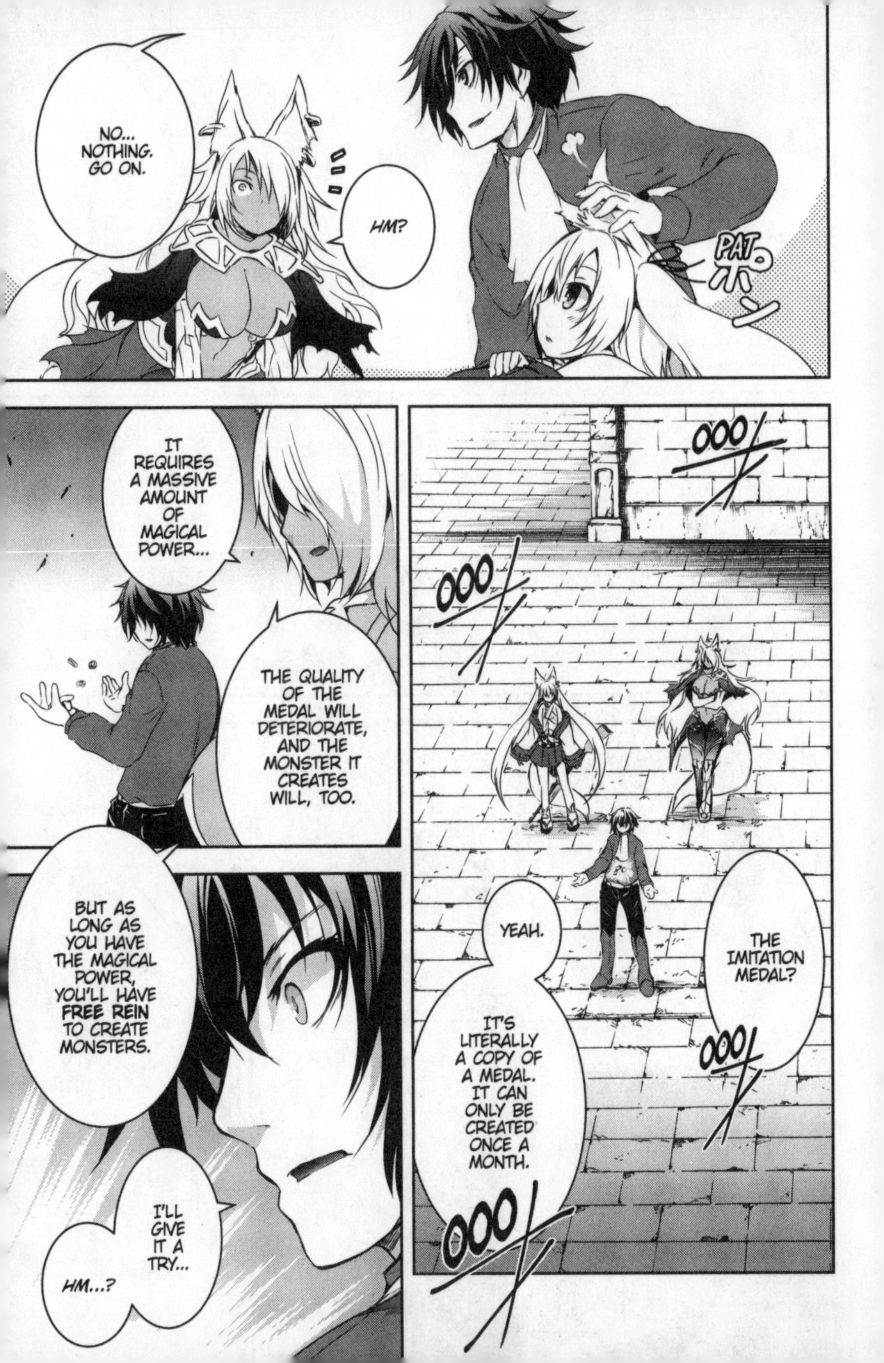
PAT ポン
HM?
NO... NOTHING. GO ON.
OOO
OOO
THE IMITATION MEDAL?
YEAH.
IT'S LITERALLY A COPY OF A MEDAL. IT CAN ONLY BE CREATED ONCE A MONTH.
OOO
OOO
IT REQUIRES A MASSIVE AMOUNT OF MAGICAL POWER...
THE QUALITY OF THE MEDAL WILL DETERIORATE, AND THE MONSTER IT CREATES WILL, TOO.
BUT AS LONG AS YOU HAVE THE MAGICAL POWER, YOU'LL HAVE FREE REIN TO CREATE MONSTERS.
I'LL GIVE IT A TRY...
HM...?

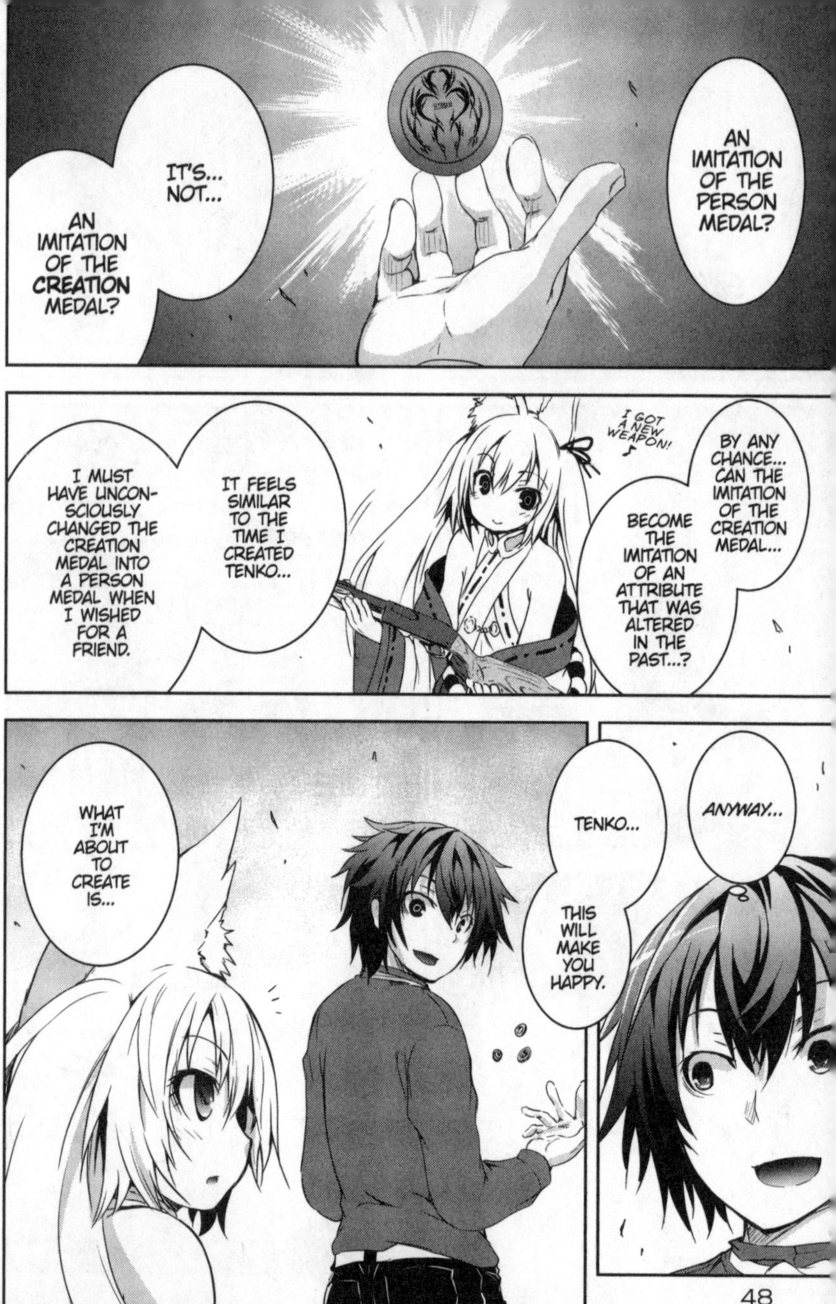
AN IMITATION OF THE PERSON MEDAL?
IT'S... NOT...
AN IMITATION OF THE CREATION MEDAL?
BY ANY CHANCE... CAN THE IMITATION OF THE CREATION MEDAL...
BECOME THE IMITATION OF AN ATTRIBUTE THAT WAS ALTERED IN THE PAST...?
I GOT A NEW WEAPON! ♪
IT FEELS SIMILAR TO THE TIME I CREATED TENKO...
I MUST HAVE UNCONSCIOUSLY CHANGED THE CREATION MEDAL INTO A PERSON MEDAL WHEN I WISHED FOR A FRIEND.
ANYWAY...
TENKO...
THIS WILL MAKE YOU HAPPY.
WHAT I'M ABOUT TO CREATE IS...

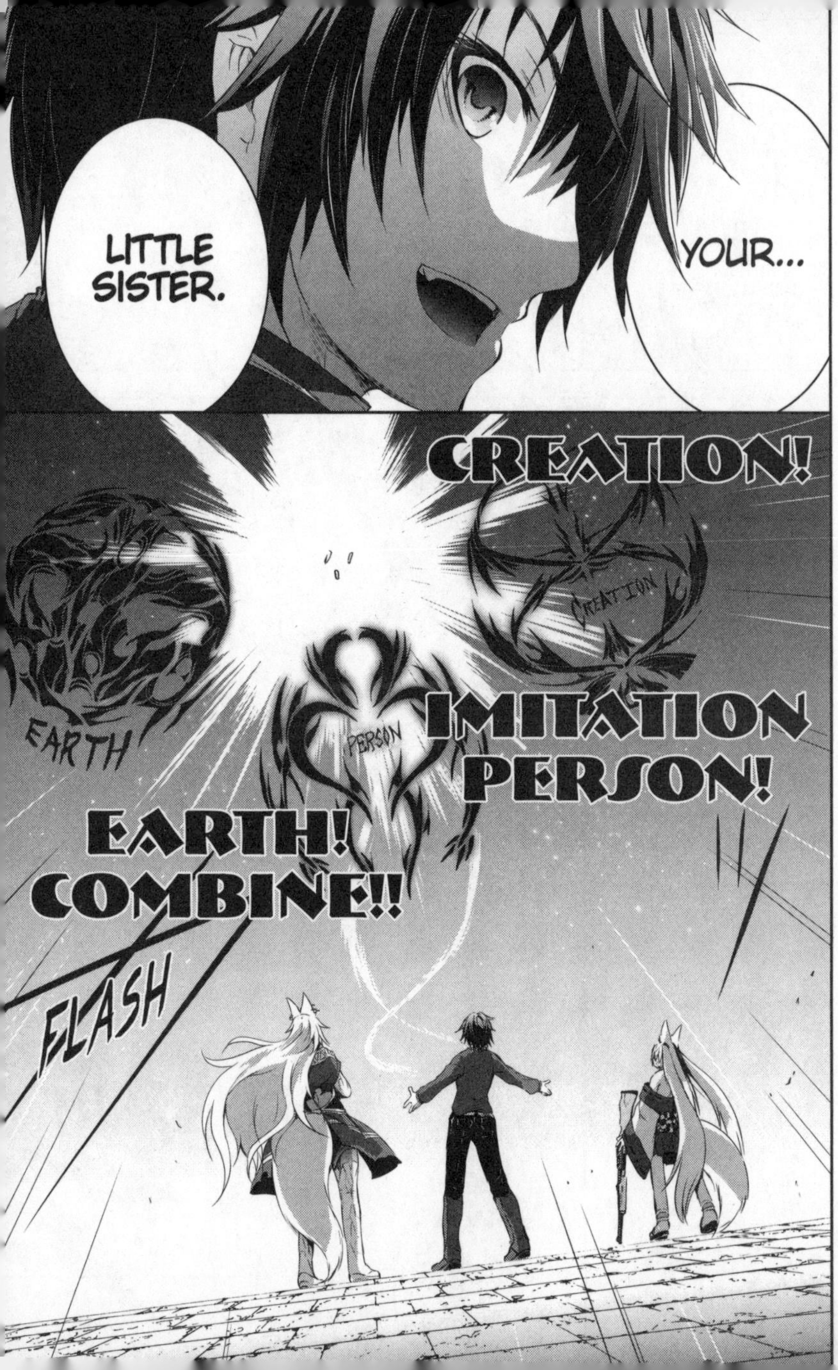
YOUR...
LITTLE SISTER.
CREATION!
CREATION
IMITATION PERSON!
PERSON
EARTH
EARTH! COMBINE!!
FLASH

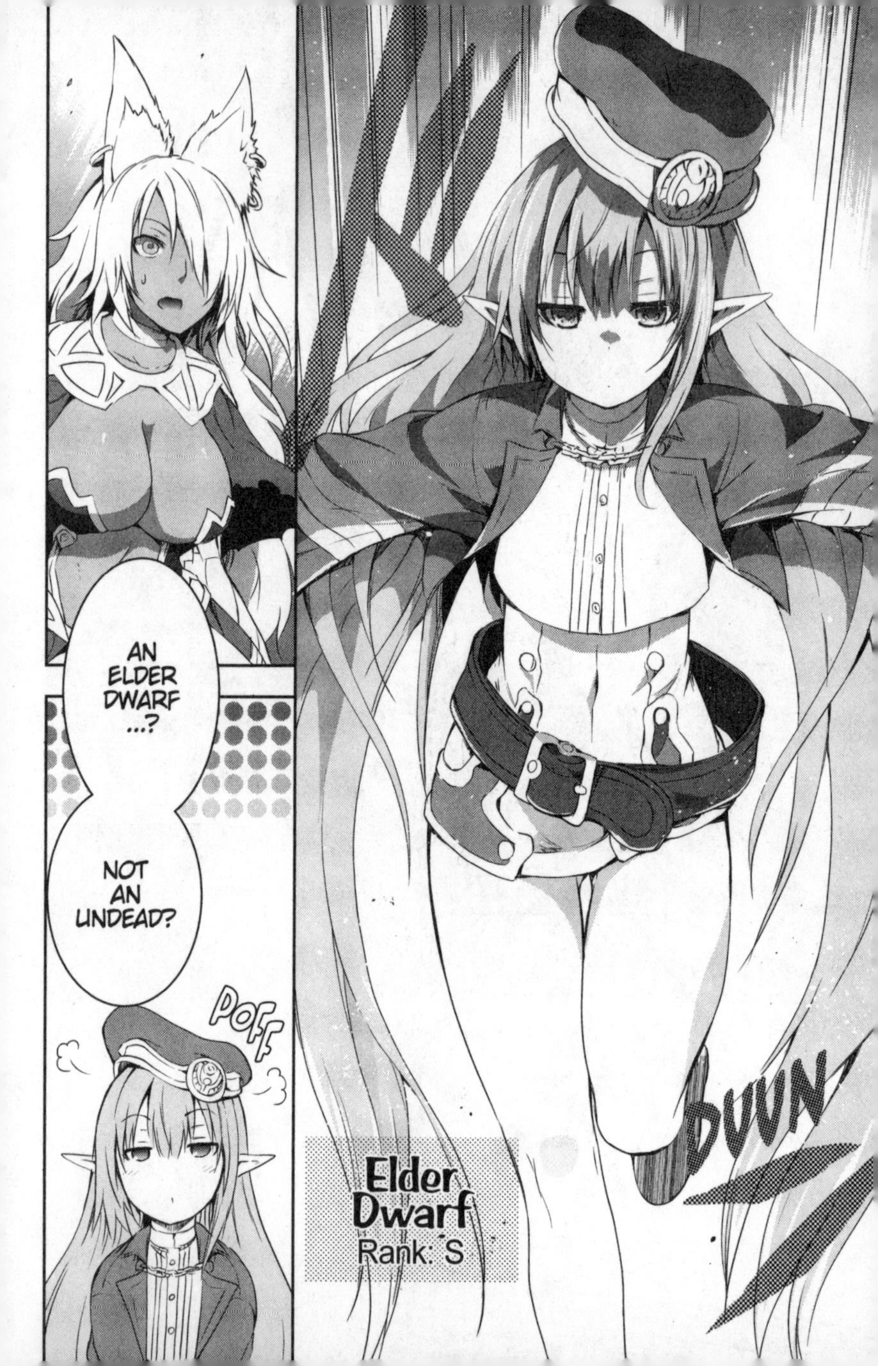
DUUN
Elder Dwarf
Rank: S
AN ELDER DWARF ...?
NOT AN UNDEAD?
POFF

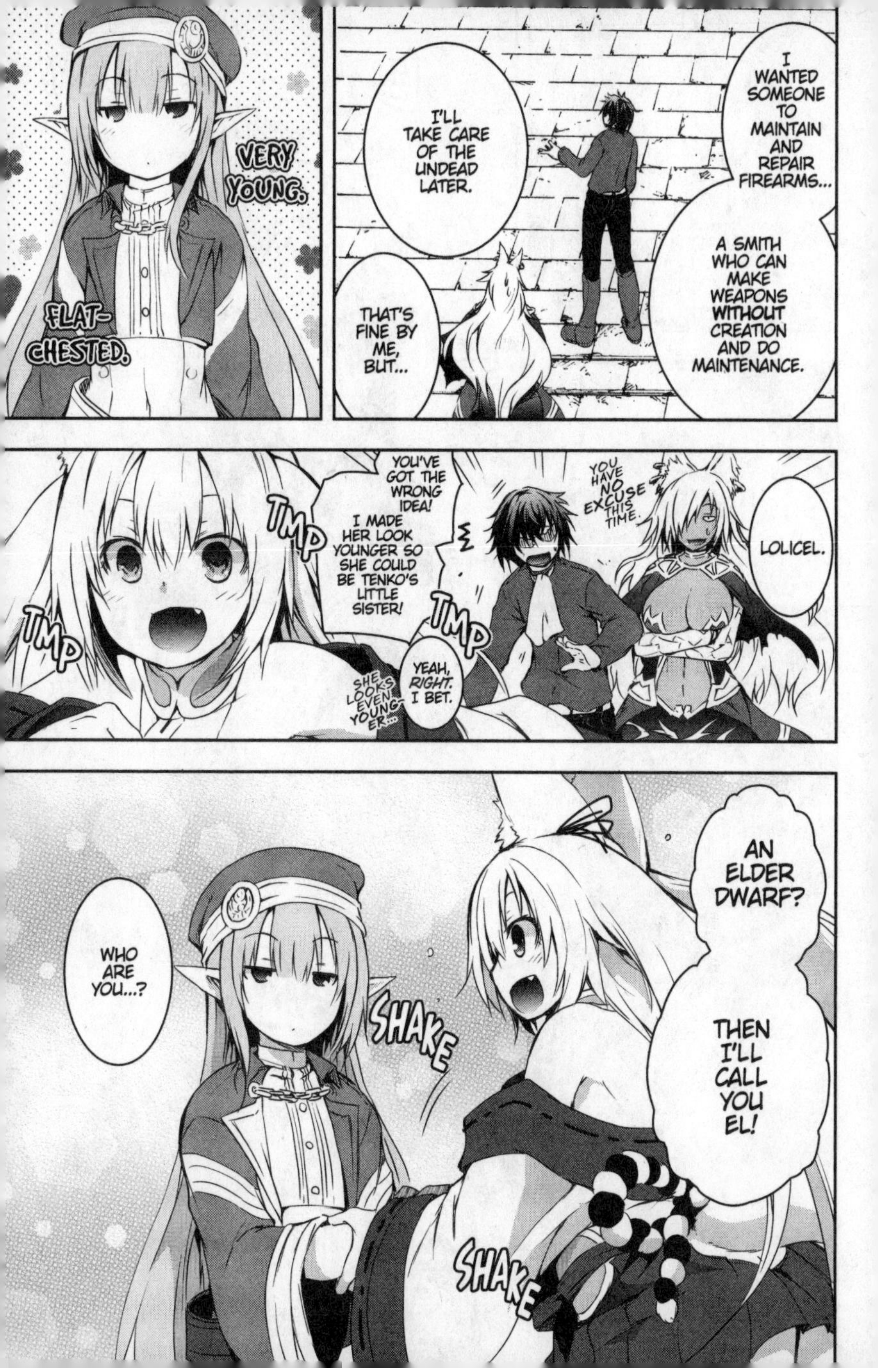
I WANTED SOMEONE TO MAINTAIN AND REPAIR FIREARMS...
A SMITH WHO CAN MAKE WEAPONS WITHOUT CREATION AND DO MAINTENANCE.
I'LL TAKE CARE OF THE UNDEAD LATER.
THAT'S FINE BY ME, BUT...
VERY YOUNG.
FLAT-CHESTED.
LOLICEL.
YOU HAVE NO EXCUSE THIS TIME.
YOU'VE GOT THE WRONG IDEA! I MADE HER LOOK YOUNGER SO SHE COULD BE TENKO'S LITTLE SISTER!
TMP
YEAH, RIGHT. I BET.
SHE LOOKS EVEN YOUNGER...
TMP
TMP
AN ELDER DWARF?
THEN I'LL CALL YOU EL!
SHAKE
WHO ARE YOU...?
SHAKE

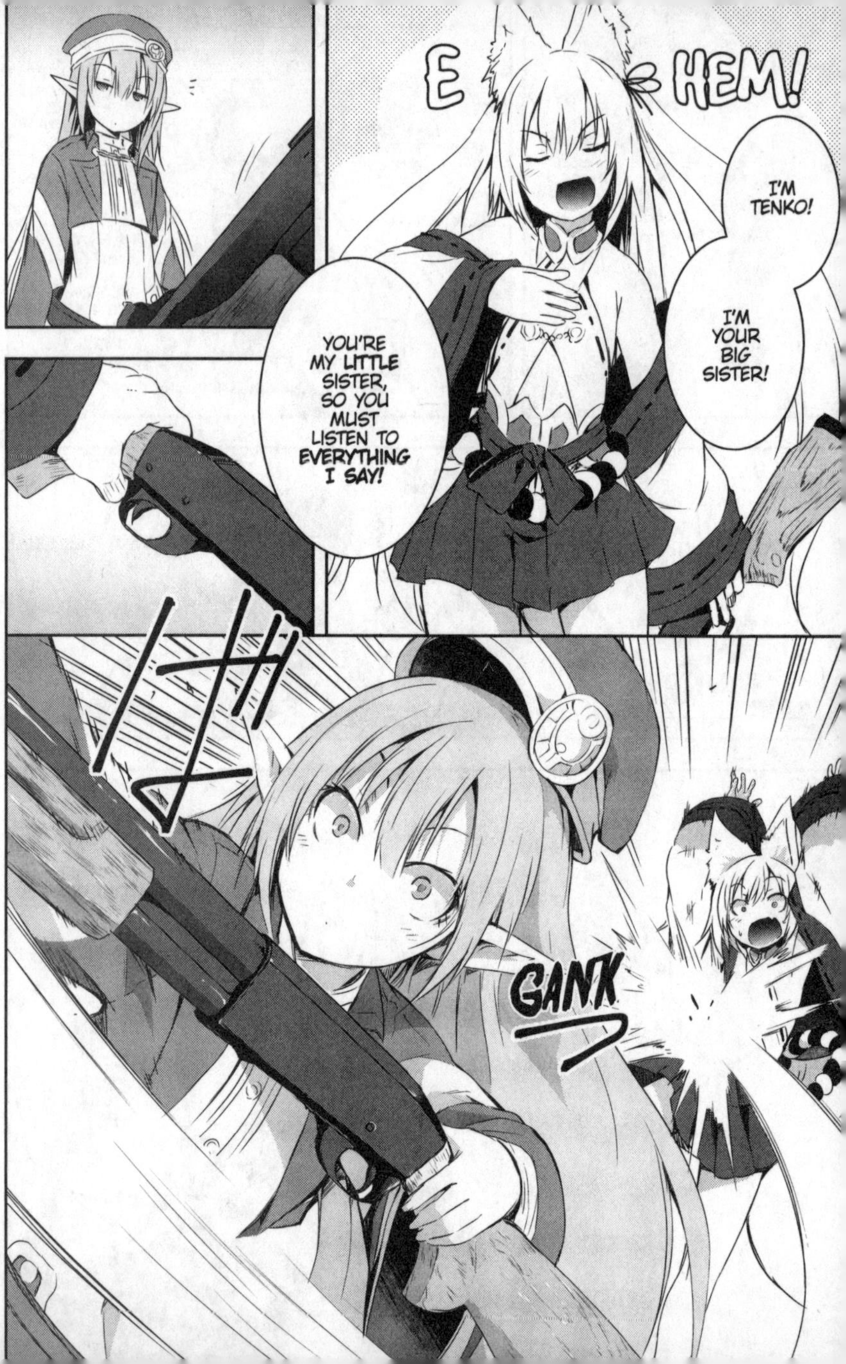

E HEM!
I'M TENKO!
I'M YOUR BIG SISTER!
YOU'RE MY LITTLE SISTER, SO YOU MUST LISTEN TO EVERYTHING I SAY!
...
GANK

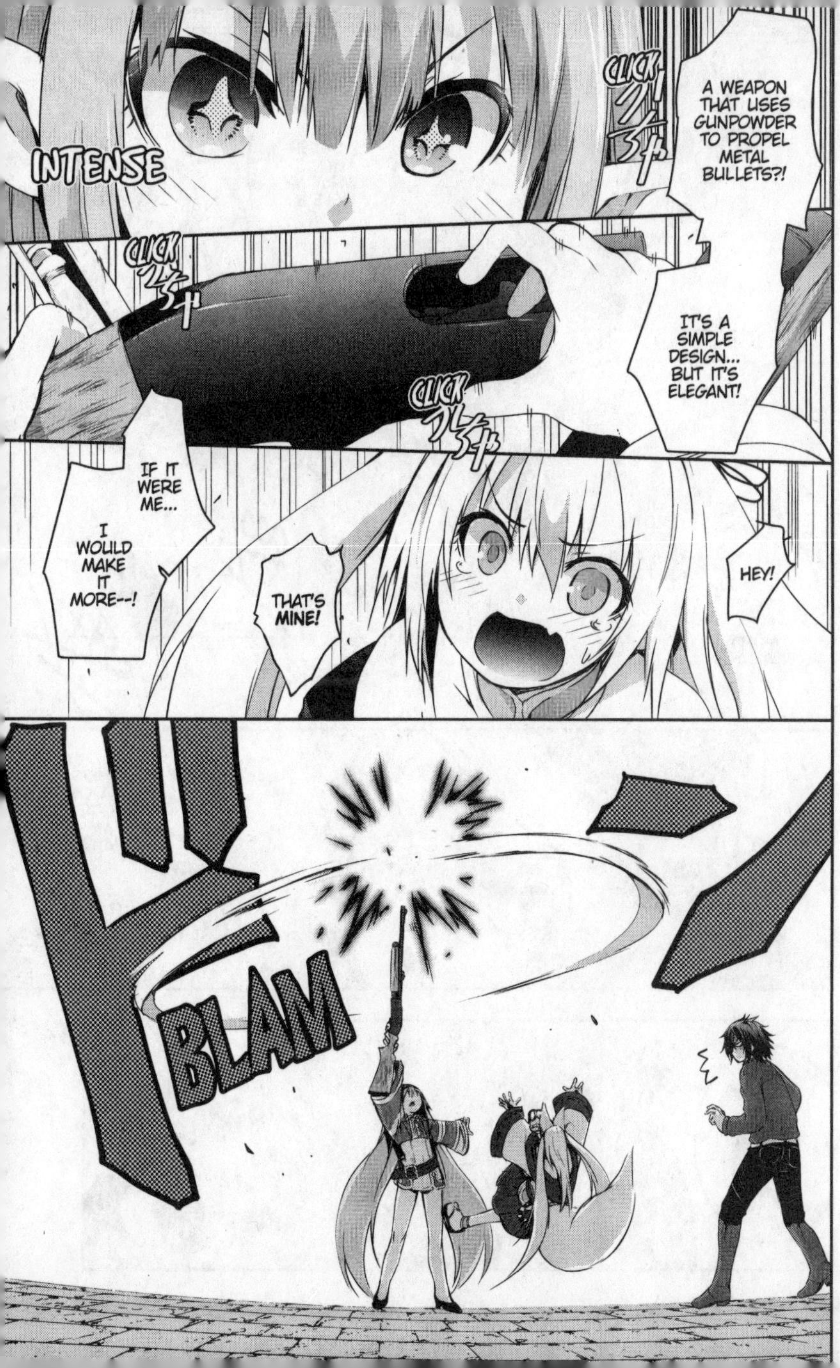
A WEAPON THAT USES GUNPOWDER TO PROPEL METAL BULLETS?!
CLICK
INTENSE
IT'S A SIMPLE DESIGN... BUT IT'S ELEGANT!
CLICK
CLICK
HEY!
THAT'S MINE!
IF IT WERE ME...
I WOULD MAKE IT MORE--!
BLAM

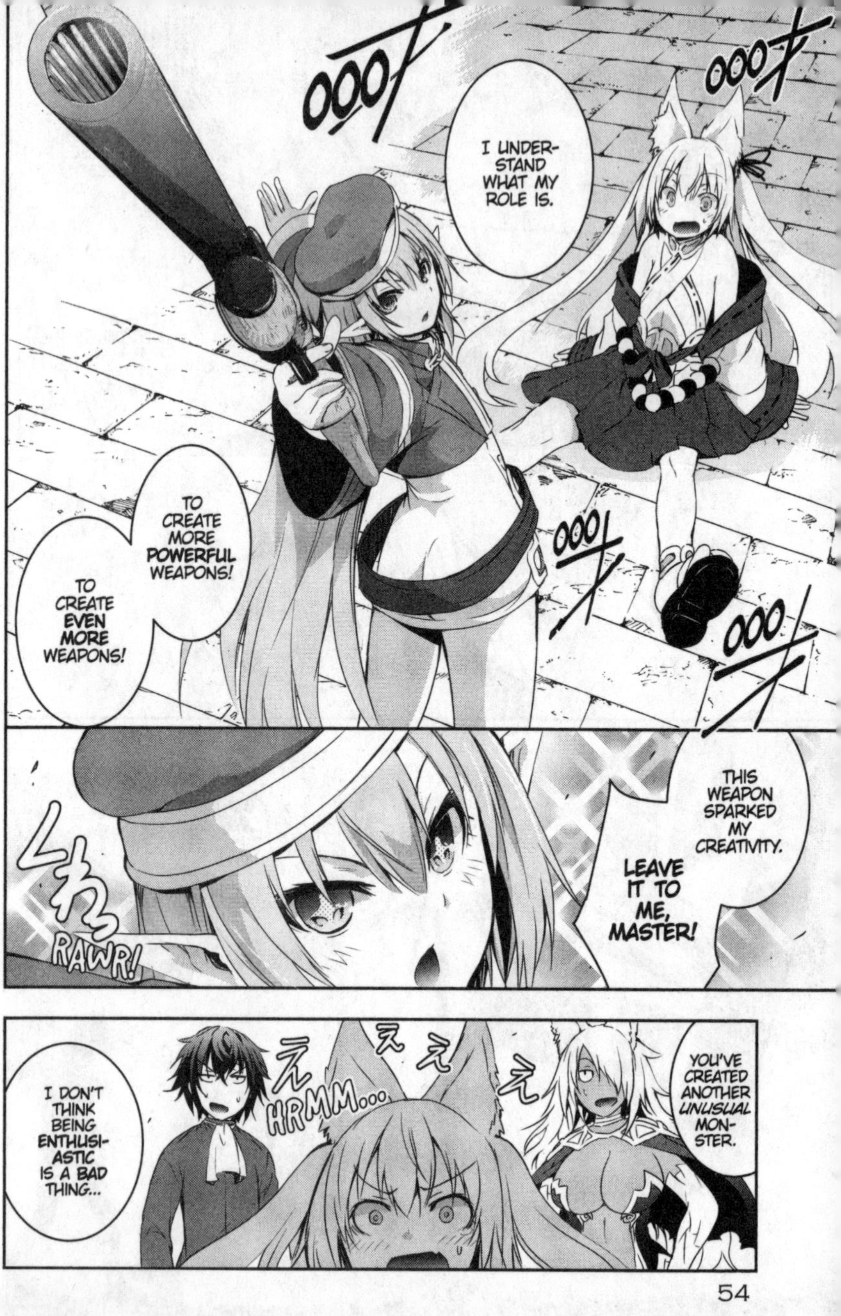
I UNDERSTAND WHAT MY ROLE IS.
TO CREATE MORE POWERFUL WEAPONS!
TO CREATE EVEN MORE WEAPONS!
THIS WEAPON SPARKED MY CREATIVITY.
LEAVE IT TO ME, MASTER!
くわ
RAWR!
YOU'VE CREATED ANOTHER UNUSUAL MONSTER.
ええええ
HRMM...
I DON'T THINK BEING ENTHUSIASTIC IS A BAD THING...

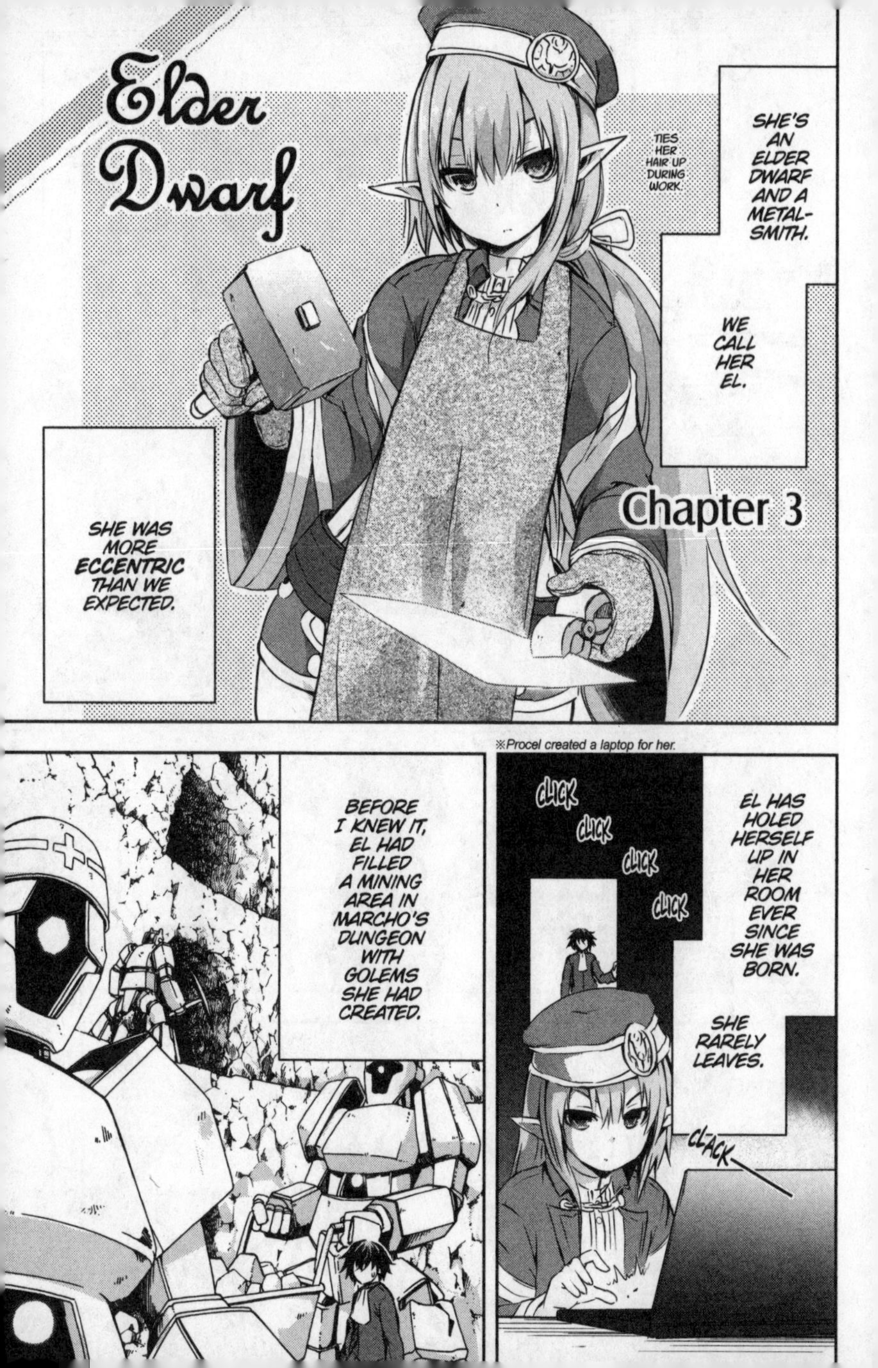
Elder Dwarf
SHE'S AN ELDER DWARF AND A METAL-SMITH.
WE CALL HER EL.
TIES HER HAIR UP DURING WORK.
Chapter 3
SHE WAS MORE ECCENTRIC THAN WE EXPECTED.
※Procel created a laptop for her.
EL HAS HOLED HERSELF UP IN HER ROOM EVER SINCE SHE WAS BORN.
CLICK
CLICK
CLICK
CLICK
SHE RARELY LEAVES.
CLACK
BEFORE I KNEW IT, EL HAD FILLED A MINING AREA IN MARCHO'S DUNGEON WITH GOLEMS SHE HAD CREATED.

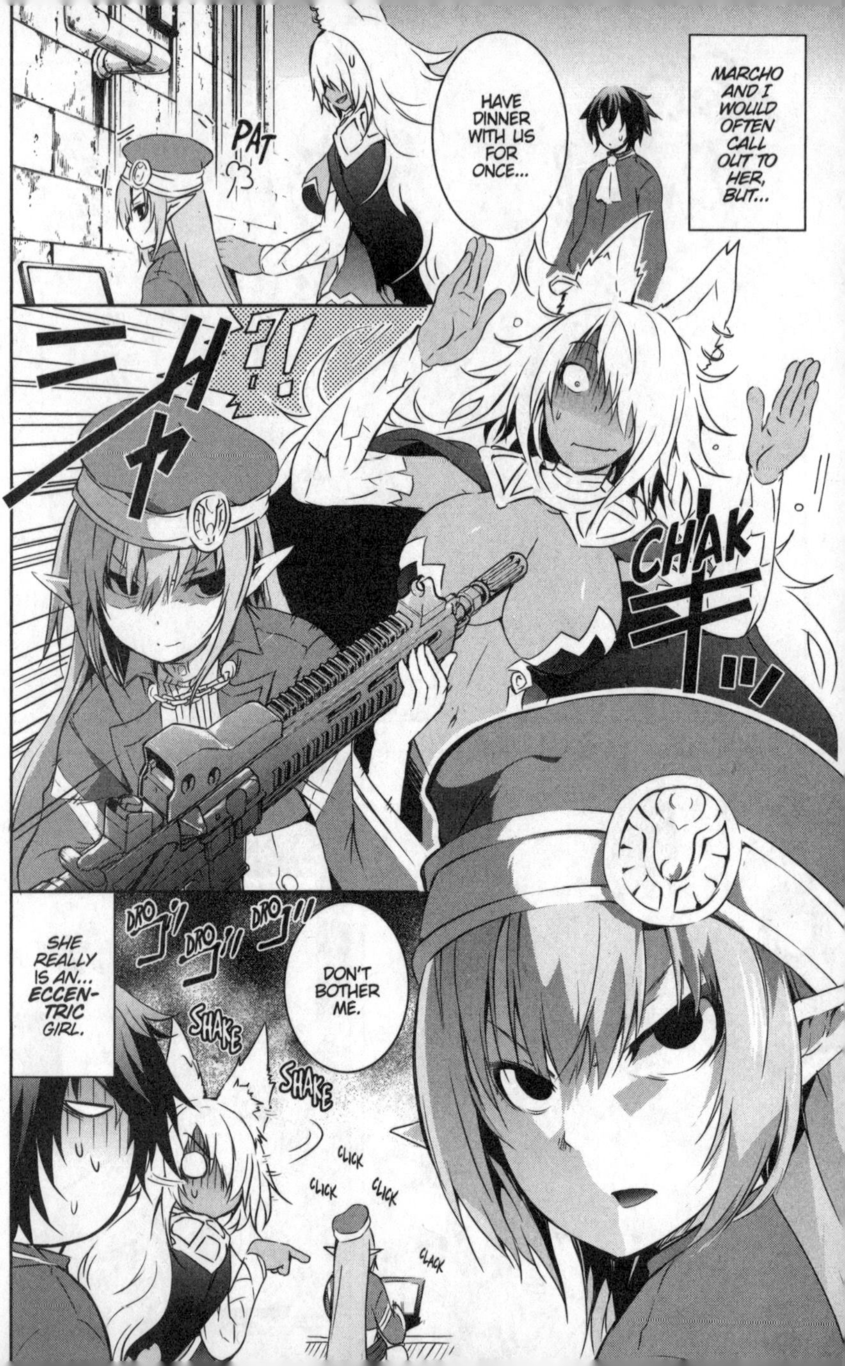
MARCHO AND I WOULD OFTEN CALL OUT TO HER, BUT...
HAVE DINNER WITH US FOR ONCE...
PAT
CHAK
?!
DON'T BOTHER ME.
DRO
DRO
DRO
SHAKE
SHAKE
SHE REALLY IS AN... ECCENTRIC GIRL.
CLICK
CLICK
CLICK
CLACK

Chapter 3:
Contracted Monsters

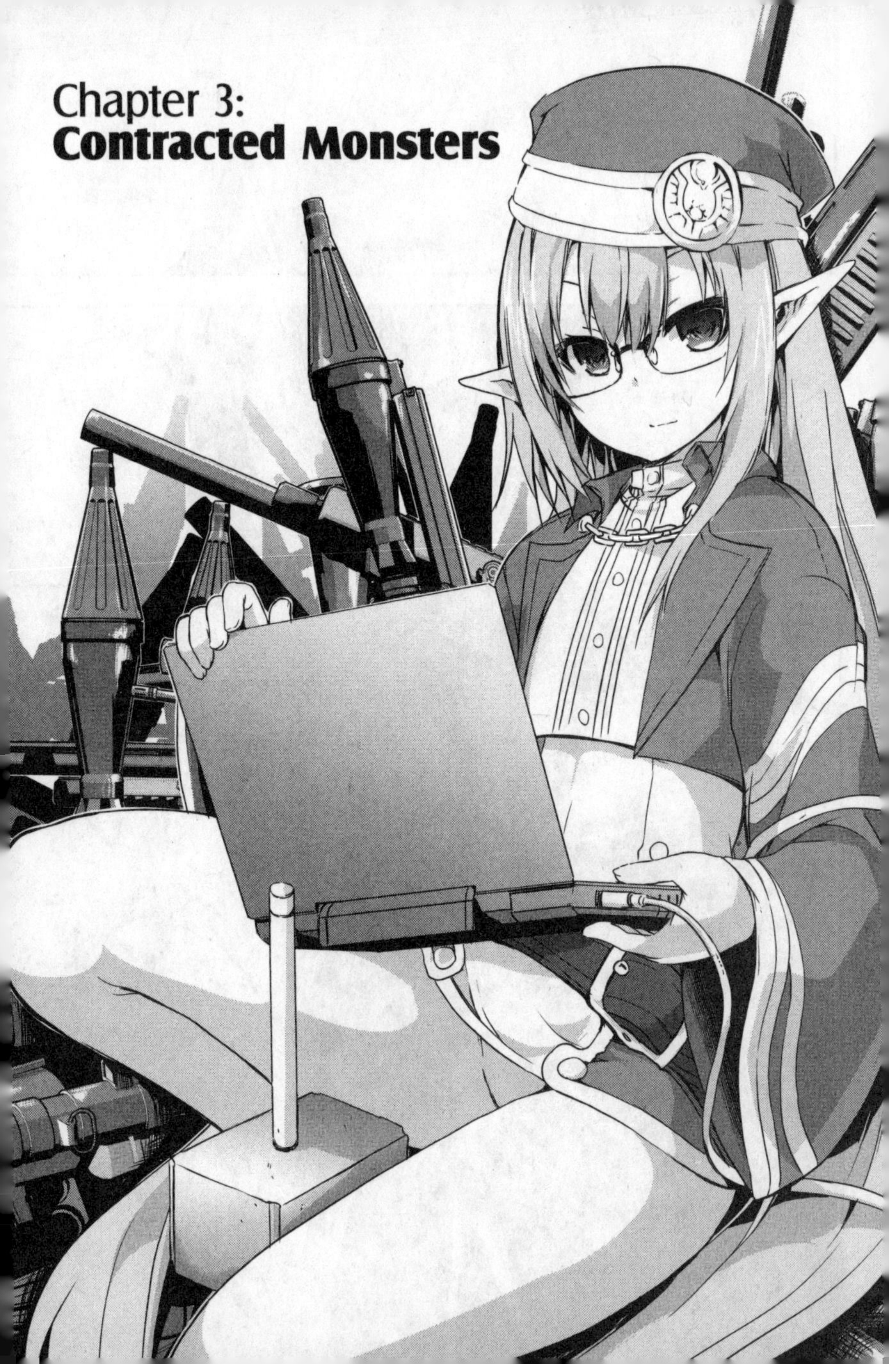

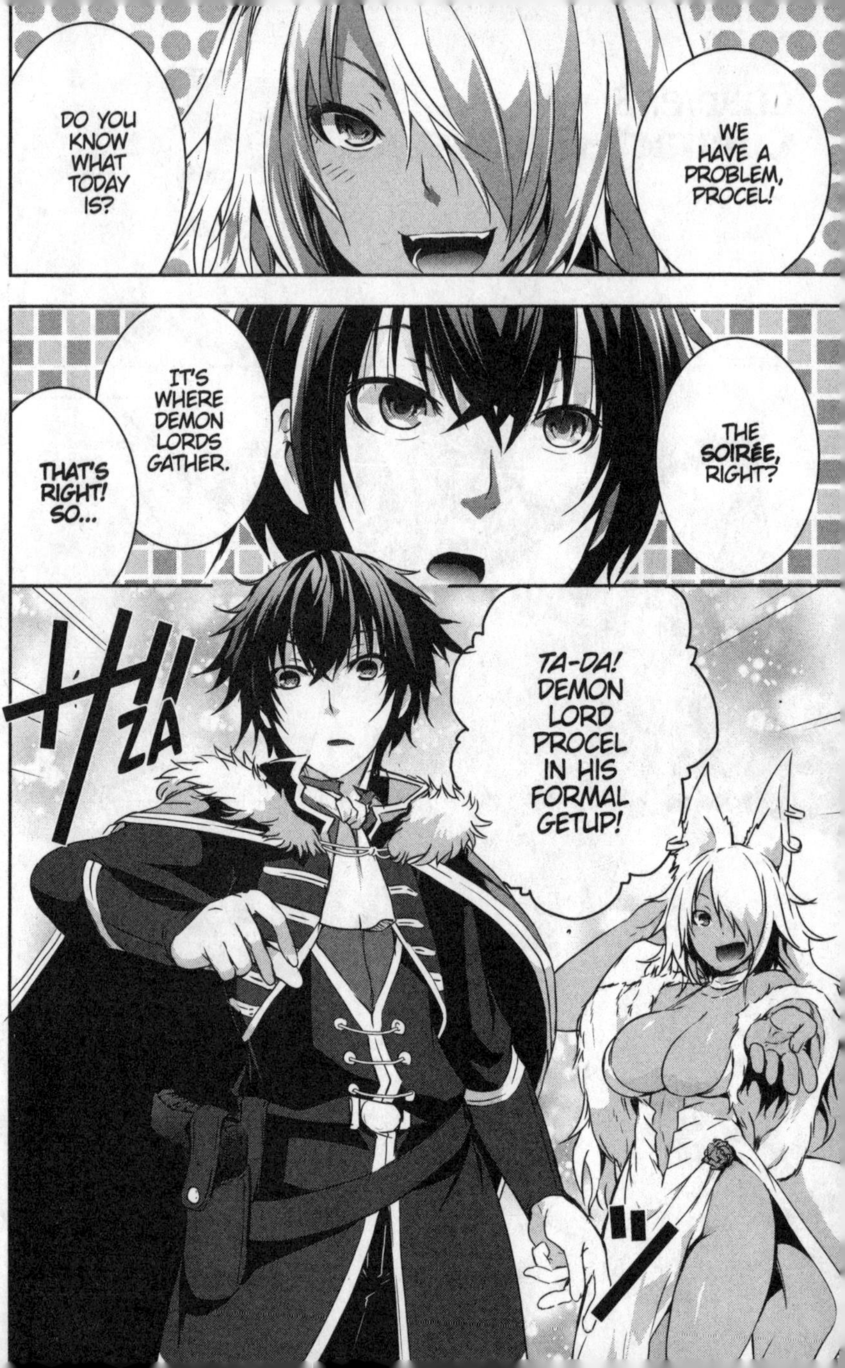
WE HAVE A PROBLEM, PROCEL!
DO YOU KNOW WHAT TODAY IS?
THE SOIRÉE, RIGHT?
IT'S WHERE DEMON LORDS GATHER.
THAT'S RIGHT! SO...
TA-DA! DEMON LORD PROCEL IN HIS FORMAL GETUP!
ZA

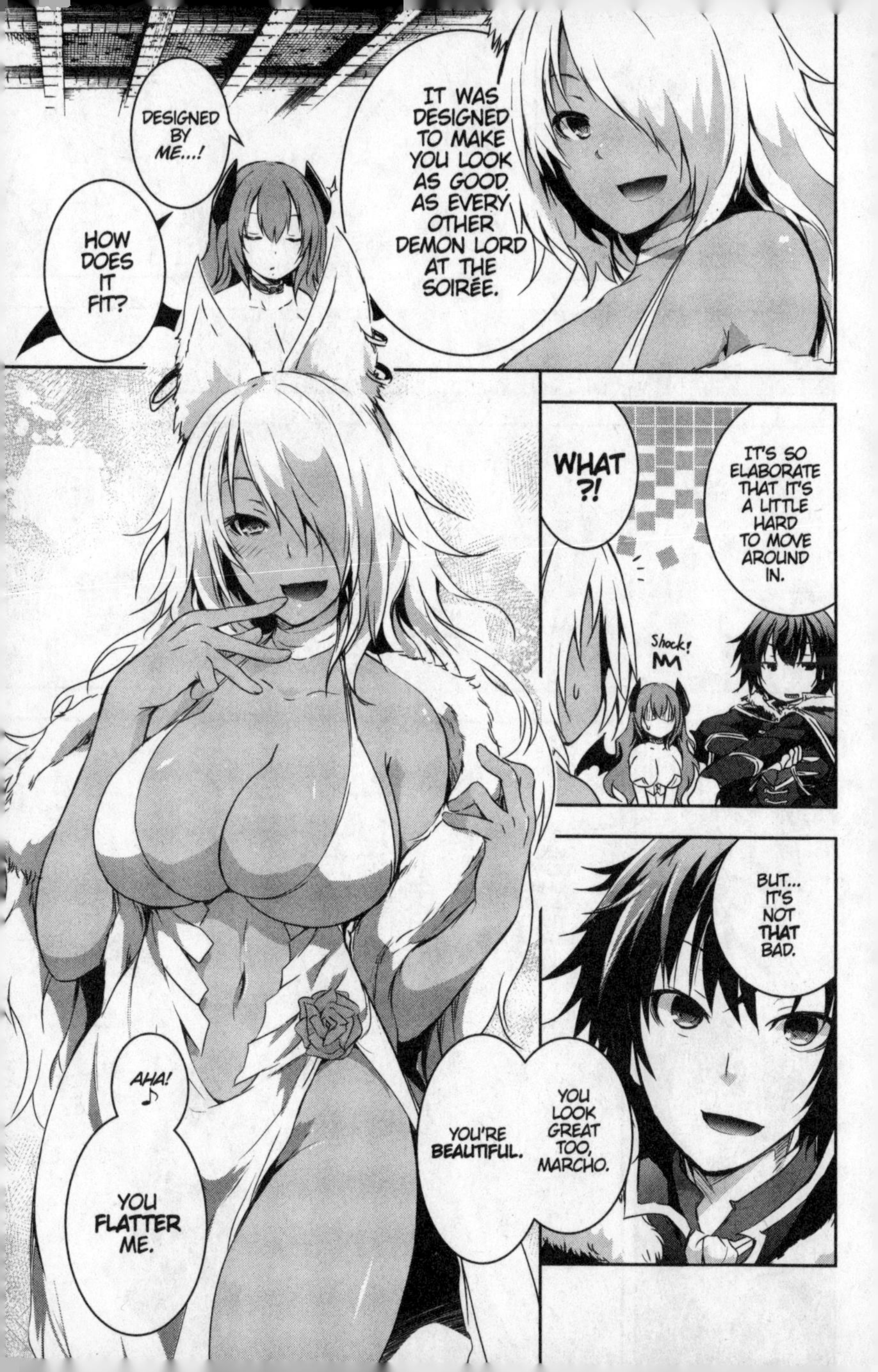
IT WAS DESIGNED TO MAKE YOU LOOK AS GOOD AS EVERY OTHER DEMON LORD AT THE SOIRÉE.
DESIGNED BY ME...!
HOW DOES IT FIT?
IT'S SO ELABORATE THAT IT'S A LITTLE HARD TO MOVE AROUND IN.
WHAT?!
Shock!
BUT... IT'S NOT THAT BAD.
YOU LOOK GREAT TOO, MARCHO.
YOU'RE BEAUTIFUL.
AHA! ♪
YOU FLATTER ME.

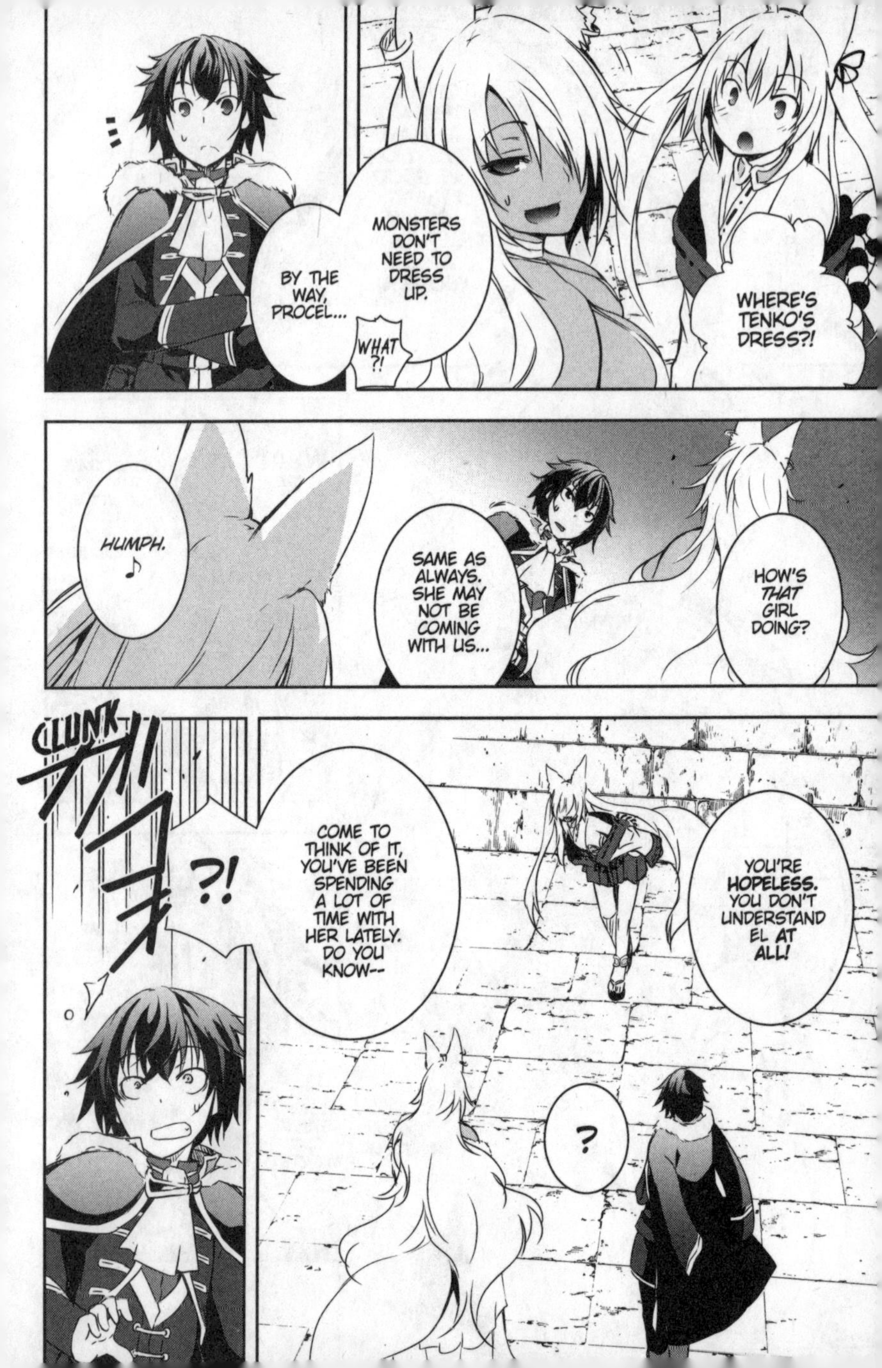
WHERE'S TENKO'S DRESS?!
MONSTERS DON'T NEED TO DRESS UP.
WHAT?!
BY THE WAY, PROCEL...
HOW'S THAT GIRL DOING?
SAME AS ALWAYS. SHE MAY NOT BE COMING WITH US...
HUMPH. ♪
YOU'RE HOPELESS. YOU DON'T UNDERSTAND EL AT ALL!
?
COME TO THINK OF IT, YOU'VE BEEN SPENDING A LOT OF TIME WITH HER LATELY. DO YOU KNOW--
CLUNK
?!

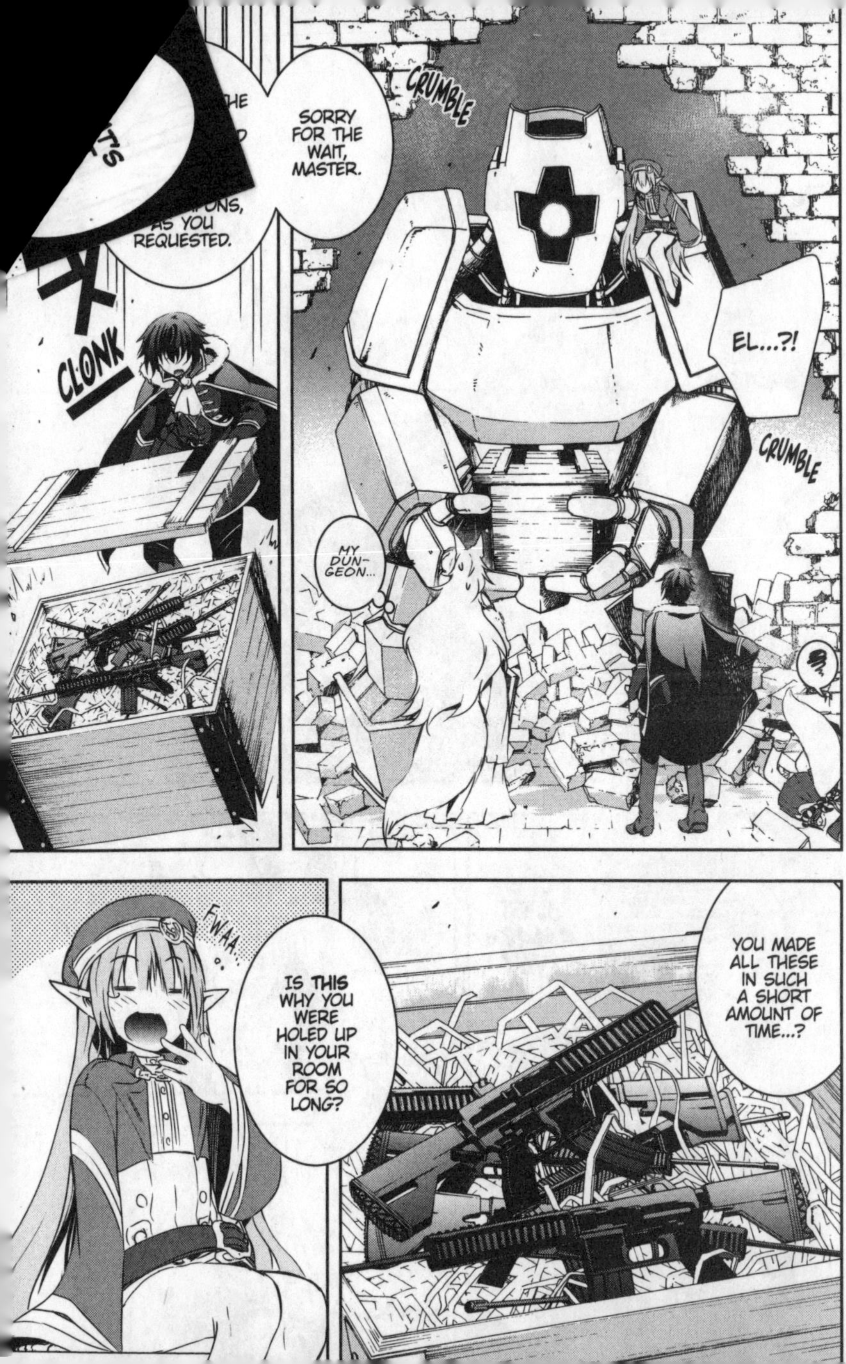
CRUMBLE
SORRY FOR THE WAIT, MASTER.
EL...?!
CRUMBLE
MY DUN-GEON...
AS YOU REQUESTED.
CLONK
YOU MADE ALL THESE IN SUCH A SHORT AMOUNT OF TIME...?
FWAA...
IS THIS WHY YOU WERE HOLED UP IN YOUR ROOM FOR SO LONG?

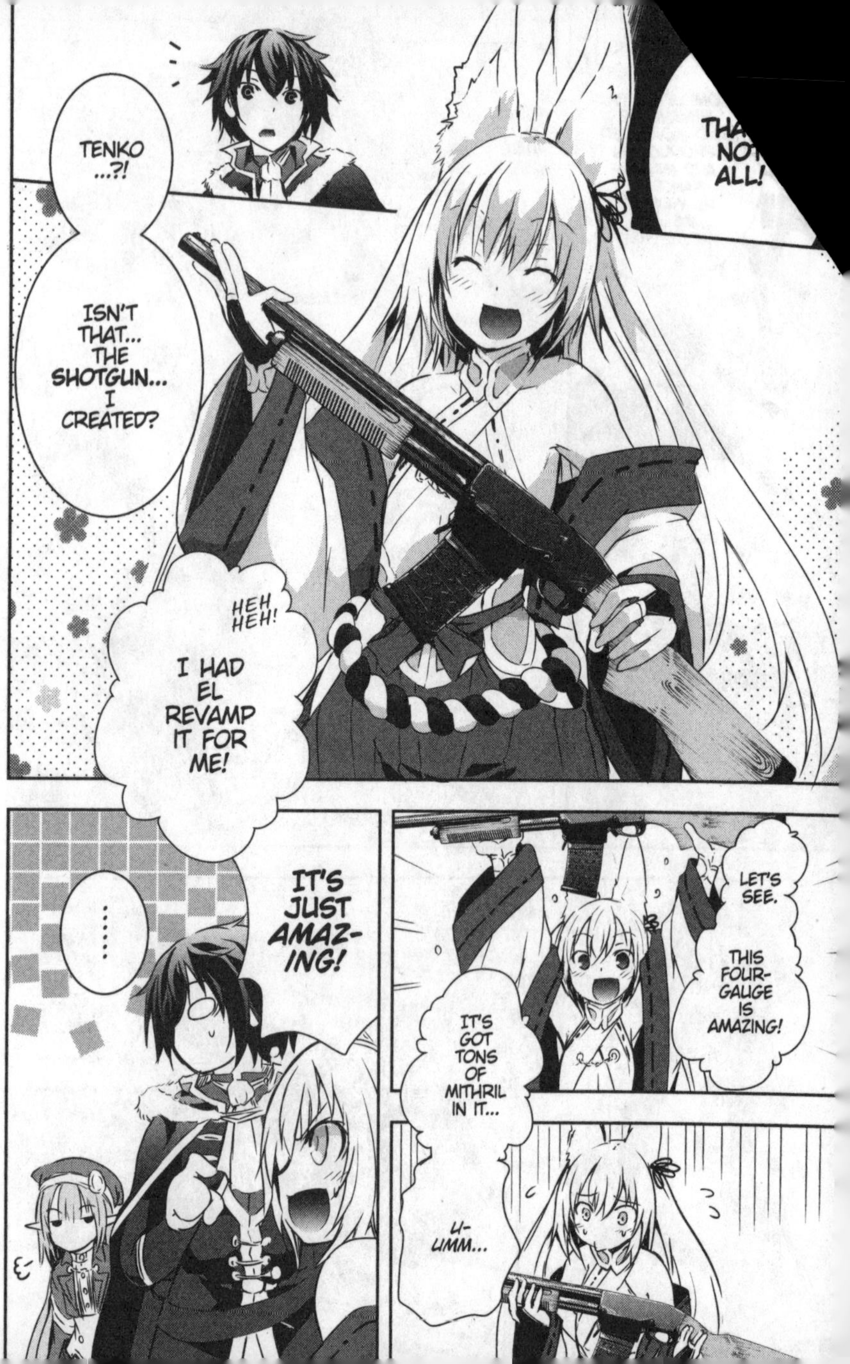
THA
NOT
ALL!
TENKO ...?!
ISN'T THAT... THE SHOTGUN... I CREATED?
HEH HEH!
I HAD EL REVAMP IT FOR ME!
LET'S SEE.
THIS FOUR-GAUGE IS AMAZING!
IT'S GOT TONS OF MITHRIL IN IT...
U-UMM...
IT'S JUST AMAZING!
......

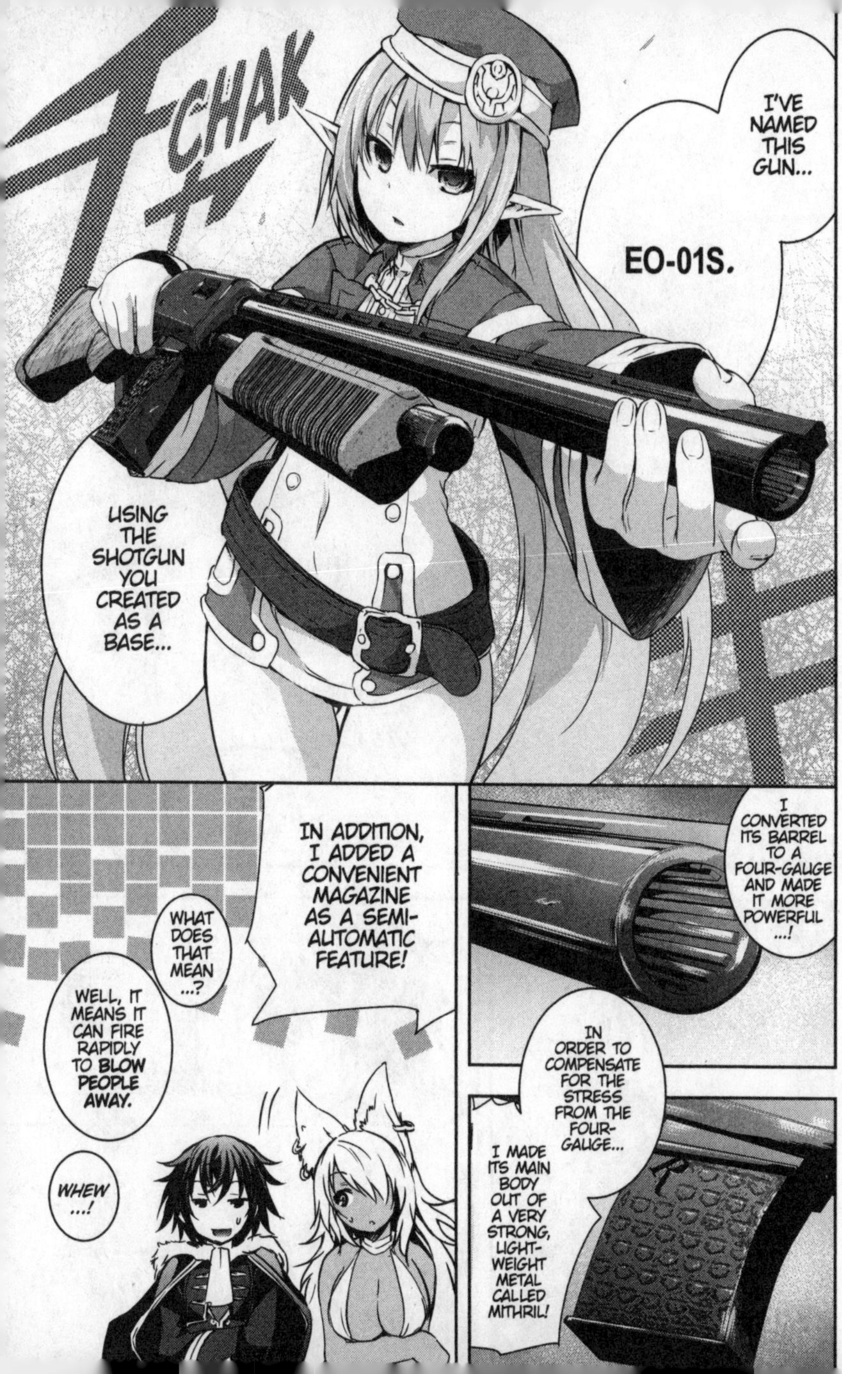
I'VE NAMED THIS GUN...
EO-01S.
CHAK
USING THE SHOTGUN YOU CREATED AS A BASE...
I CONVERTED ITS BARREL TO A FOUR-GAUGE AND MADE IT MORE POWERFUL ...!
IN ORDER TO COMPENSATE FOR THE STRESS FROM THE FOUR-GAUGE...
I MADE ITS MAIN BODY OUT OF A VERY STRONG, LIGHT-WEIGHT METAL CALLED MITHRIL!
IN ADDITION, I ADDED A CONVENIENT MAGAZINE AS A SEMI-AUTOMATIC FEATURE!
WHAT DOES THAT MEAN ...?
WELL, IT MEANS IT CAN FIRE RAPIDLY TO BLOW PEOPLE AWAY.
WHEW ...!

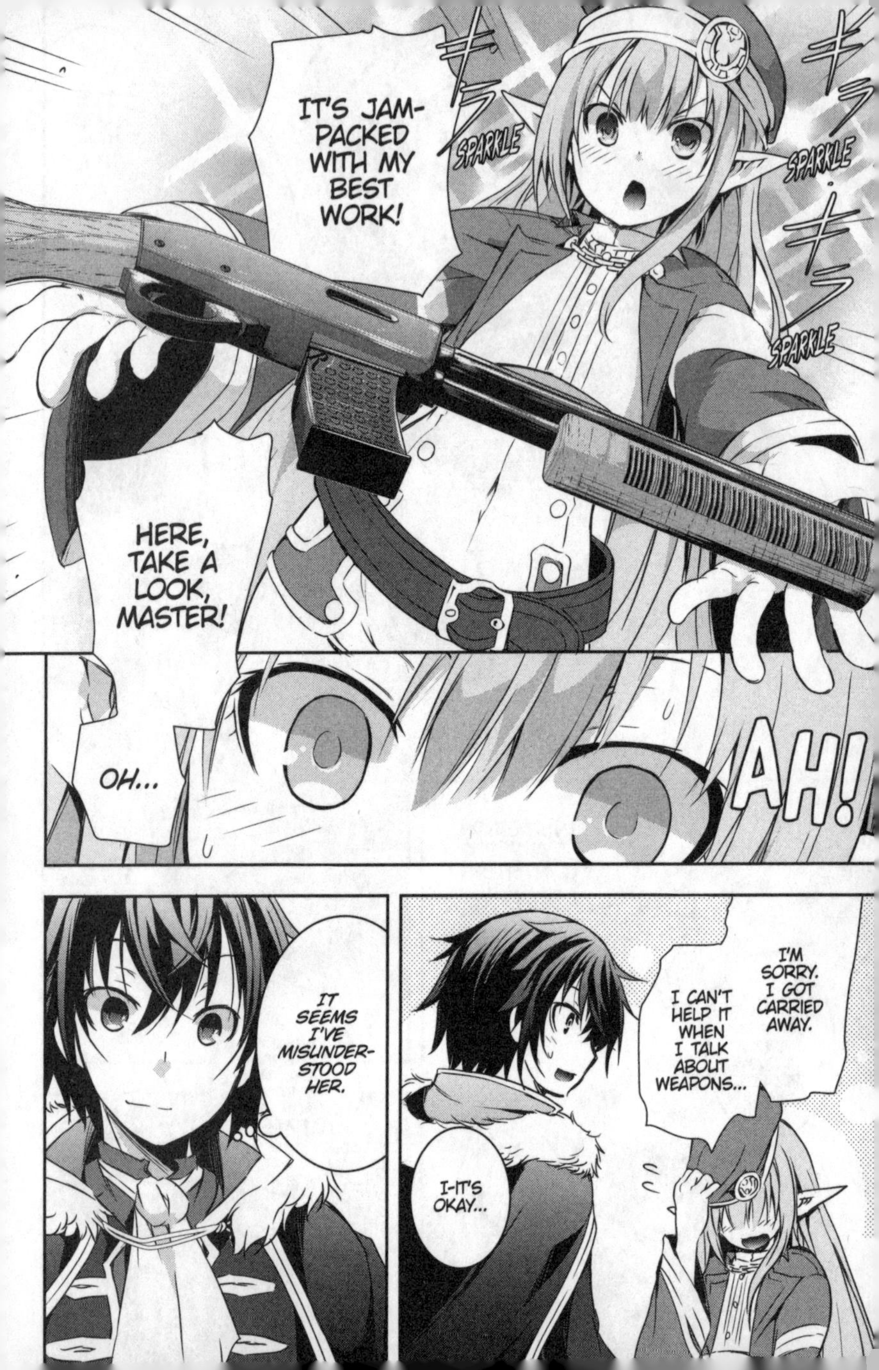
SPARKLE
SPARKLE
SPARKLE
IT'S JAM-PACKED WITH MY BEST WORK!
HERE, TAKE A LOOK, MASTER!
AH!
OH...
I'M SORRY. I GOT CARRIED AWAY.
I CAN'T HELP IT WHEN I TALK ABOUT WEAPONS...
I-IT'S OKAY...
IT SEEMS I'VE MISUNDERSTOOD HER.

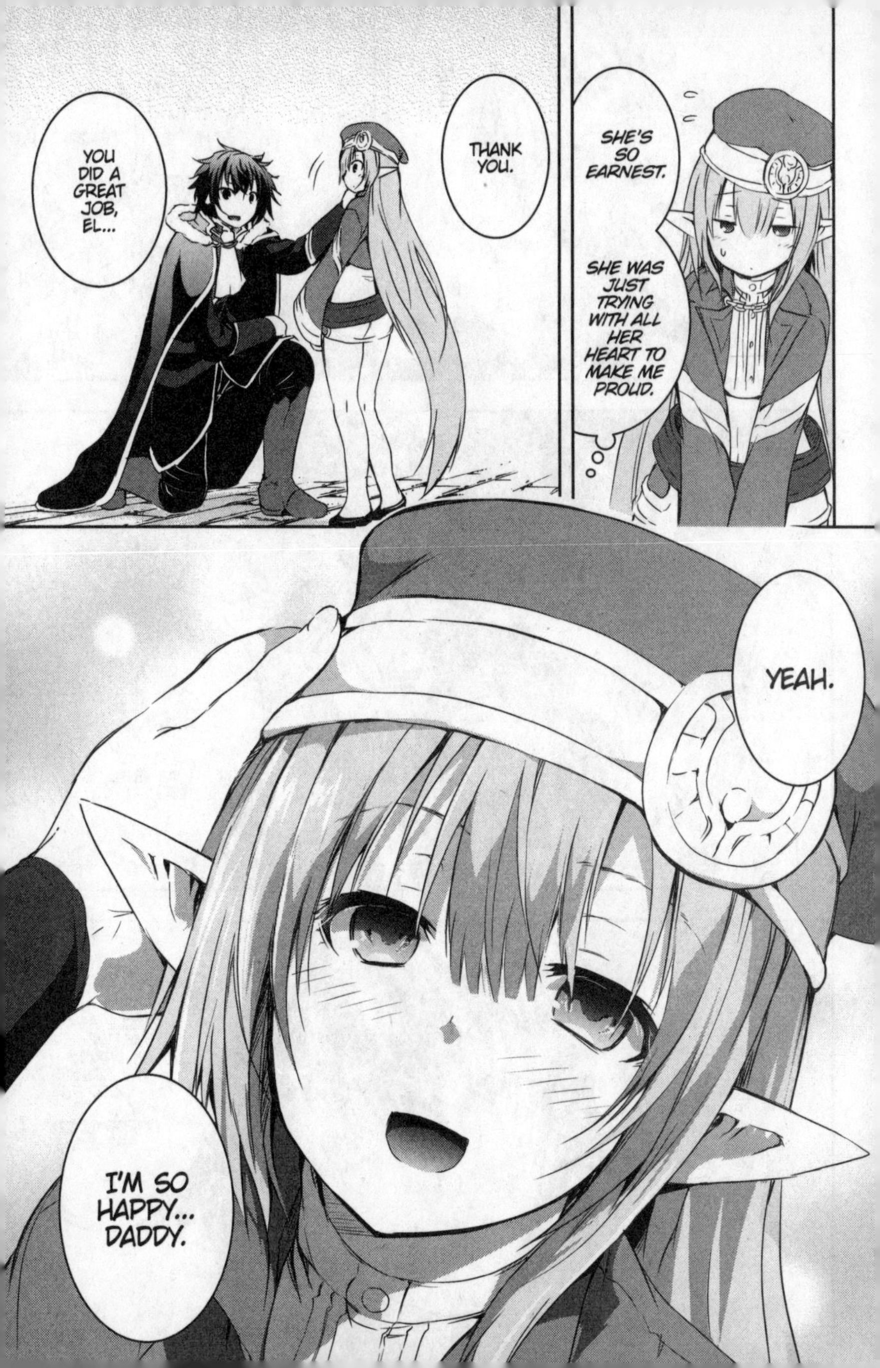
SHE'S SO EARNEST.
SHE WAS JUST TRYING WITH ALL HER HEART TO MAKE ME PROUD.
THANK YOU.
YOU DID A GREAT JOB, EL...
YEAH.
I'M SO HAPPY... DADDY.

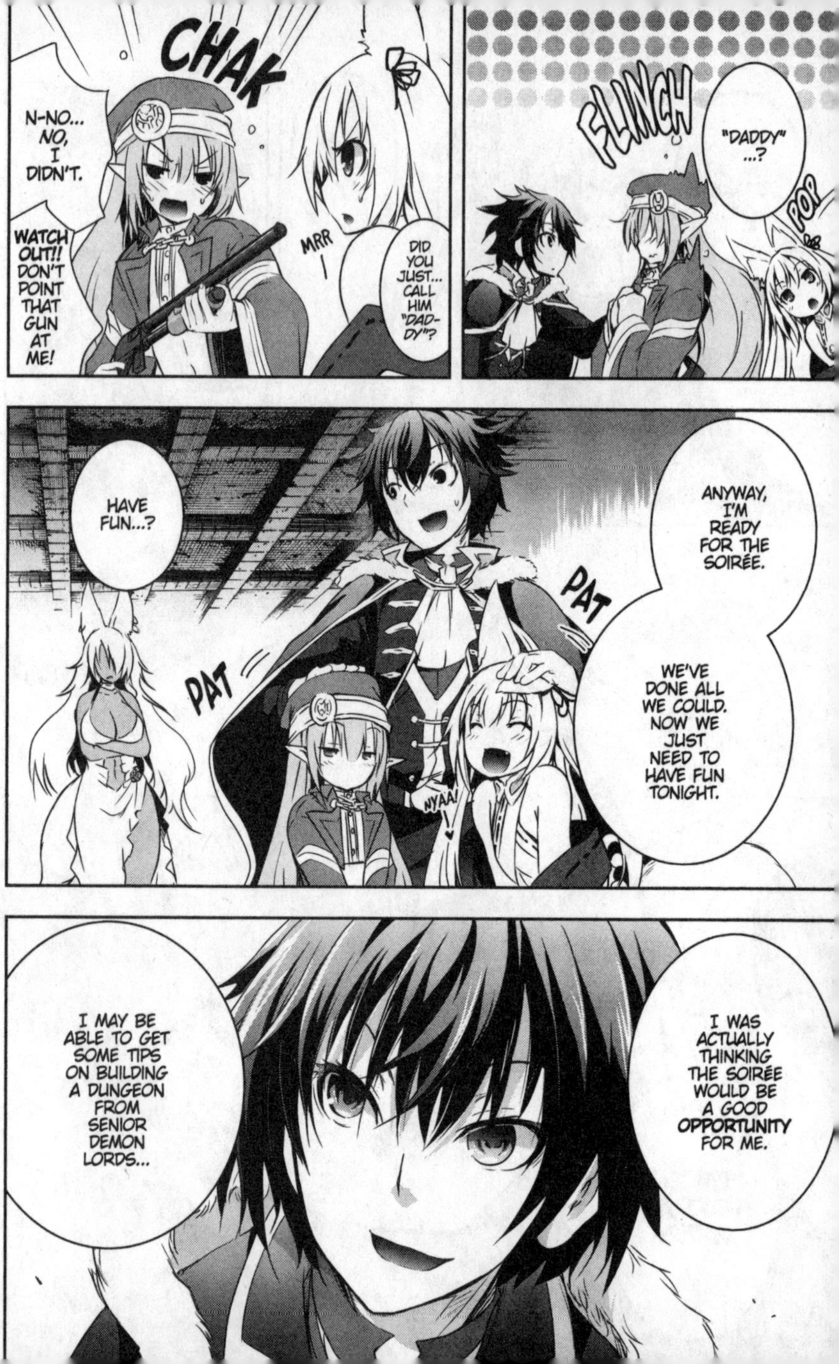
FLINCH
"DADDY" ...?
POP
CHAK
DID YOU JUST... CALL HIM "DADDY"?
MRR
N-NO... NO, I DIDN'T.
WATCH OUT!! DON'T POINT THAT GUN AT ME!
ANYWAY, I'M READY FOR THE SOIRÉE.
WE'VE DONE ALL WE COULD. NOW WE JUST NEED TO HAVE FUN TONIGHT.
PAT
HAVE FUN...?
PAT
NYAA!
I WAS ACTUALLY THINKING THE SOIRÉE WOULD BE A GOOD OPPORTUNITY FOR ME.
I MAY BE ABLE TO GET SOME TIPS ON BUILDING A DUNGEON FROM SENIOR DEMON LORDS...

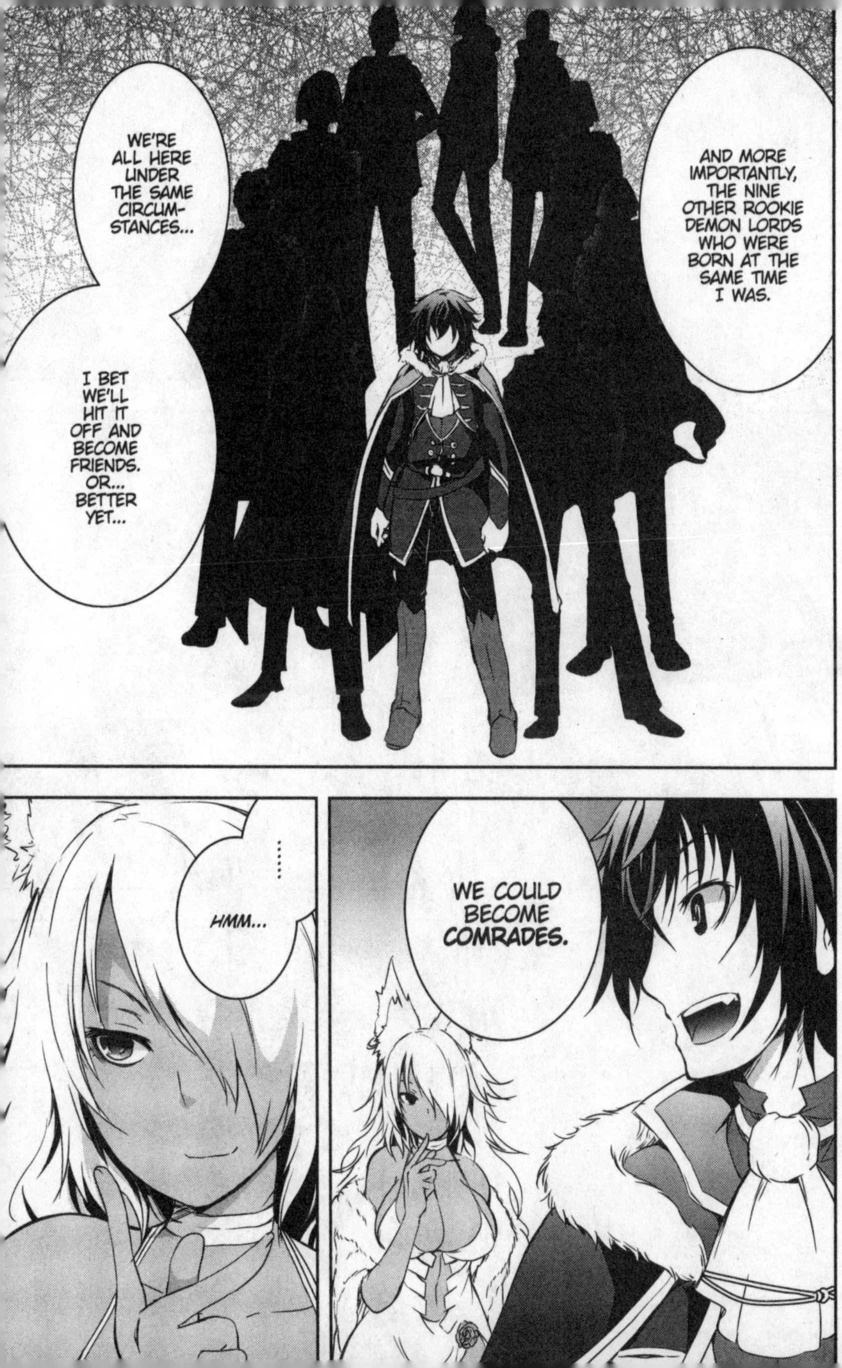
AND MORE IMPORTANTLY, THE NINE OTHER ROOKIE DEMON LORDS WHO WERE BORN AT THE SAME TIME I WAS.
WE'RE ALL HERE UNDER THE SAME CIRCUM-STANCES...
I BET WE'LL HIT IT OFF AND BECOME FRIENDS. OR... BETTER YET...
WE COULD BECOME COMRADES.
......
HMM...

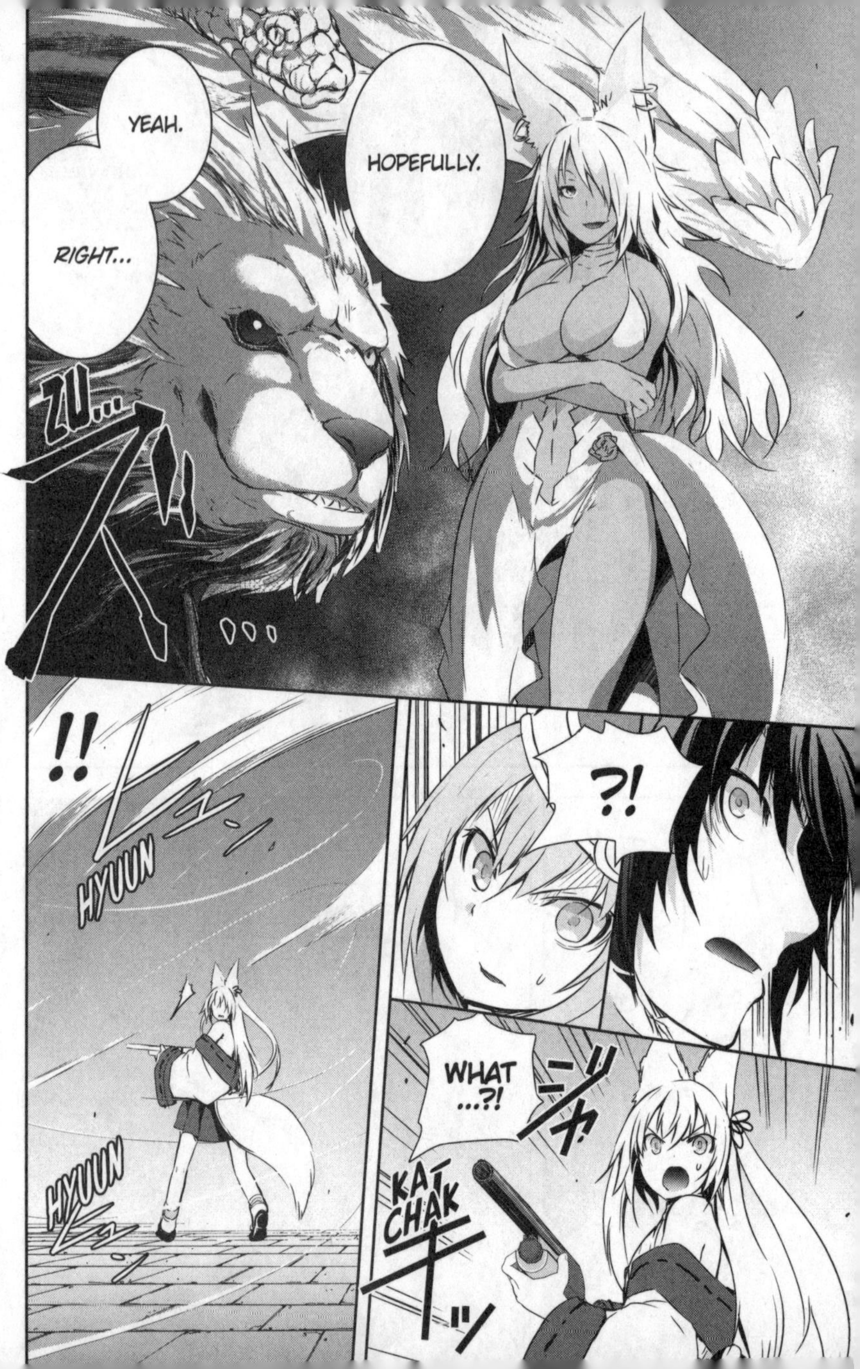
HOPEFULLY.
YEAH.
RIGHT...
ZU...
?!
WHAT ...?!
KA-CHAK
!!
HYUUN
HYUUN

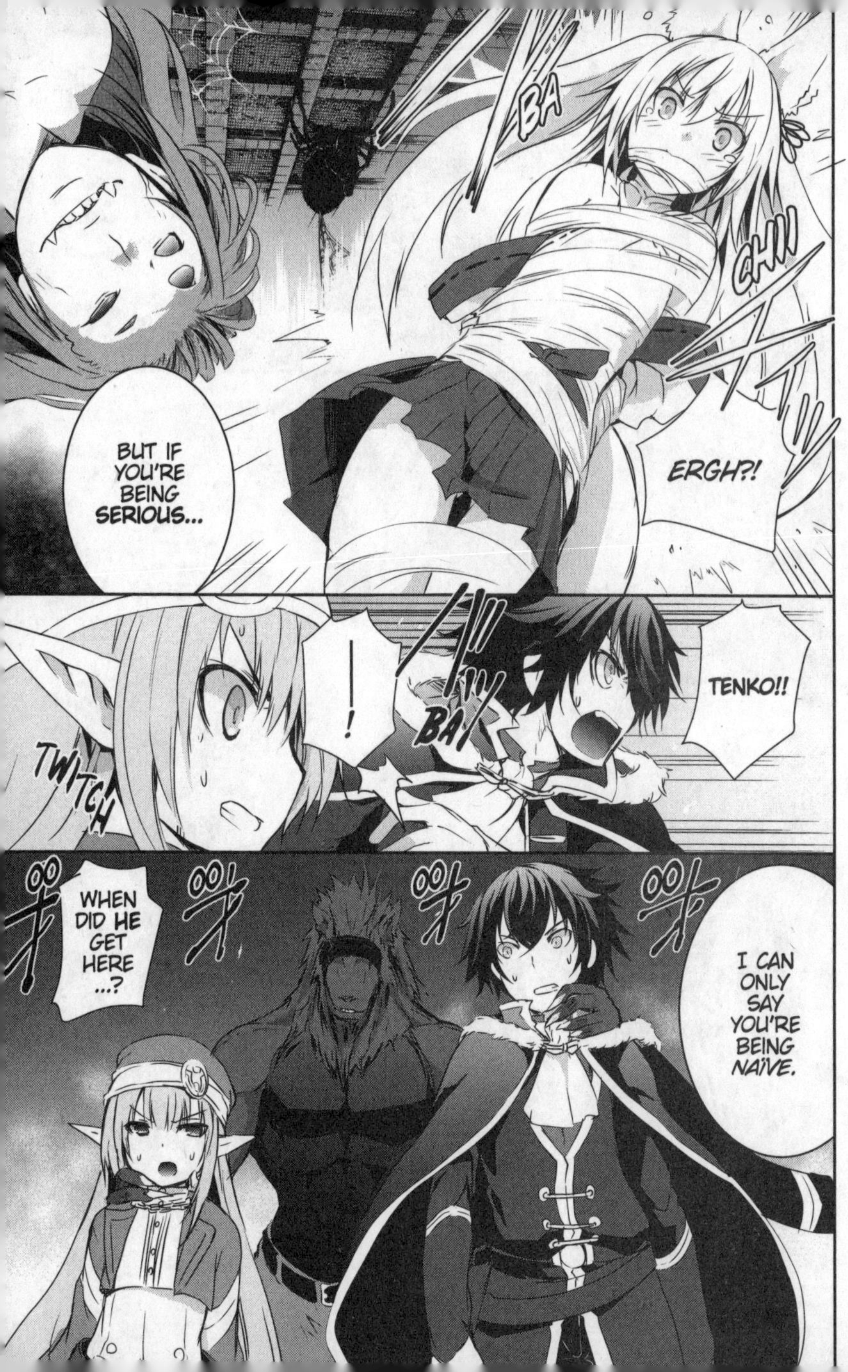
BA
CHIII
ERGH?!
BUT IF YOU'RE BEING SERIOUS...
TENKO!!
BA
!
TWITCH
I CAN ONLY SAY YOU'RE BEING NAÏVE.
WHEN DID HE GET HERE ...?

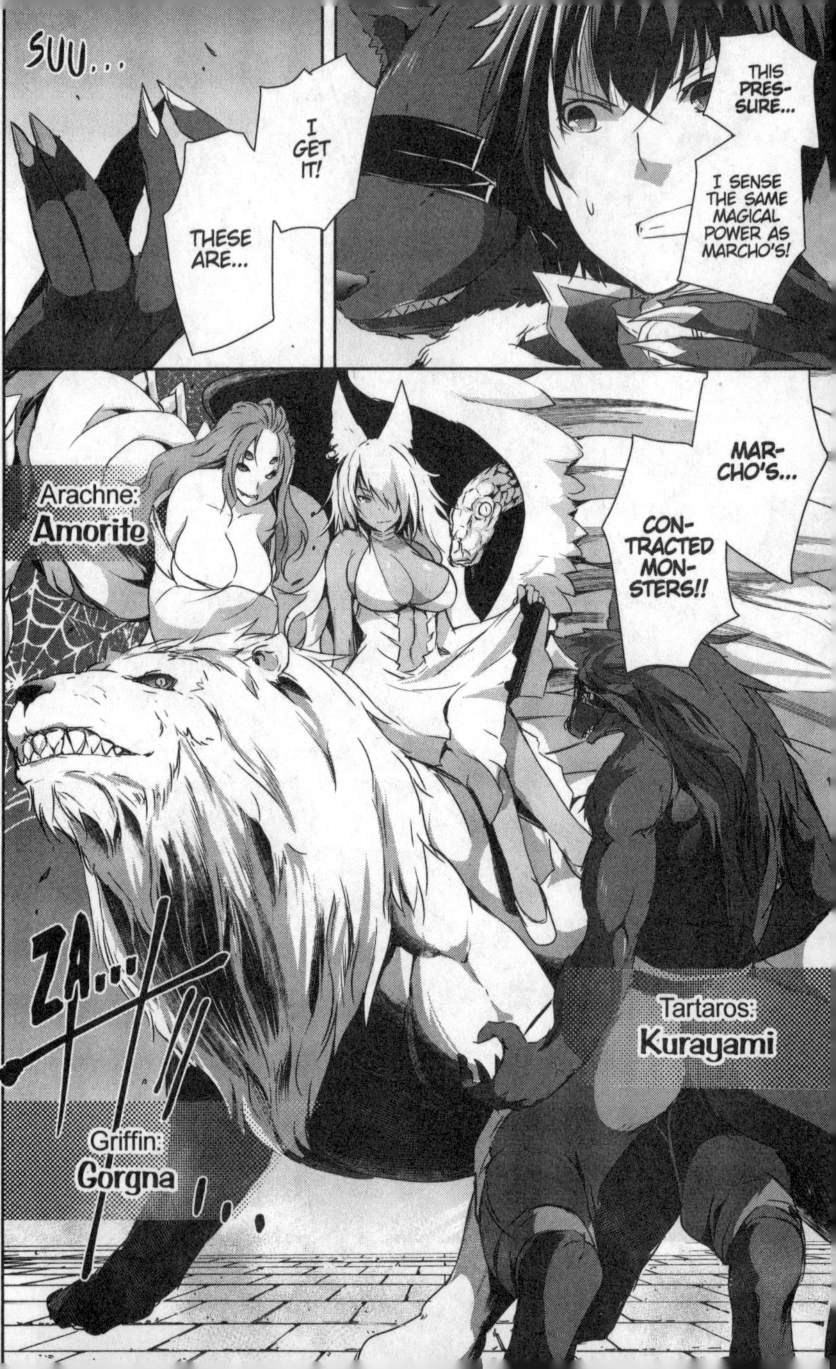
THIS PRES-SURE...
I SENSE THE SAME MAGICAL POWER AS MARCHO'S!
SUU...
I GET IT!
THESE ARE...
MAR-CHO'S...
CON-TRACTED MON-STERS!!
Arachne: Amorite
Tartaros: Kurayami
ZA...
Griffin: Gorgna

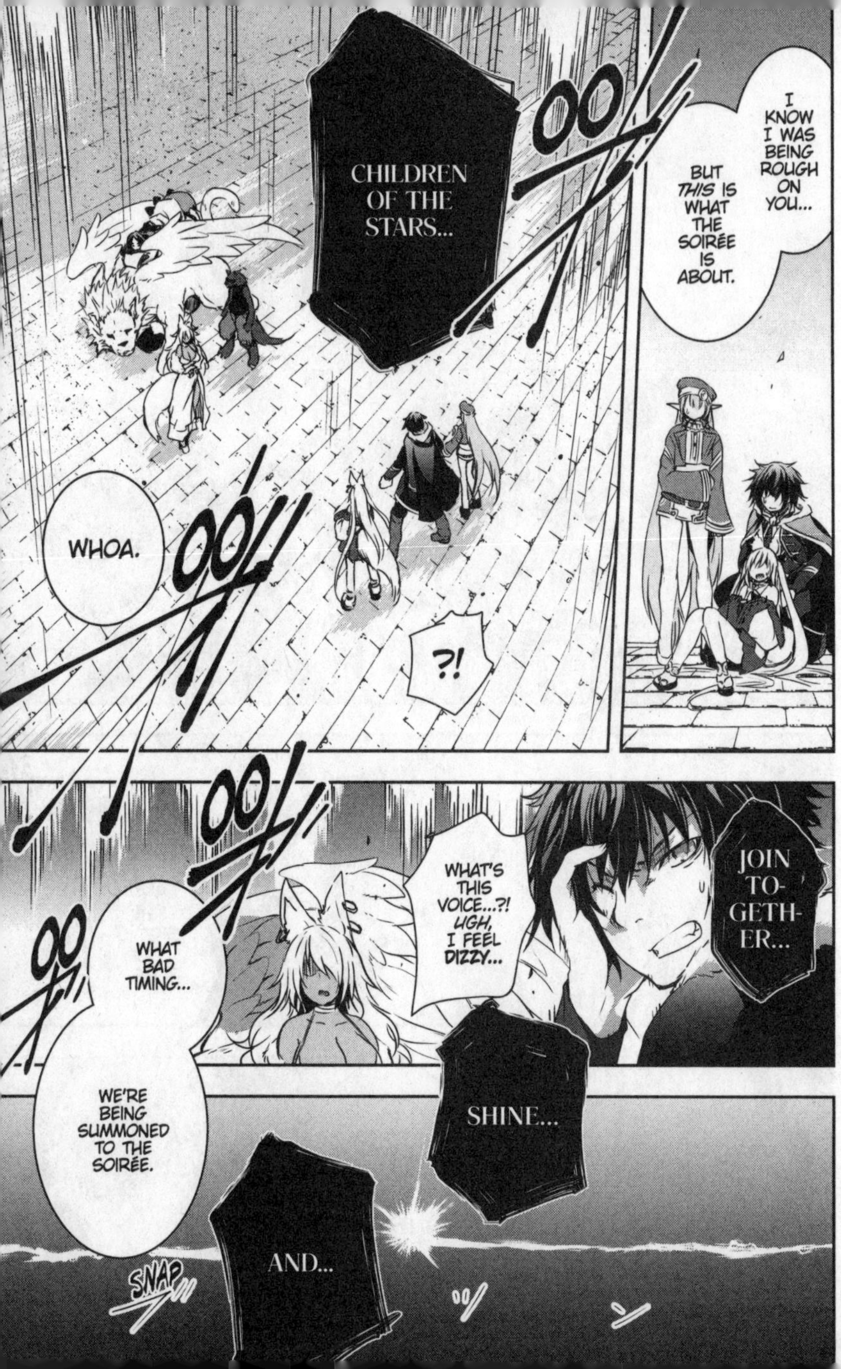
I KNOW I WAS BEING ROUGH ON YOU...
BUT *THIS* IS WHAT THE SOIRÉE IS ABOUT.
CHILDREN OF THE STARS...
OO
?!
WHOA.
OO
JOIN TO-GETH-ER...
WHAT'S THIS VOICE...?! *UGH*, I FEEL DIZZY...
OO
WHAT BAD TIMING...
OO
SHINE...
WE'RE BEING SUMMONED TO THE SOIRÉE.
AND...
SNAP

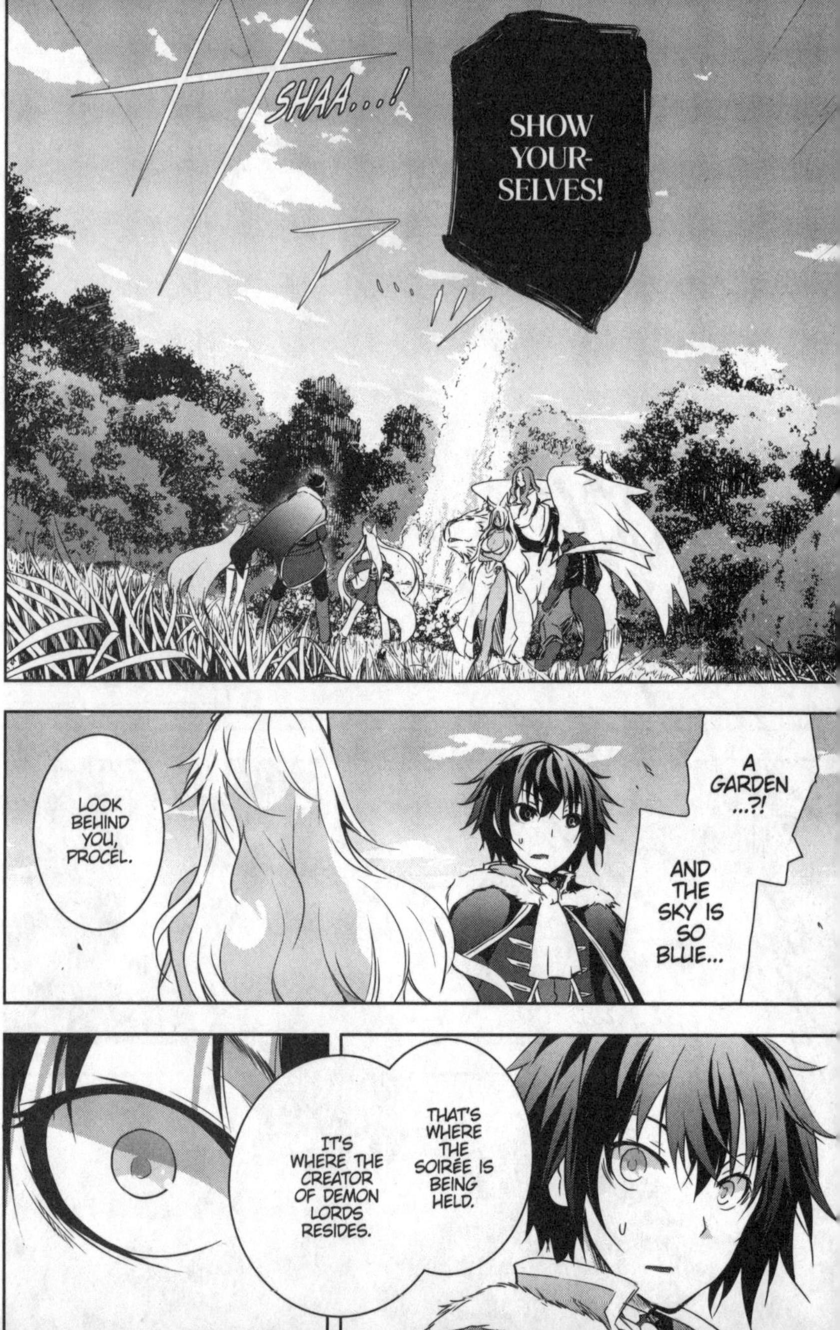
SHOW YOUR-SELVES!
SHAA...!
A GARDEN ...?!
AND THE SKY IS SO BLUE...
LOOK BEHIND YOU, PROCEL.
THAT'S WHERE THE SOIRÉE IS BEING HELD.
IT'S WHERE THE CREATOR OF DEMON LORDS RESIDES.

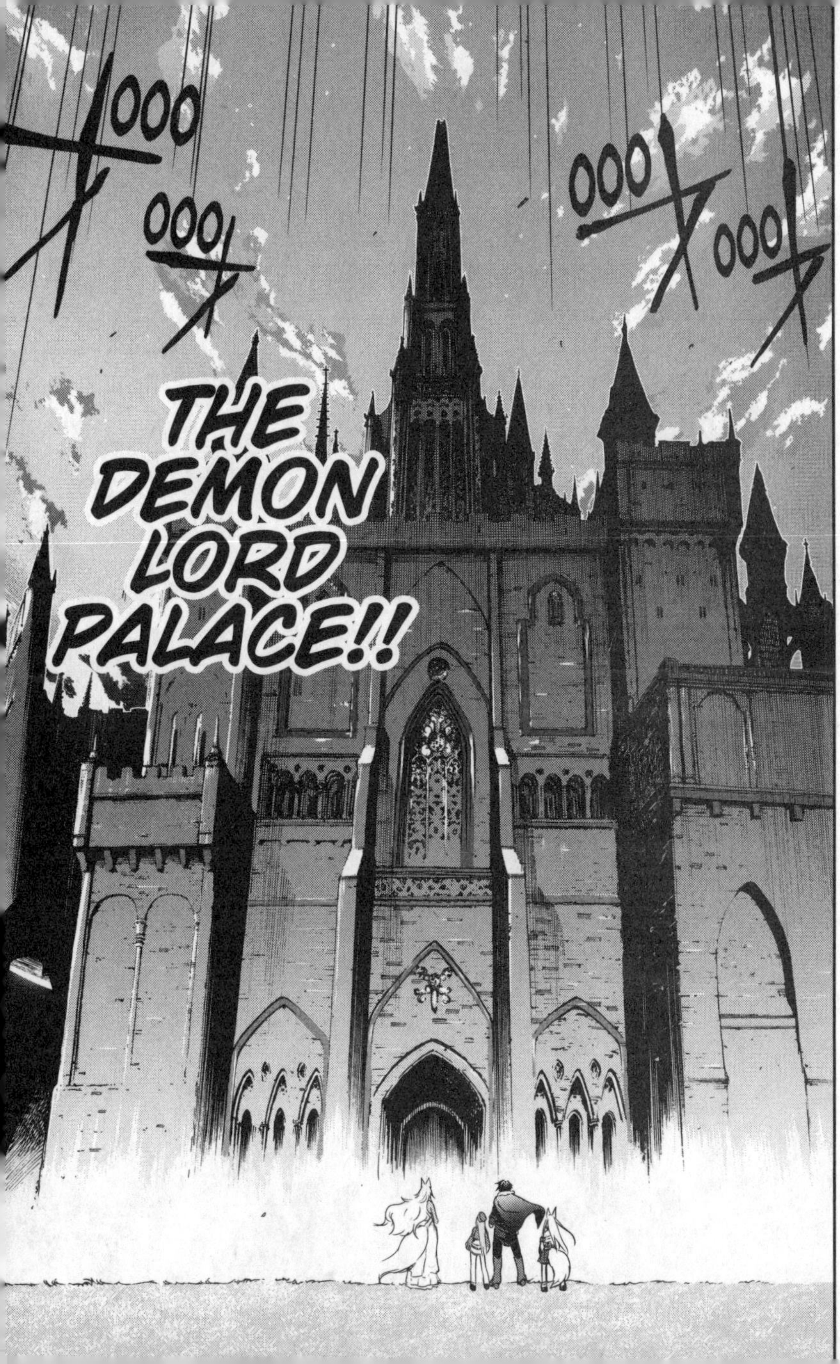
THE DEMON LORD PALACE!!

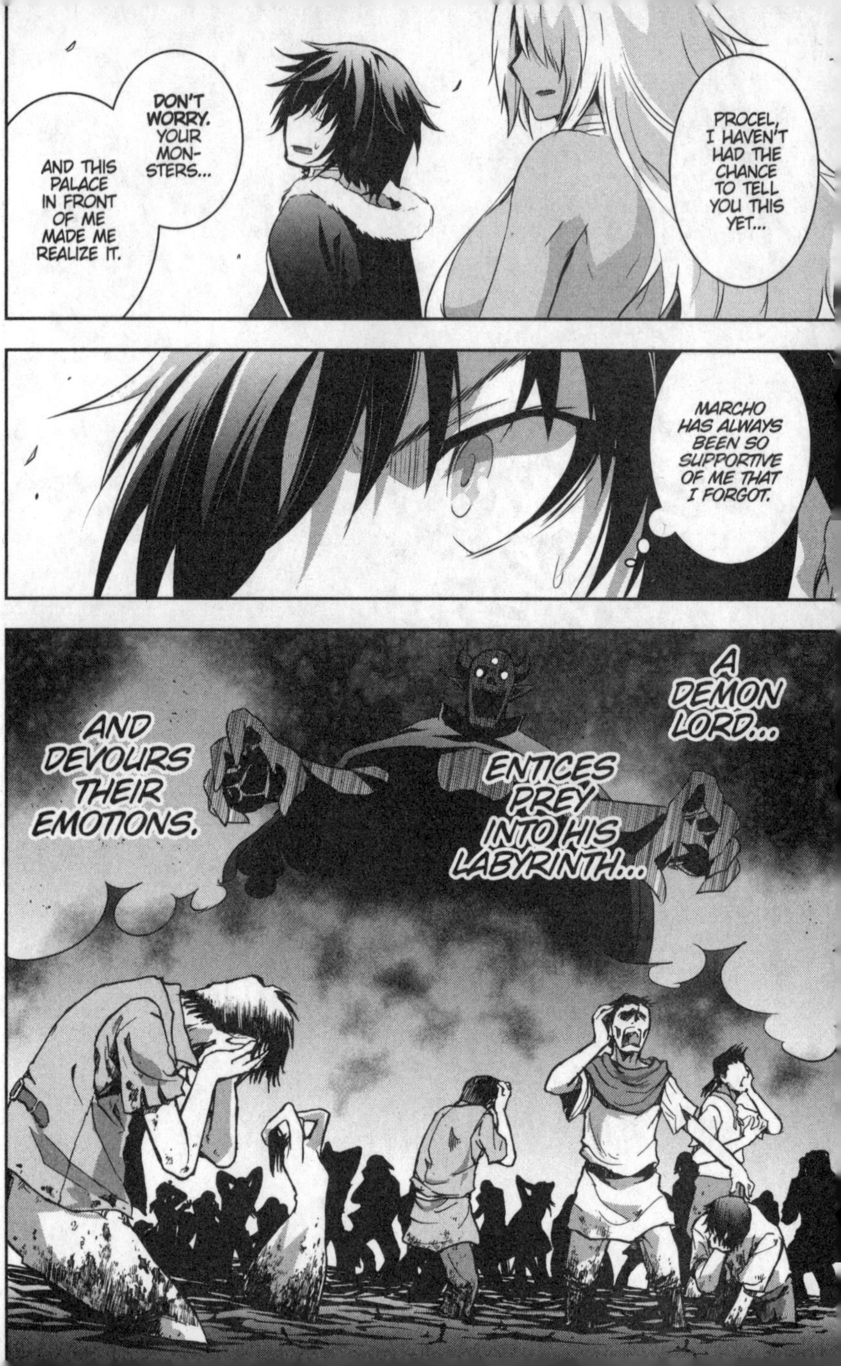
PROCEL, I HAVEN'T HAD THE CHANCE TO TELL YOU THIS YET...
DON'T WORRY. YOUR MON-STERS...
AND THIS PALACE IN FRONT OF ME MADE ME REALIZE IT.
MARCHO HAS ALWAYS BEEN SO SUPPORTIVE OF ME THAT I FORGOT.
A DEMON LORD...
ENTICES PREY INTO HIS LABYRINTH...
AND DEVOURS THEIR EMOTIONS.

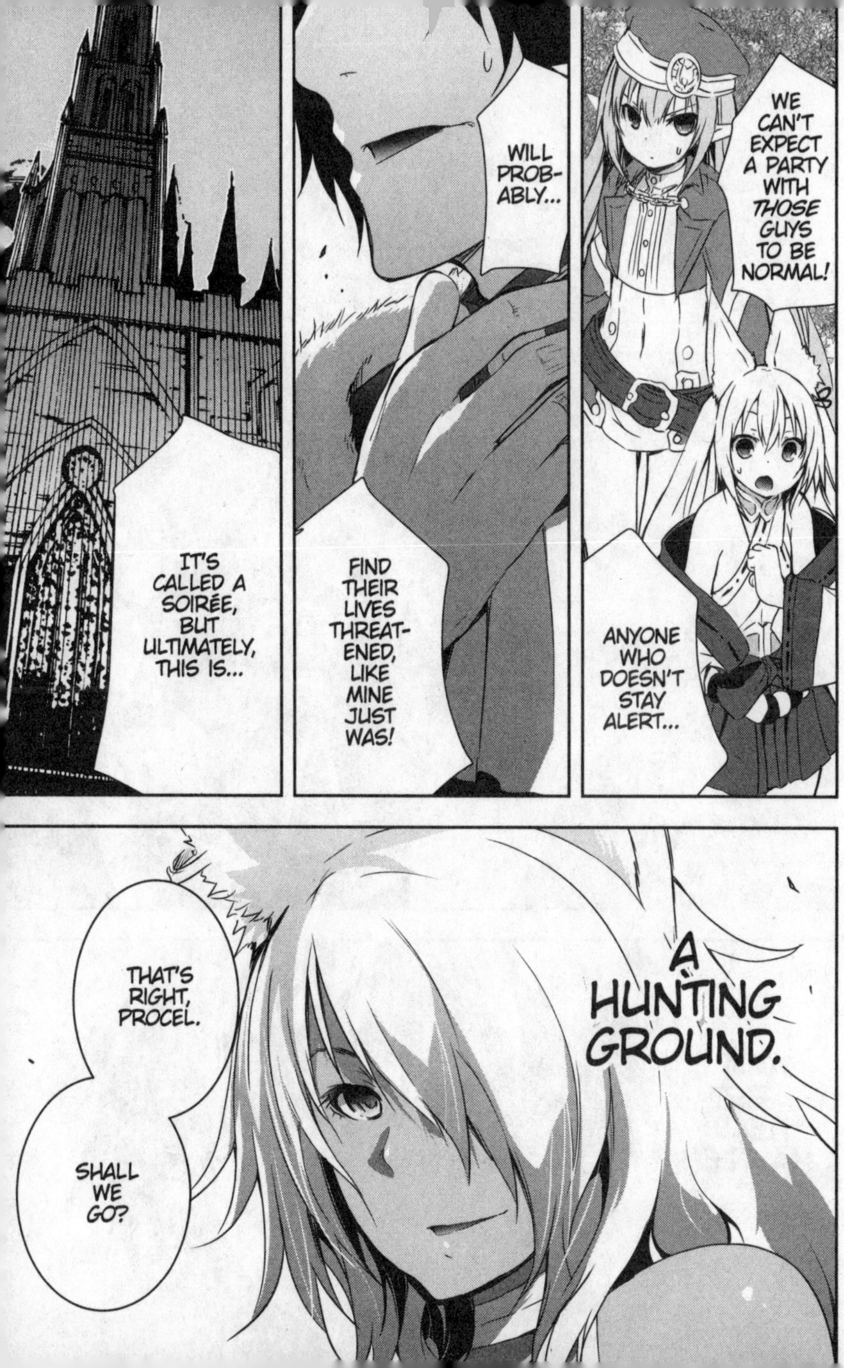
WE CAN'T EXPECT A PARTY WITH *THOSE* GUYS TO BE NORMAL!
ANYONE WHO DOESN'T STAY ALERT...
WILL PROBABLY...
FIND THEIR LIVES THREATENED, LIKE MINE JUST WAS!
IT'S CALLED A SOIRÉE, BUT ULTIMATELY, THIS IS...
A HUNTING GROUND.
THAT'S RIGHT, PROCEL.
SHALL WE GO?

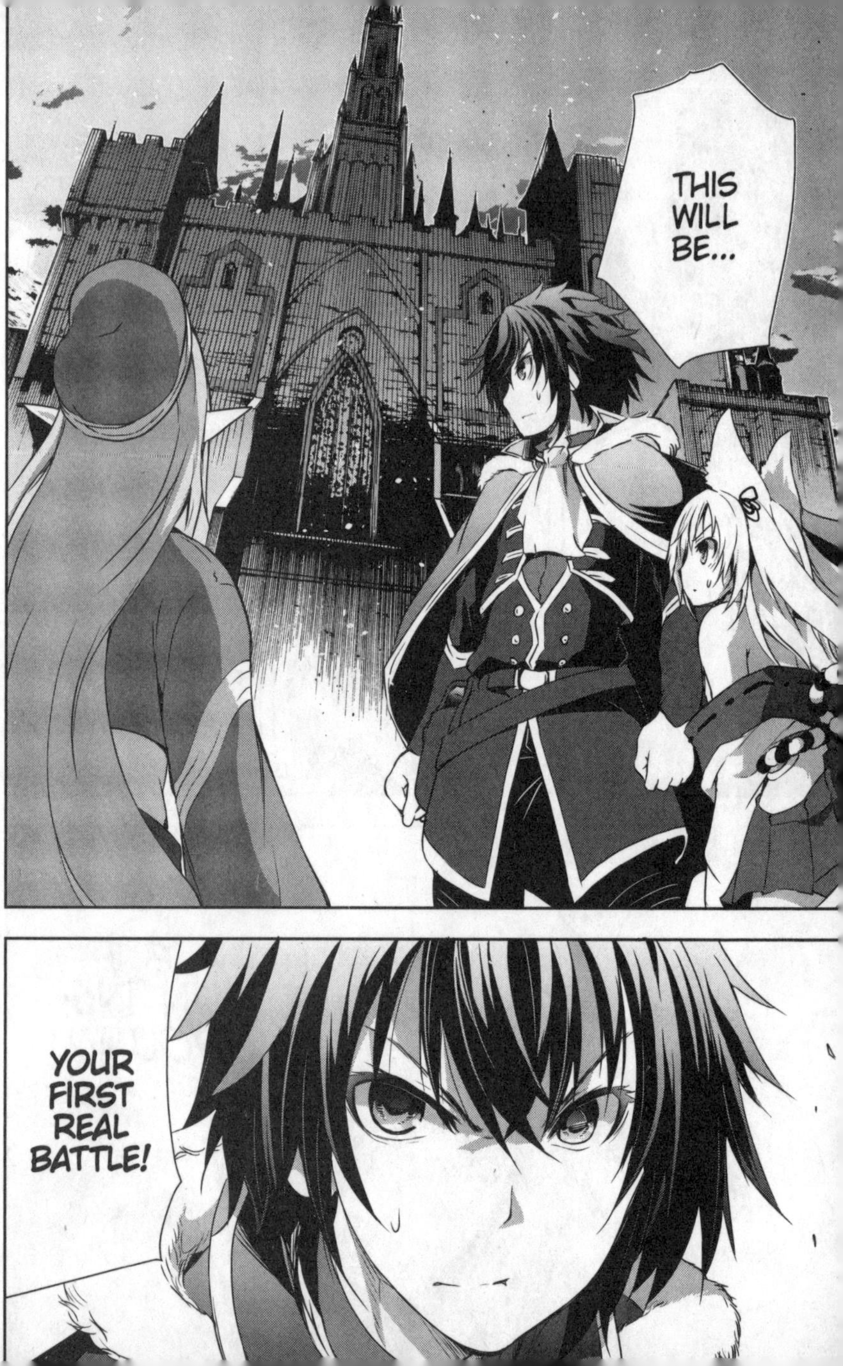
THIS WILL BE...
YOUR FIRST REAL BATTLE!

Chapter 4

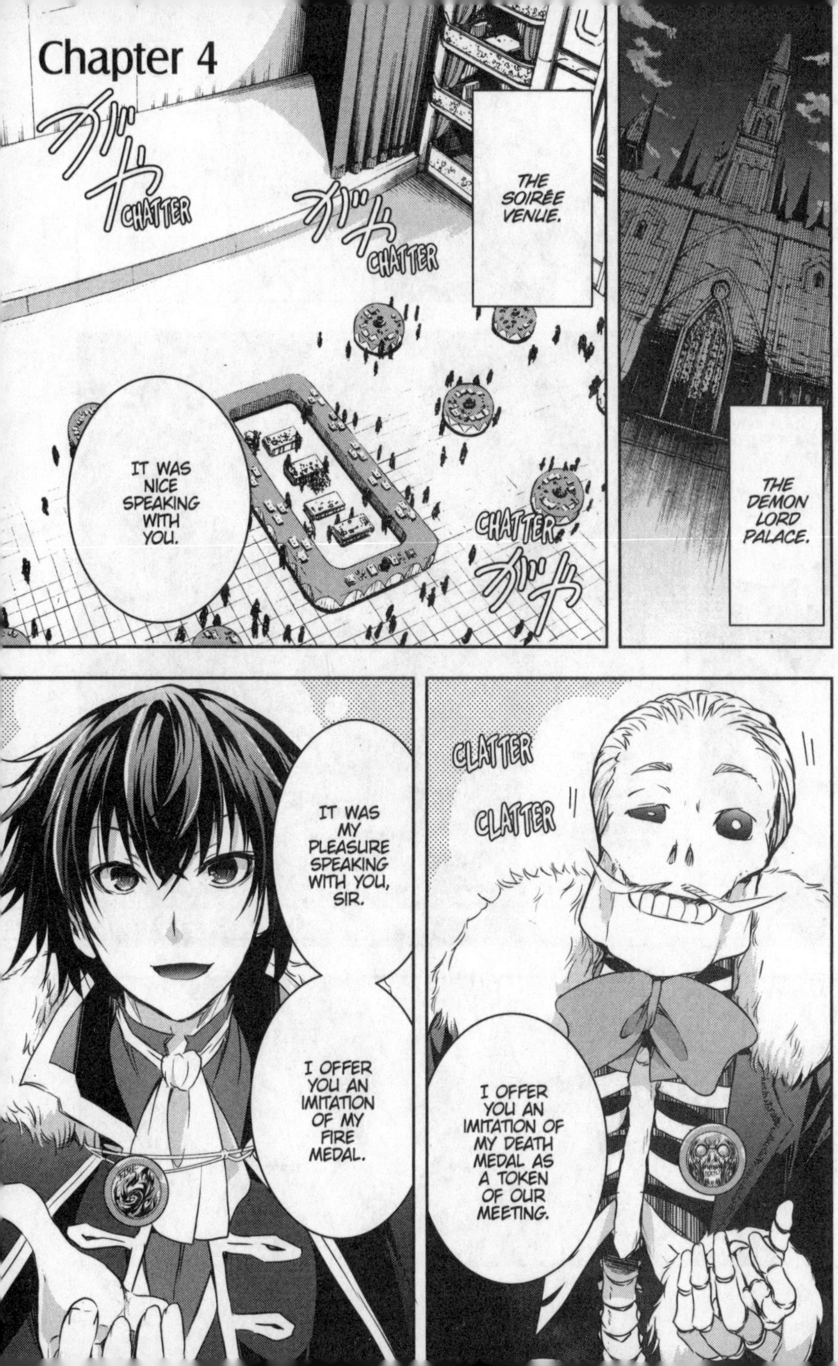
THE DEMON LORD PALACE.
THE SOIRÉE VENUE.
CHATTER
CHATTER
CHATTER
IT WAS NICE SPEAKING WITH YOU.
CLATTER
CLATTER
I OFFER YOU AN IMITATION OF MY DEATH MEDAL AS A TOKEN OF OUR MEETING.
IT WAS MY PLEASURE SPEAKING WITH YOU, SIR.
I OFFER YOU AN IMITATION OF MY FIRE MEDAL.

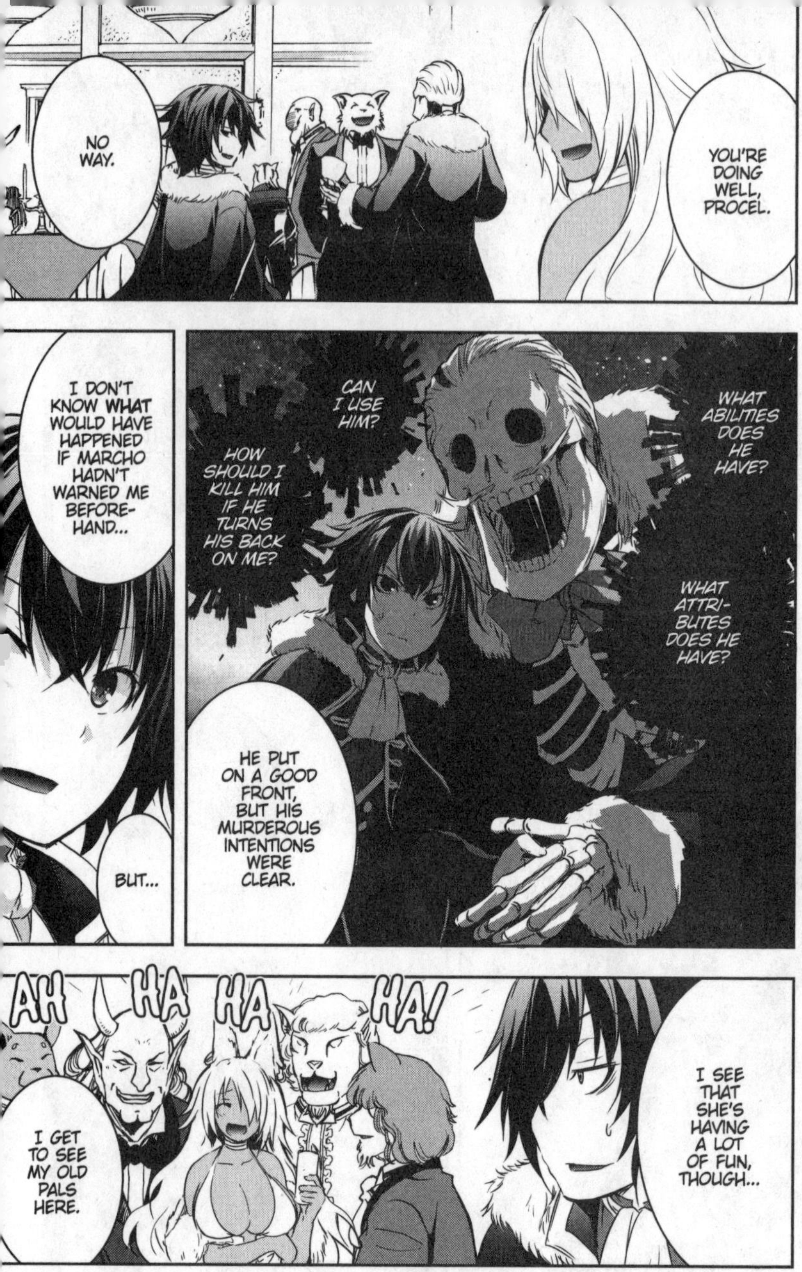
YOU'RE DOING WELL, PROCEL.
NO WAY.
WHAT ABILITIES DOES HE HAVE?
CAN I USE HIM?
WHAT ATTRIBUTES DOES HE HAVE?
HOW SHOULD I KILL HIM IF HE TURNS HIS BACK ON ME?
HE PUT ON A GOOD FRONT, BUT HIS MURDEROUS INTENTIONS WERE CLEAR.
I DON'T KNOW WHAT WOULD HAVE HAPPENED IF MARCHO HADN'T WARNED ME BEFORE-HAND...
BUT...
I SEE THAT SHE'S HAVING A LOT OF FUN, THOUGH...
AH HA HA HA!
I GET TO SEE MY OLD PALS HERE.

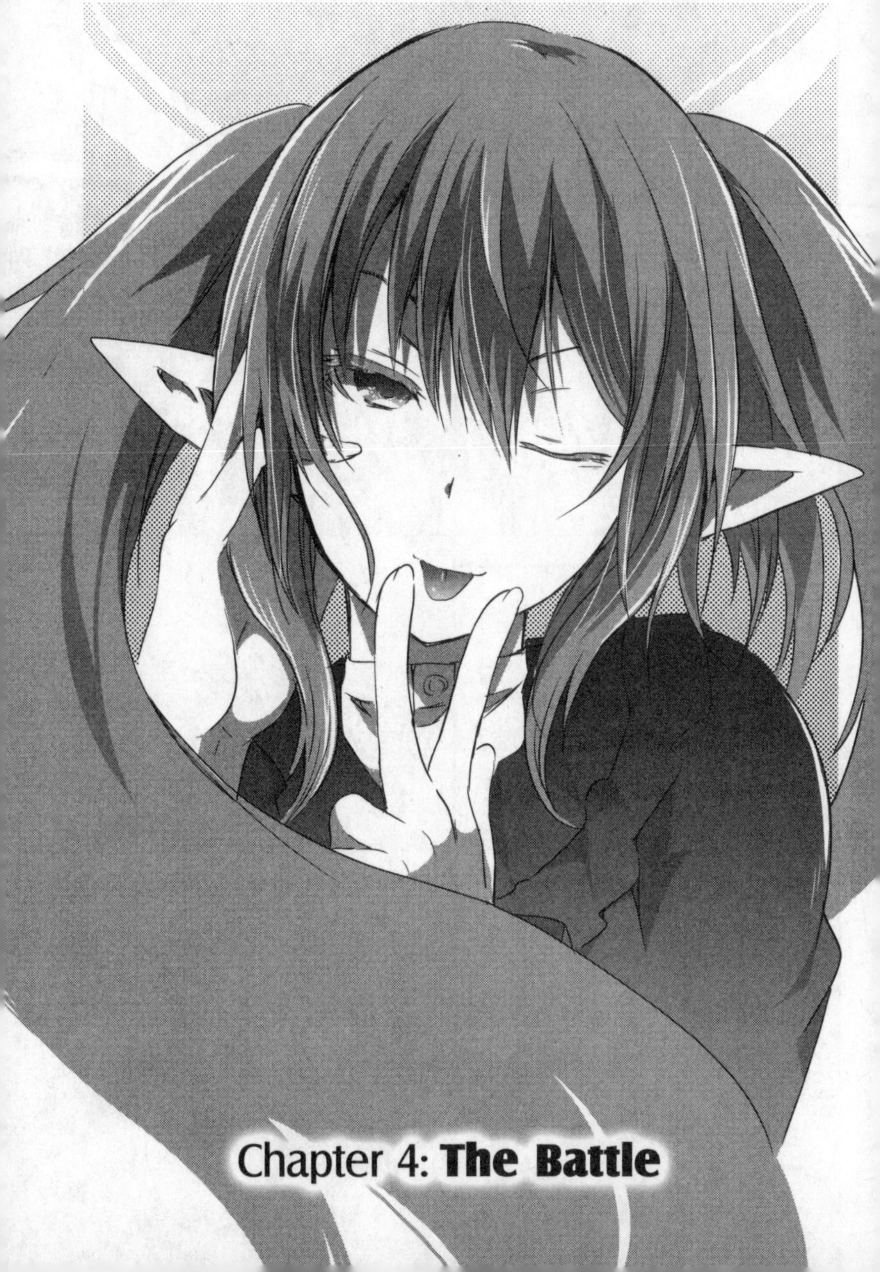

Chapter 4: **The Battle**

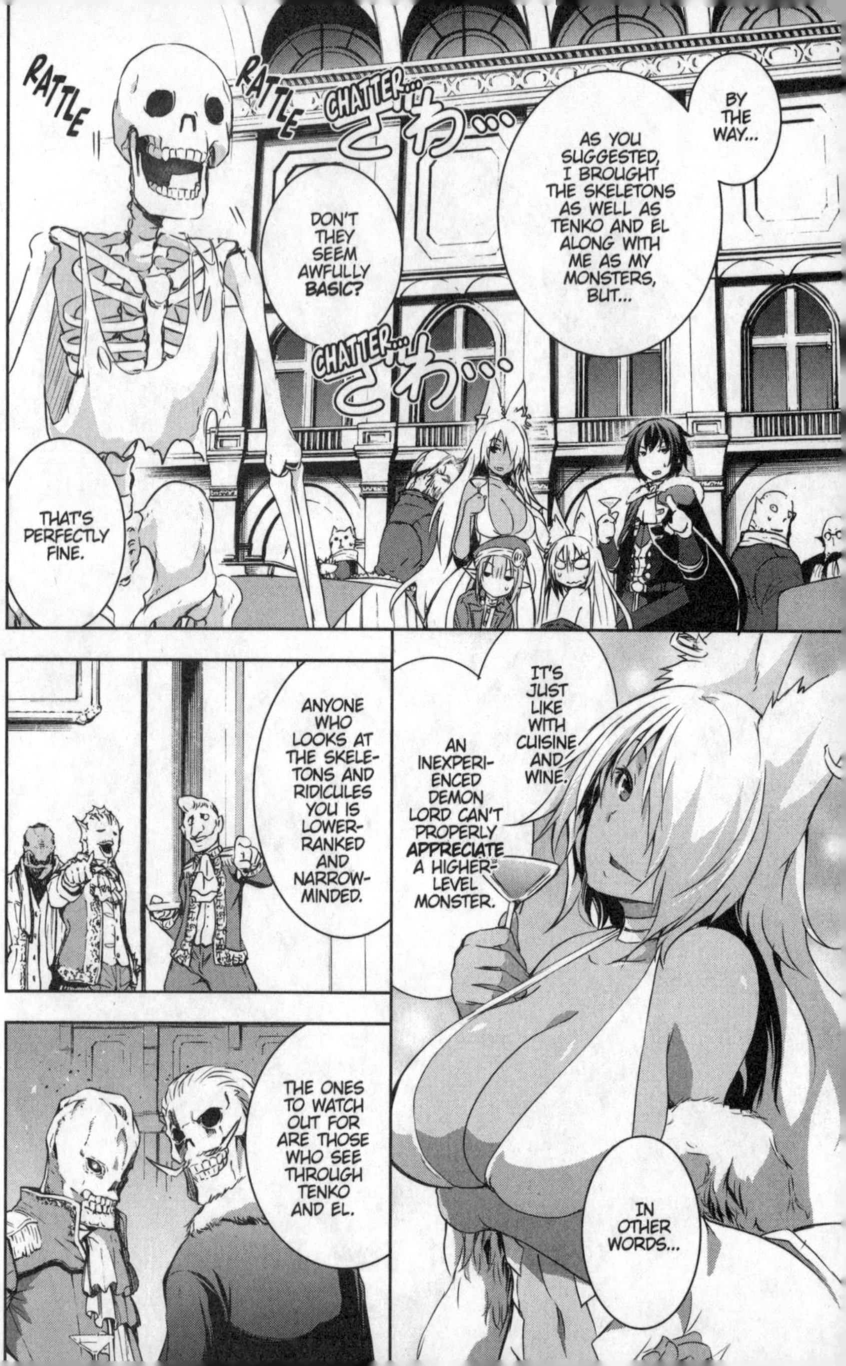
BY THE WAY...
AS YOU SUGGESTED, I BROUGHT THE SKELETONS AS WELL AS TENKO AND EL ALONG WITH ME AS MY MONSTERS, BUT...
CHATTER... ざわ…
RATTLE RATTLE
DON'T THEY SEEM AWFULLY BASIC?
CHATTER... ざわ…
THAT'S PERFECTLY FINE.
IT'S JUST LIKE WITH CUISINE AND WINE.
AN INEXPERIENCED DEMON LORD CAN'T PROPERLY APPRECIATE A HIGHER-LEVEL MONSTER.
IN OTHER WORDS...
ANYONE WHO LOOKS AT THE SKELETONS AND RIDICULES YOU IS LOWER-RANKED AND NARROW-MINDED.
THE ONES TO WATCH OUT FOR ARE THOSE WHO SEE THROUGH TENKO AND EL.

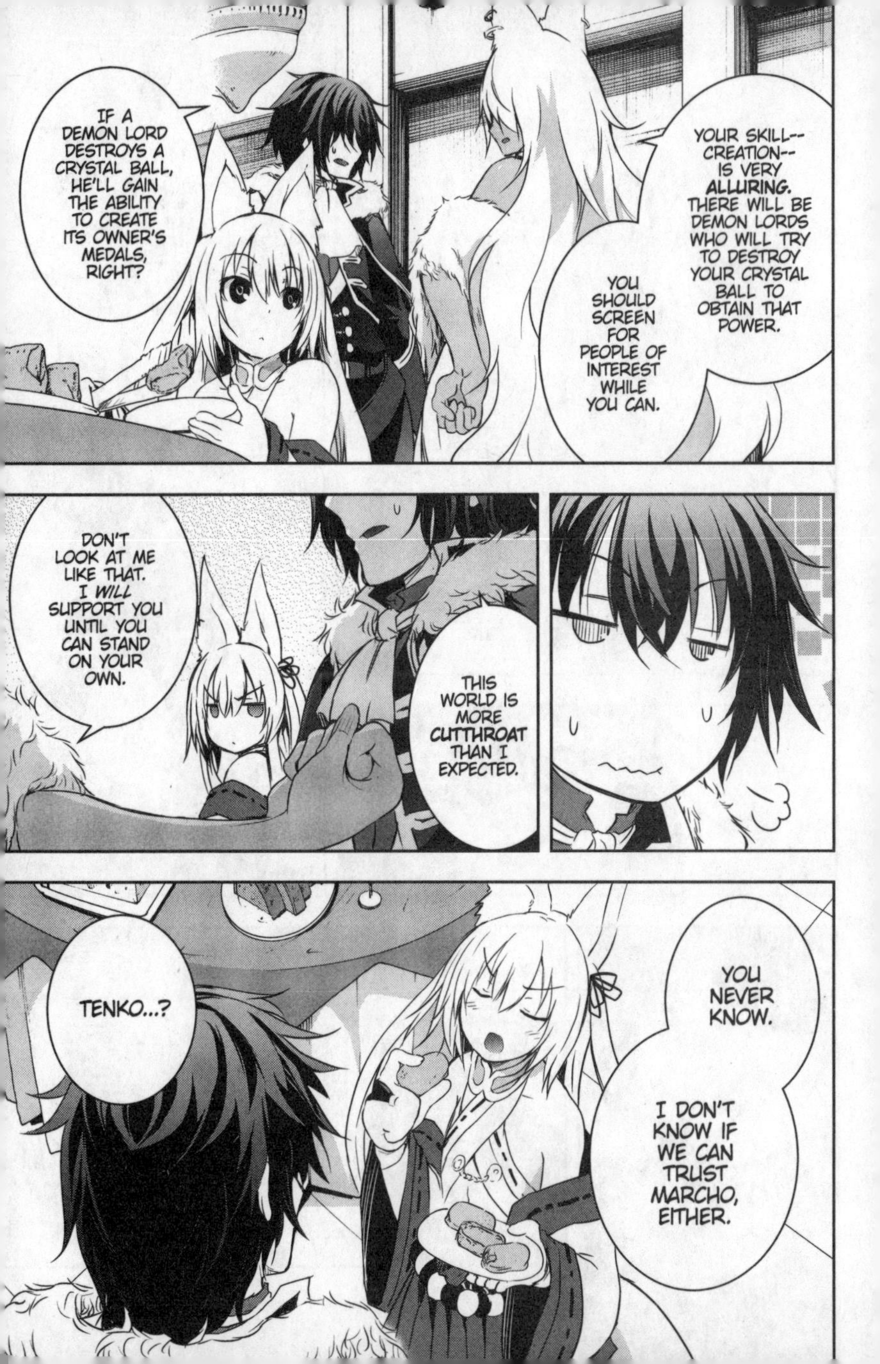
IF A DEMON LORD DESTROYS A CRYSTAL BALL, HE'LL GAIN THE ABILITY TO CREATE ITS OWNER'S MEDALS, RIGHT?
YOUR SKILL-- CREATION-- IS VERY ALLURING. THERE WILL BE DEMON LORDS WHO WILL TRY TO DESTROY YOUR CRYSTAL BALL TO OBTAIN THAT POWER.
YOU SHOULD SCREEN FOR PEOPLE OF INTEREST WHILE YOU CAN.
THIS WORLD IS MORE CUTTHROAT THAN I EXPECTED.
DON'T LOOK AT ME LIKE THAT. I WILL SUPPORT YOU UNTIL YOU CAN STAND ON YOUR OWN.
YOU NEVER KNOW.
I DON'T KNOW IF WE CAN TRUST MARCHO, EITHER.
TENKO...?

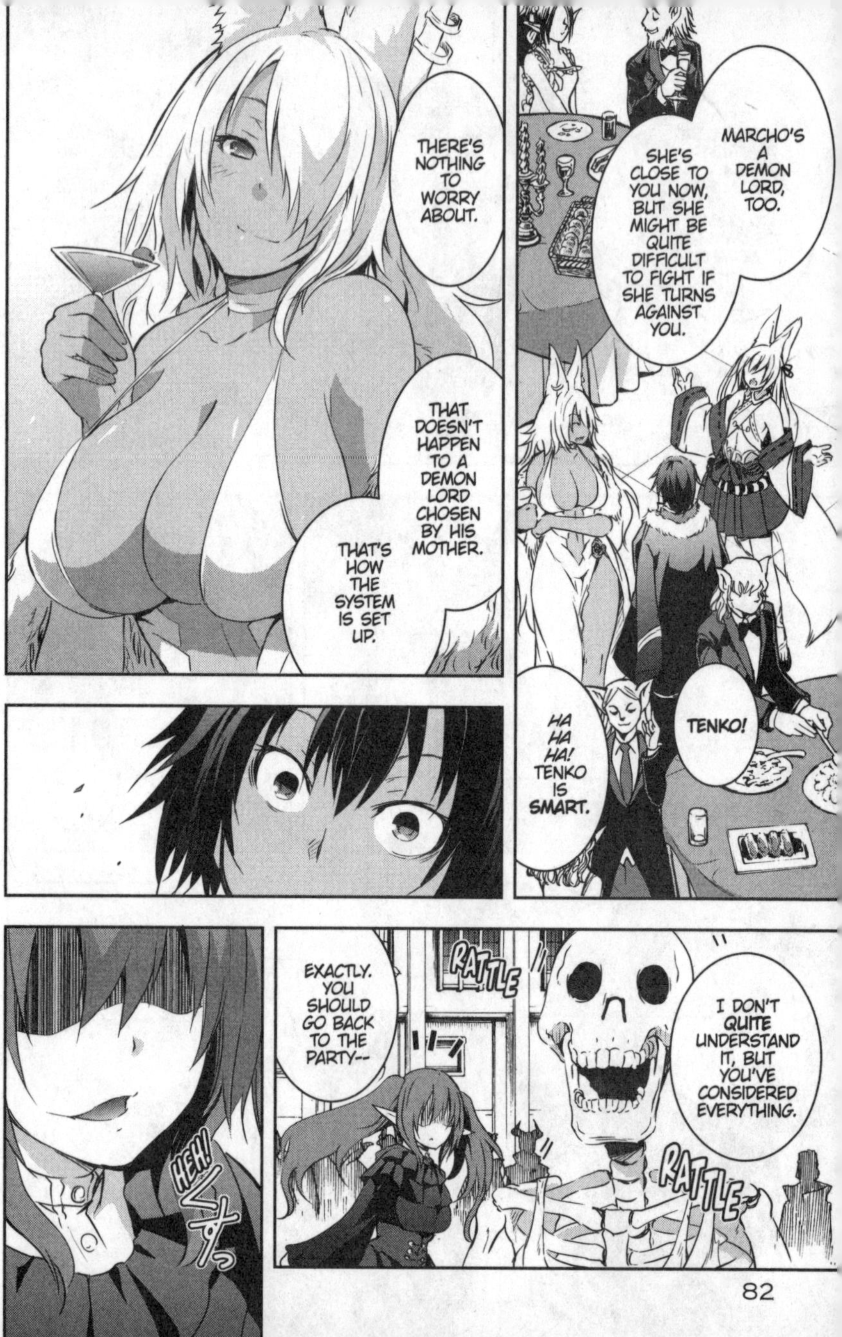
MARCHO'S A DEMON LORD, TOO.
SHE'S CLOSE TO YOU NOW, BUT SHE MIGHT BE QUITE DIFFICULT TO FIGHT IF SHE TURNS AGAINST YOU.
TENKO!
HA HA HA! TENKO IS SMART.
THERE'S NOTHING TO WORRY ABOUT.
THAT DOESN'T HAPPEN TO A DEMON LORD CHOSEN BY HIS MOTHER.
THAT'S HOW THE SYSTEM IS SET UP.
RATTLE
I DON'T QUITE UNDERSTAND IT, BUT YOU'VE CONSIDERED EVERYTHING.
RATTLE
EXACTLY. YOU SHOULD GO BACK TO THE PARTY--
HEH!
くすっ

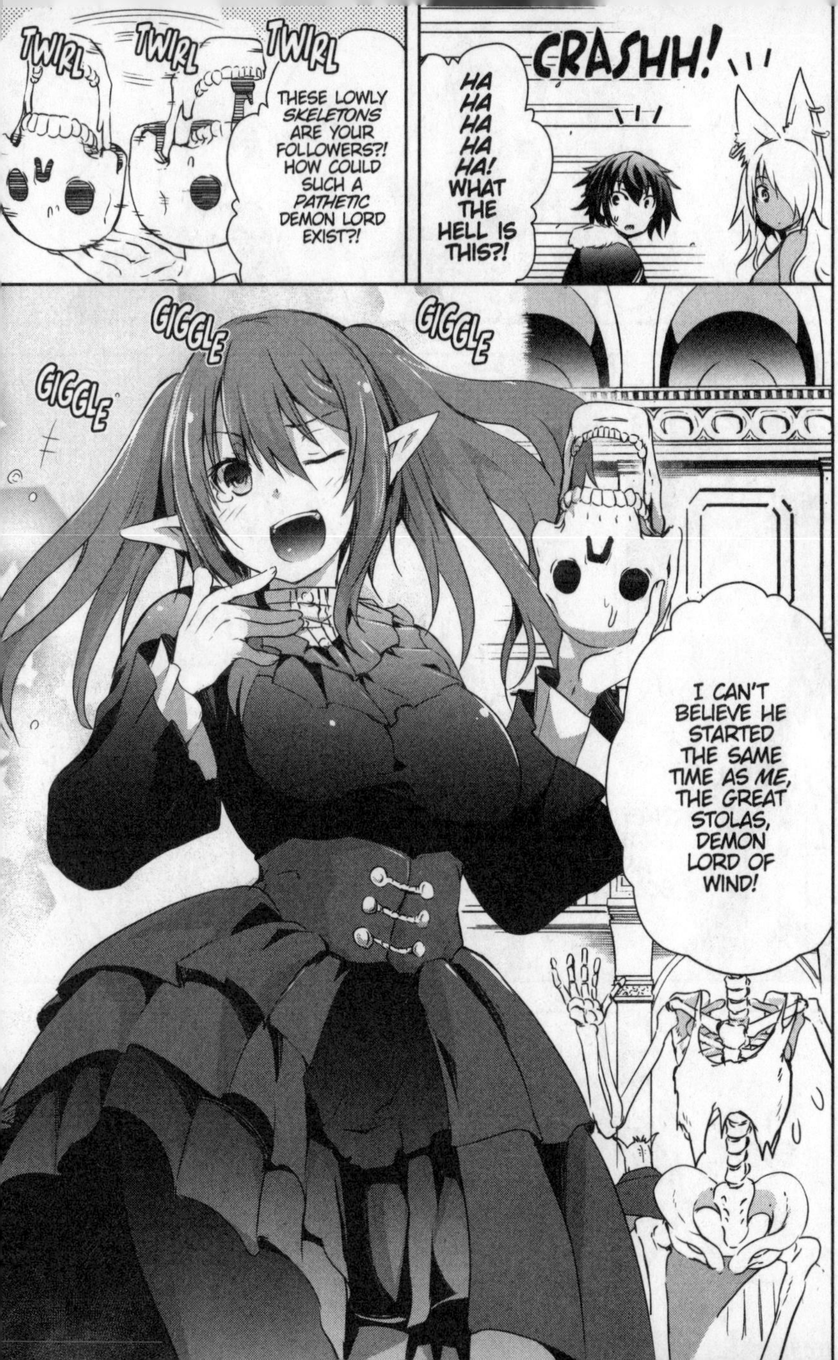
CRASHH!
HA HA HA HA HA HA! WHAT THE HELL IS THIS?!
TWIRL
TWIRL
TWIRL
THESE LOWLY *SKELETONS* ARE YOUR FOLLOWERS?! HOW COULD SUCH A *PATHETIC* DEMON LORD EXIST?!
I CAN'T BELIEVE HE STARTED THE SAME TIME AS *ME*, THE GREAT STOLAS, DEMON LORD OF WIND!
GIGGLE
GIGGLE
GIGGLE

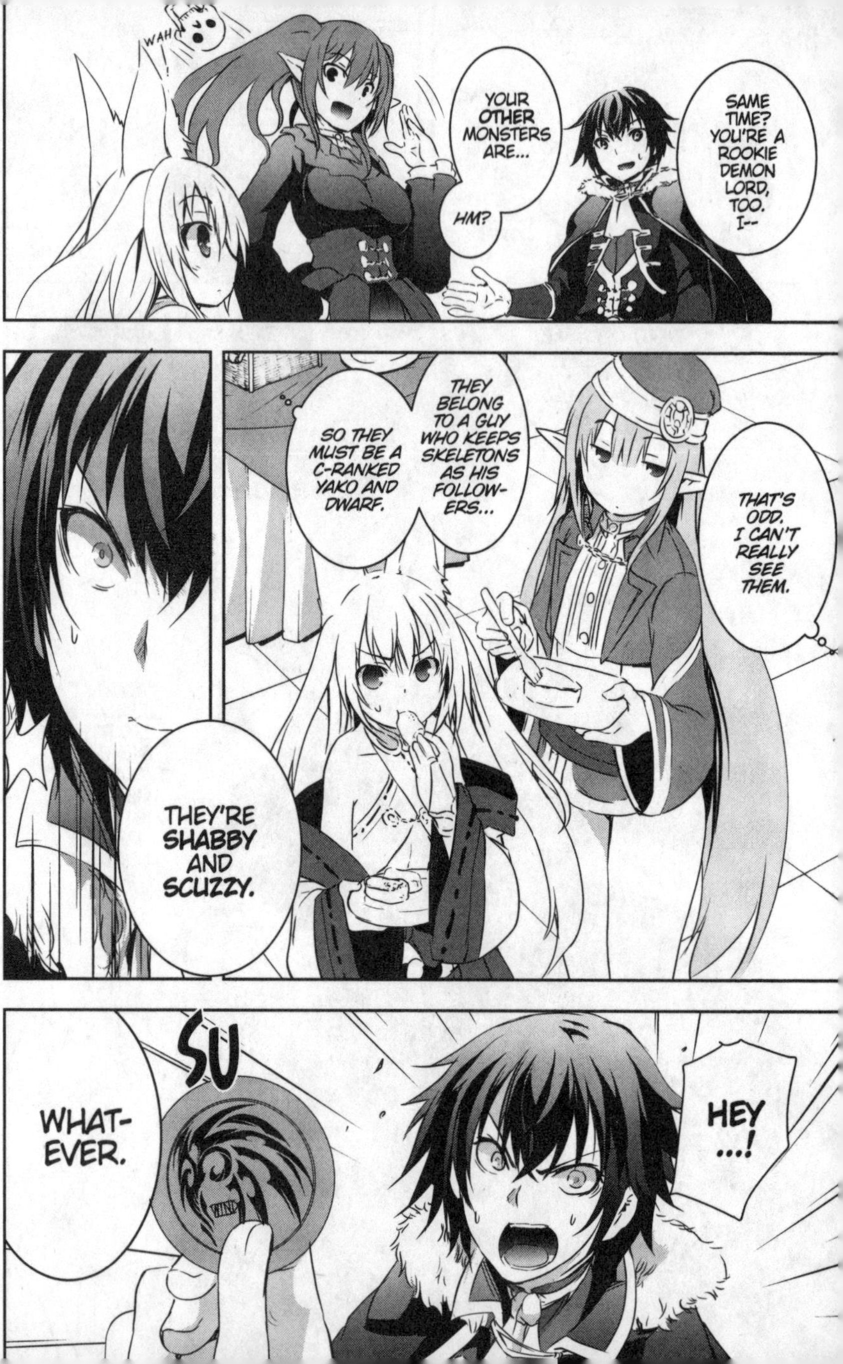
SAME TIME? YOU'RE A ROOKIE DEMON LORD, TOO. I--
YOUR OTHER MONSTERS ARE...
HM?
WAH
THAT'S ODD. I CAN'T REALLY SEE THEM.
THEY BELONG TO A GUY WHO KEEPS SKELETONS AS HIS FOLLOWERS...
SO THEY MUST BE A C-RANKED YAKO AND DWARF.
THEY'RE SHABBY AND SCUZZY.
HEY ...!
SU
WHAT-EVER.

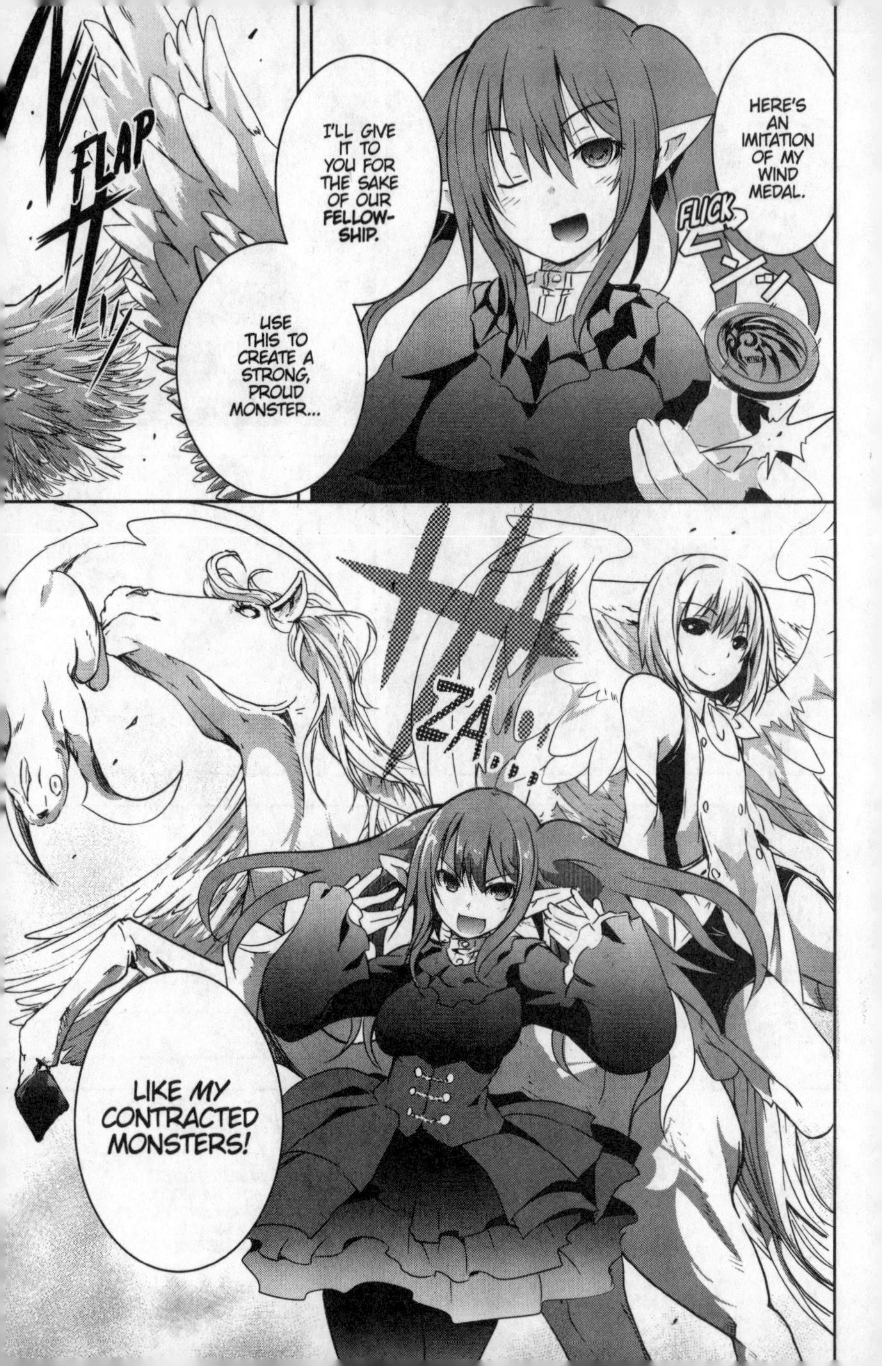
HERE'S AN IMITATION OF MY WIND MEDAL.
FLICK
I'LL GIVE IT TO YOU FOR THE SAKE OF OUR FELLOW-SHIP.
USE THIS TO CREATE A STRONG, PROUD MONSTER...
FLAP
ZA
LIKE MY CONTRACTED MONSTERS!

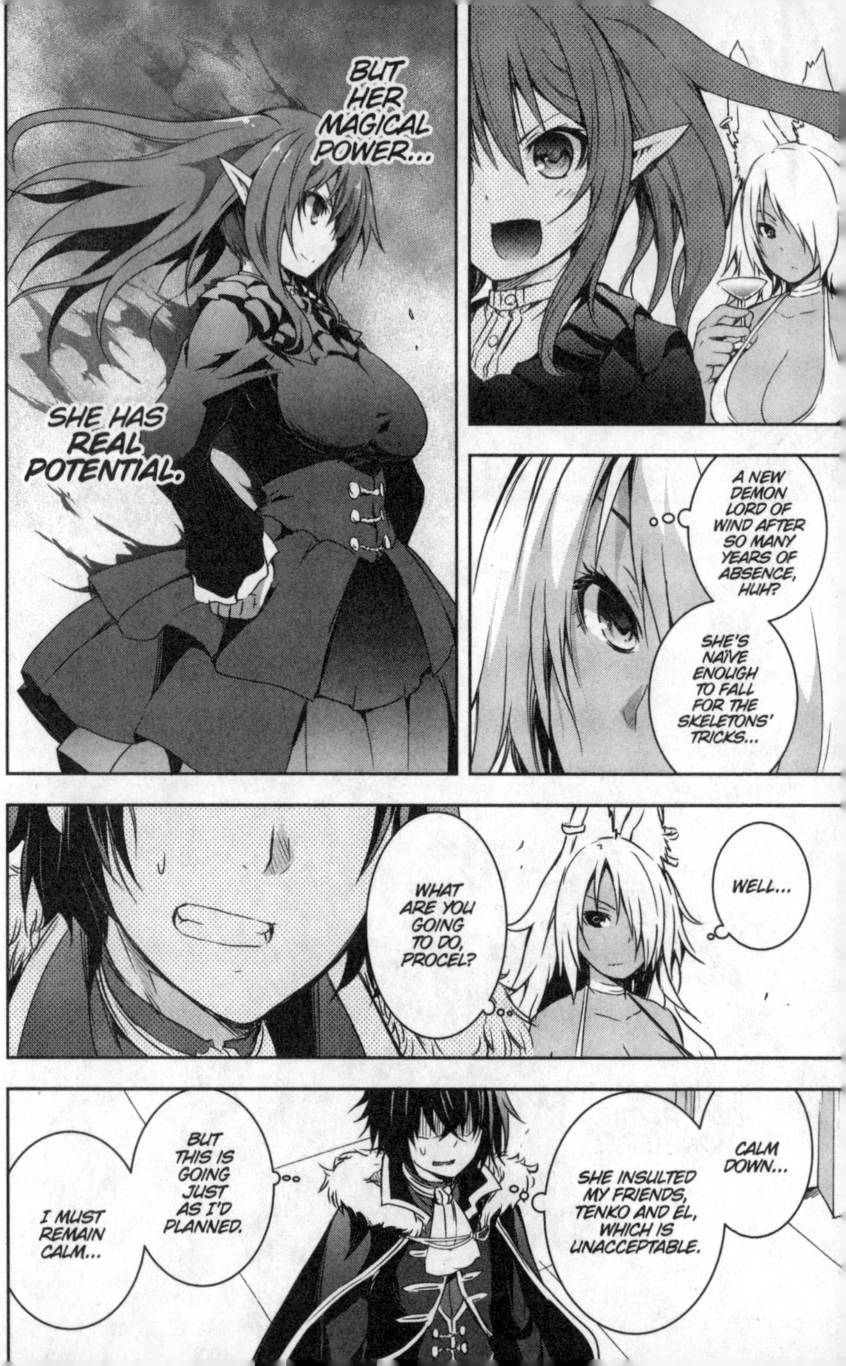
A NEW DEMON LORD OF WIND AFTER SO MANY YEARS OF ABSENCE, HUH?
SHE'S NAÏVE ENOUGH TO FALL FOR THE SKELETONS' TRICKS...
BUT HER MAGICAL POWER...
SHE HAS REAL POTENTIAL.
WELL...
WHAT ARE YOU GOING TO DO, PROCEL?
CALM DOWN...
SHE INSULTED MY FRIENDS, TENKO AND EL, WHICH IS UNACCEPTABLE.
BUT THIS IS GOING JUST AS I'D PLANNED.
I MUST REMAIN CALM...

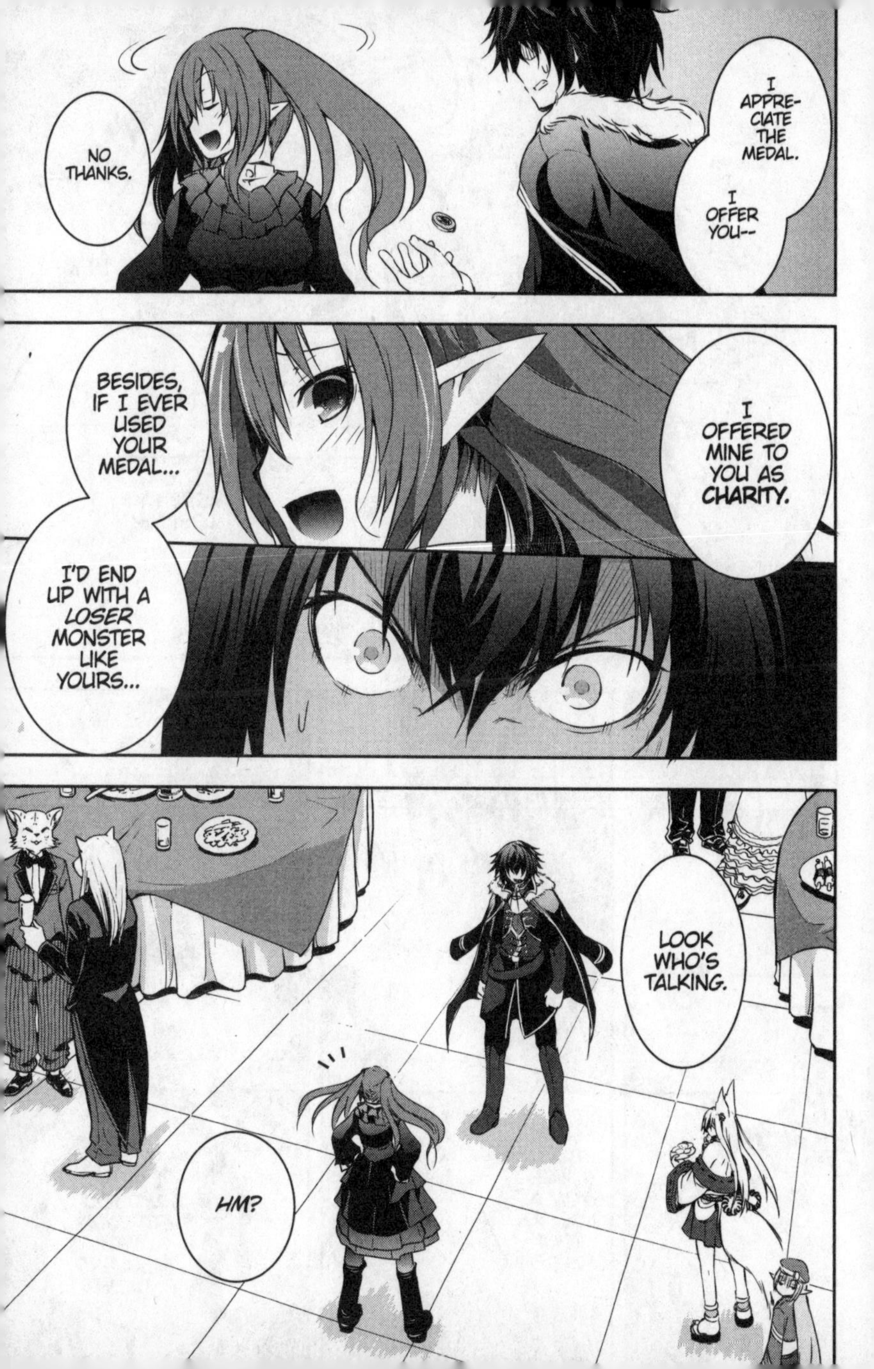
I APPRE-CIATE THE MEDAL.
I OFFER YOU--
NO THANKS.
I OFFERED MINE TO YOU AS CHARITY.
BESIDES, IF I EVER USED YOUR MEDAL...
I'D END UP WITH A *LOSER* MONSTER LIKE YOURS...
LOOK WHO'S TALKING.
HM?

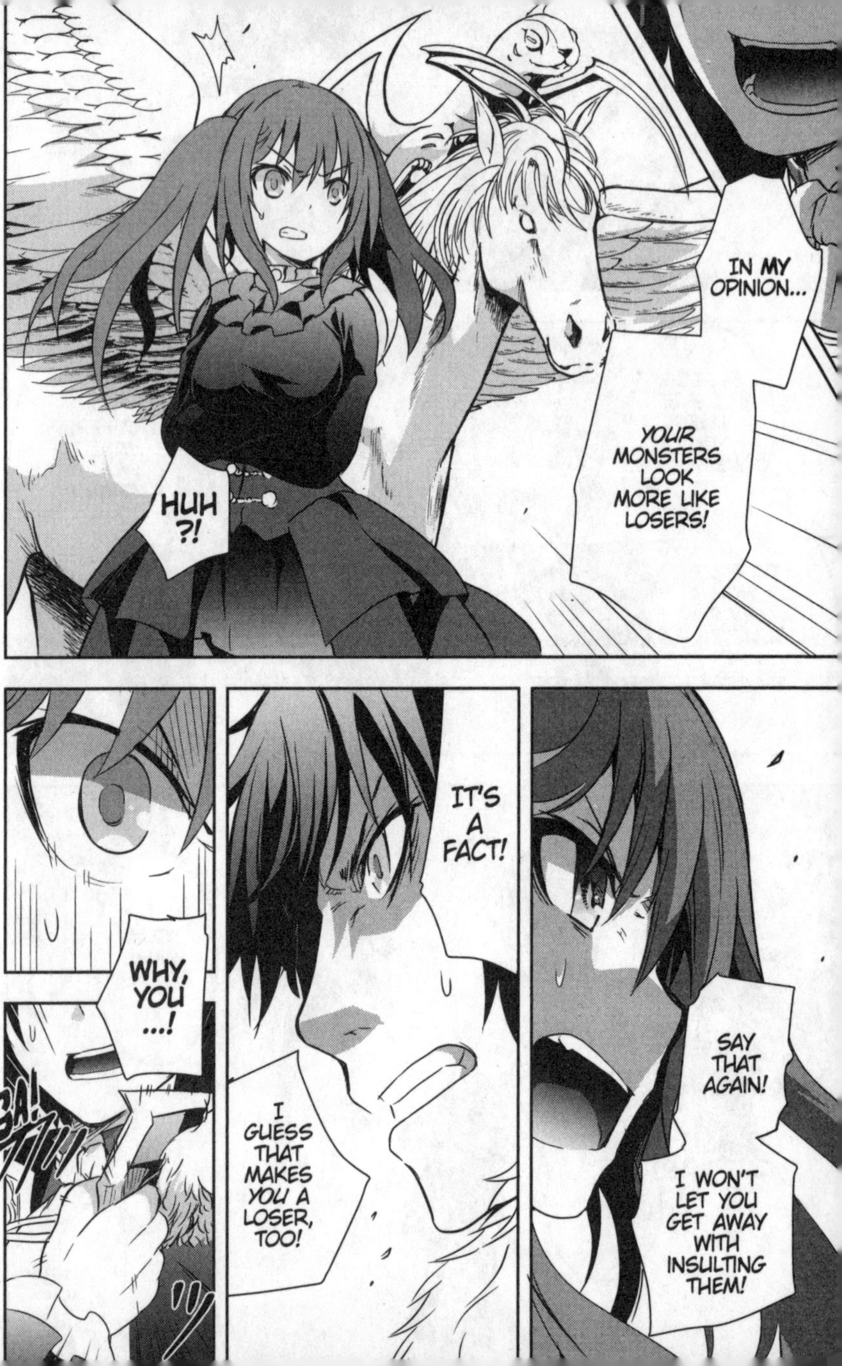
IN MY OPINION...
YOUR MONSTERS LOOK MORE LIKE LOSERS!
HUH ?!
SAY THAT AGAIN!
I WON'T LET YOU GET AWAY WITH INSULTING THEM!
IT'S A FACT!
I GUESS THAT MAKES YOU A LOSER, TOO!
WHY, YOU ...!
GA!

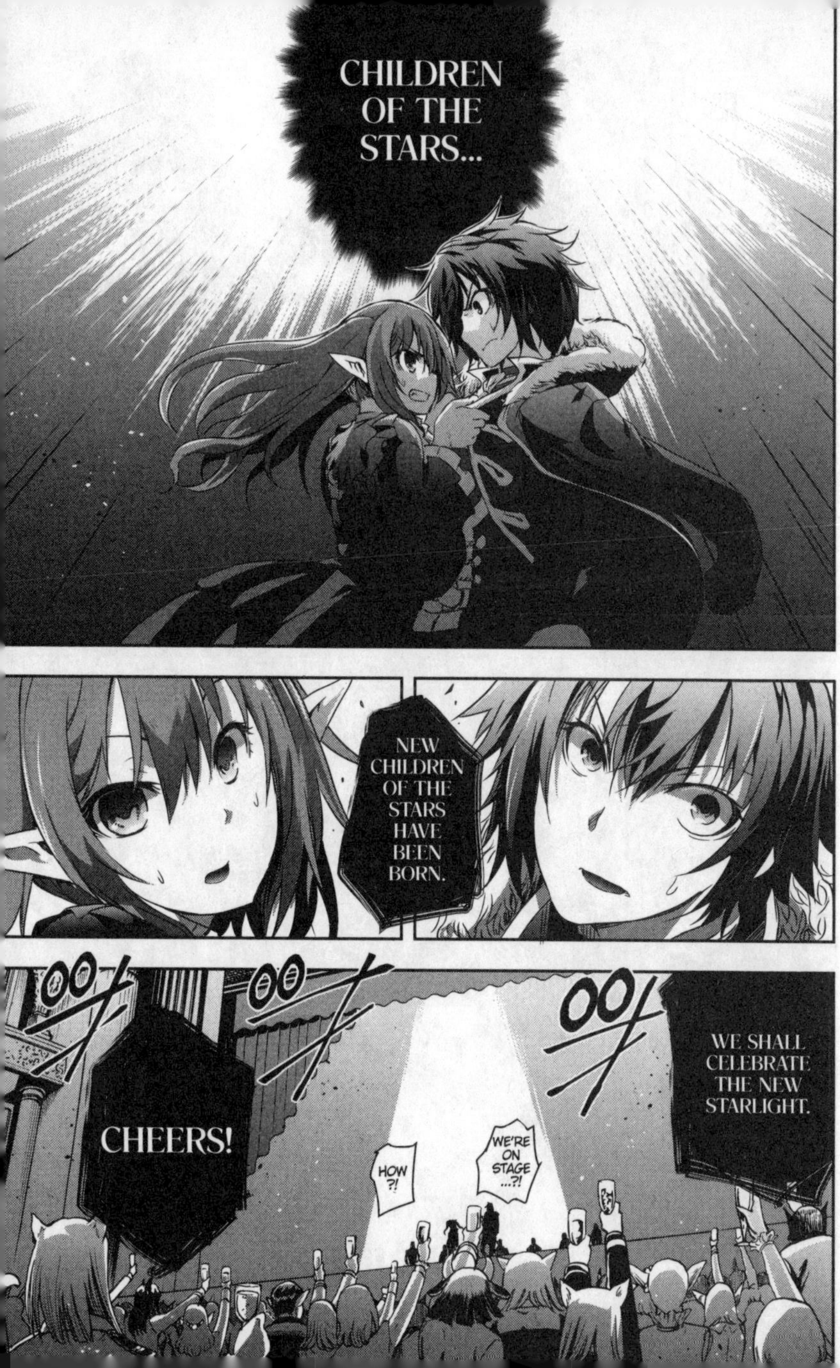
CHILDREN OF THE STARS...
NEW CHILDREN OF THE STARS HAVE BEEN BORN.
WE SHALL CELEBRATE THE NEW STARLIGHT.
OO
WE'RE ON STAGE ...?!
HOW?!
OO
CHEERS!
OO

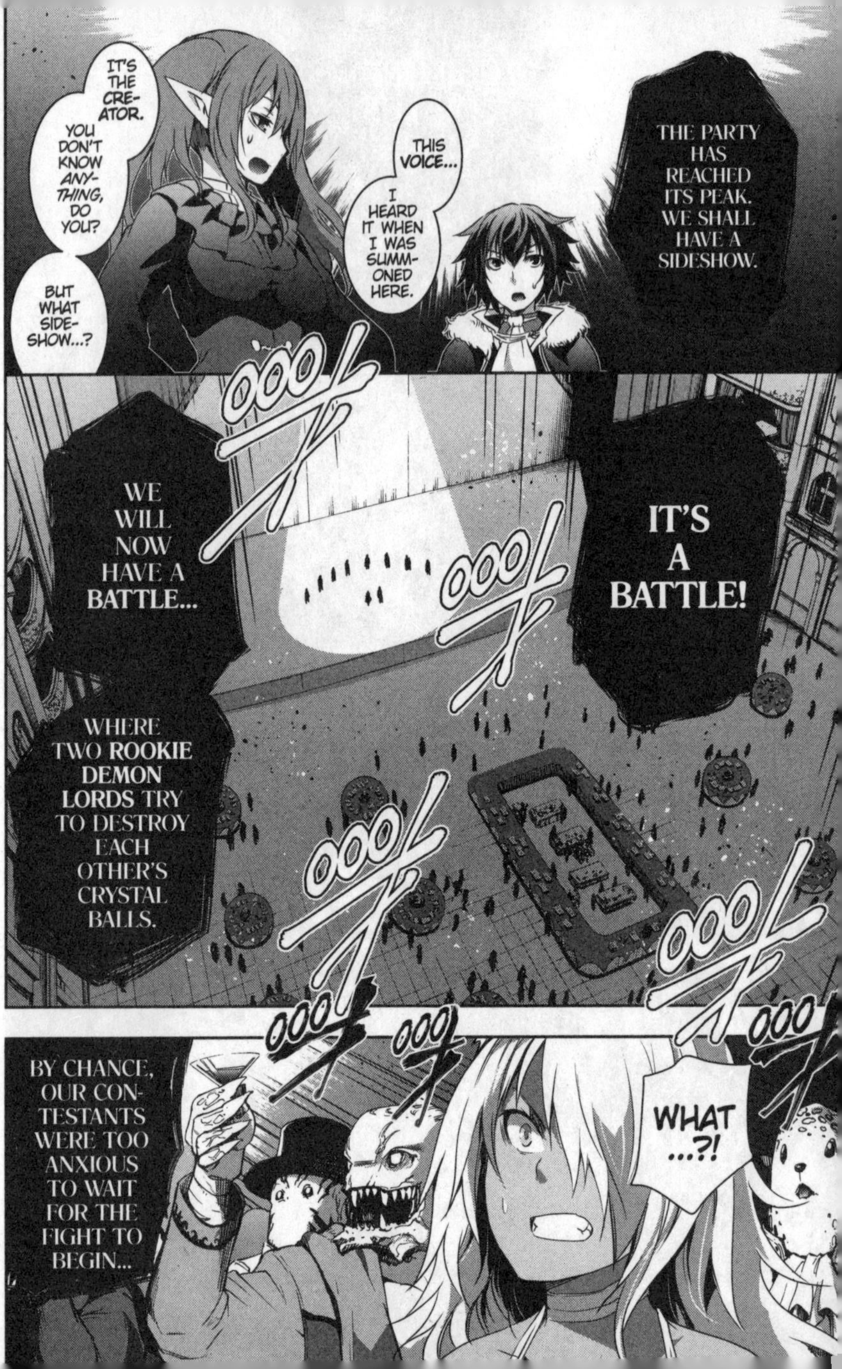
THE PARTY HAS REACHED ITS PEAK. WE SHALL HAVE A SIDESHOW.
THIS VOICE...
I HEARD IT WHEN I WAS SUMMONED HERE.
IT'S THE CREATOR. YOU DON'T KNOW ANYTHING, DO YOU?
BUT WHAT SIDESHOW...?
OOOH
IT'S A BATTLE!
OOOH
WE WILL NOW HAVE A BATTLE...
OOOH
OOOH
WHERE TWO ROOKIE DEMON LORDS TRY TO DESTROY EACH OTHER'S CRYSTAL BALLS.
OOO
WHAT ...?!
OOO
OOO
BY CHANCE, OUR CONTESTANTS WERE TOO ANXIOUS TO WAIT FOR THE FIGHT TO BEGIN...

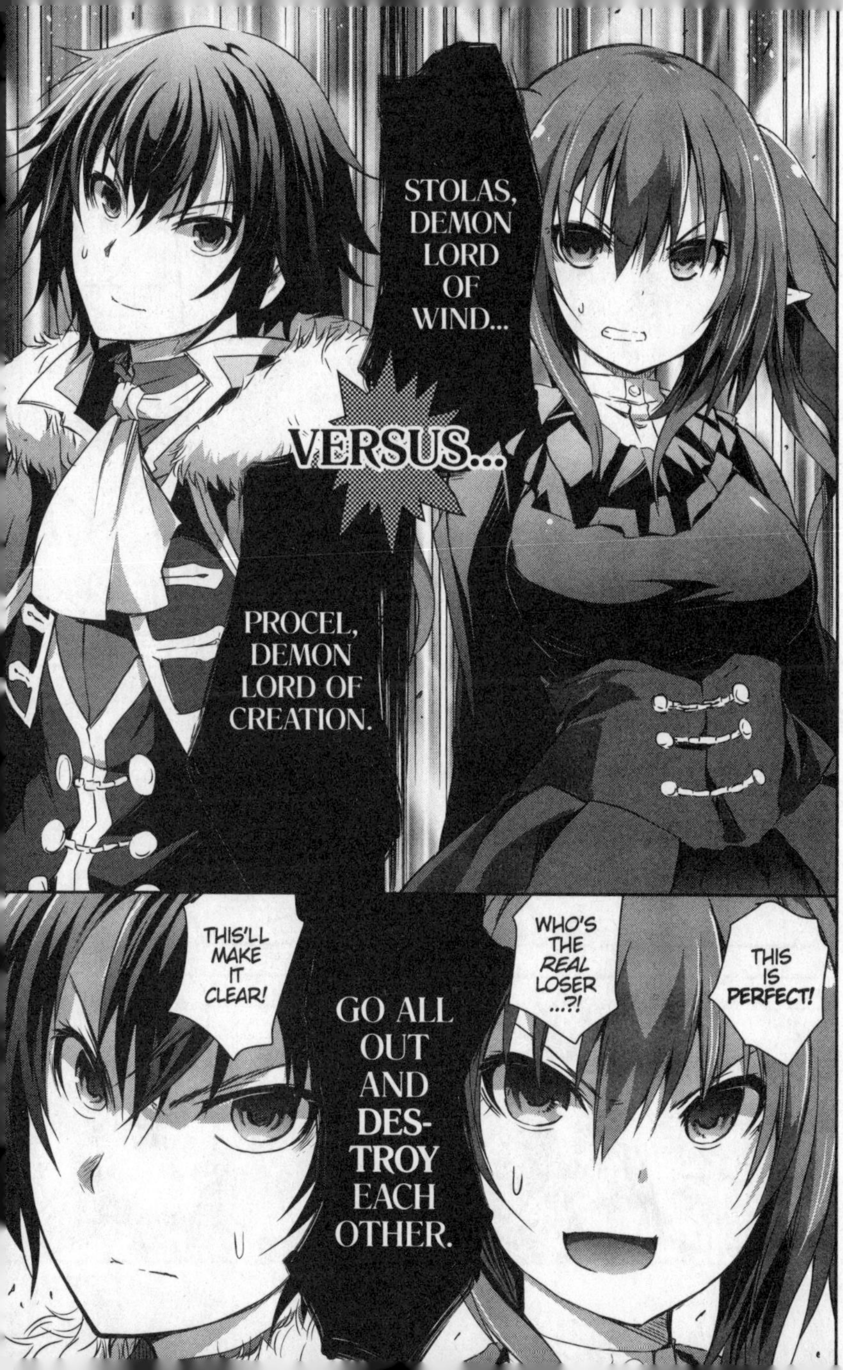
STOLAS, DEMON LORD OF WIND...
VERSUS...
PROCEL, DEMON LORD OF CREATION.
THIS IS PERFECT!
WHO'S THE *REAL* LOSER ...?!
GO ALL OUT AND DES-TROY EACH OTHER.
THIS'LL MAKE IT CLEAR!

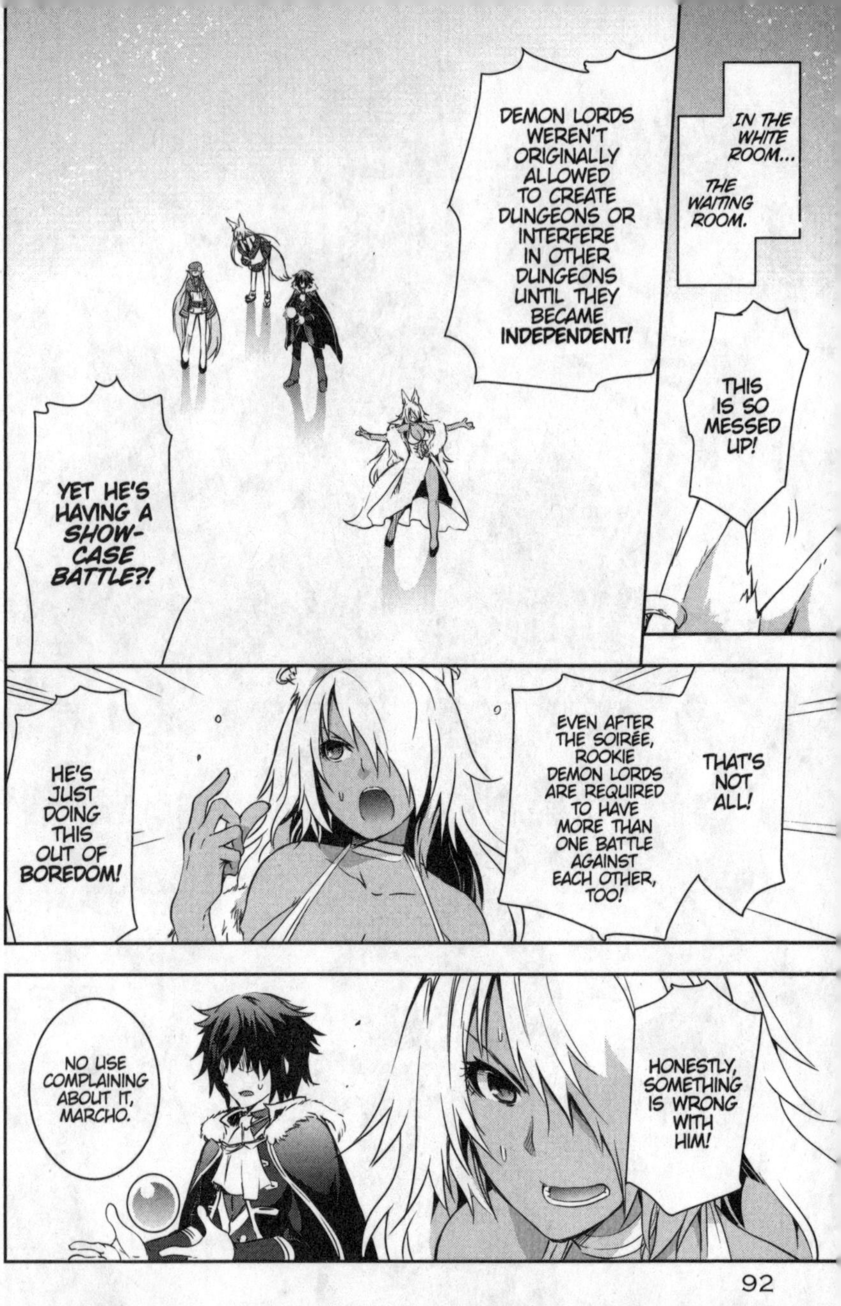
IN THE WHITE ROOM... THE WAITING ROOM.
THIS IS SO MESSED UP!
DEMON LORDS WEREN'T ORIGINALLY ALLOWED TO CREATE DUNGEONS OR INTERFERE IN OTHER DUNGEONS UNTIL THEY BECAME INDEPENDENT!
YET HE'S HAVING A SHOW-CASE BATTLE?!
THAT'S NOT ALL!
EVEN AFTER THE SOIRÉE, ROOKIE DEMON LORDS ARE REQUIRED TO HAVE MORE THAN ONE BATTLE AGAINST EACH OTHER, TOO!
HE'S JUST DOING THIS OUT OF BOREDOM!
HONESTLY, SOMETHING IS WRONG WITH HIM!
NO USE COMPLAINING ABOUT IT, MARCHO.

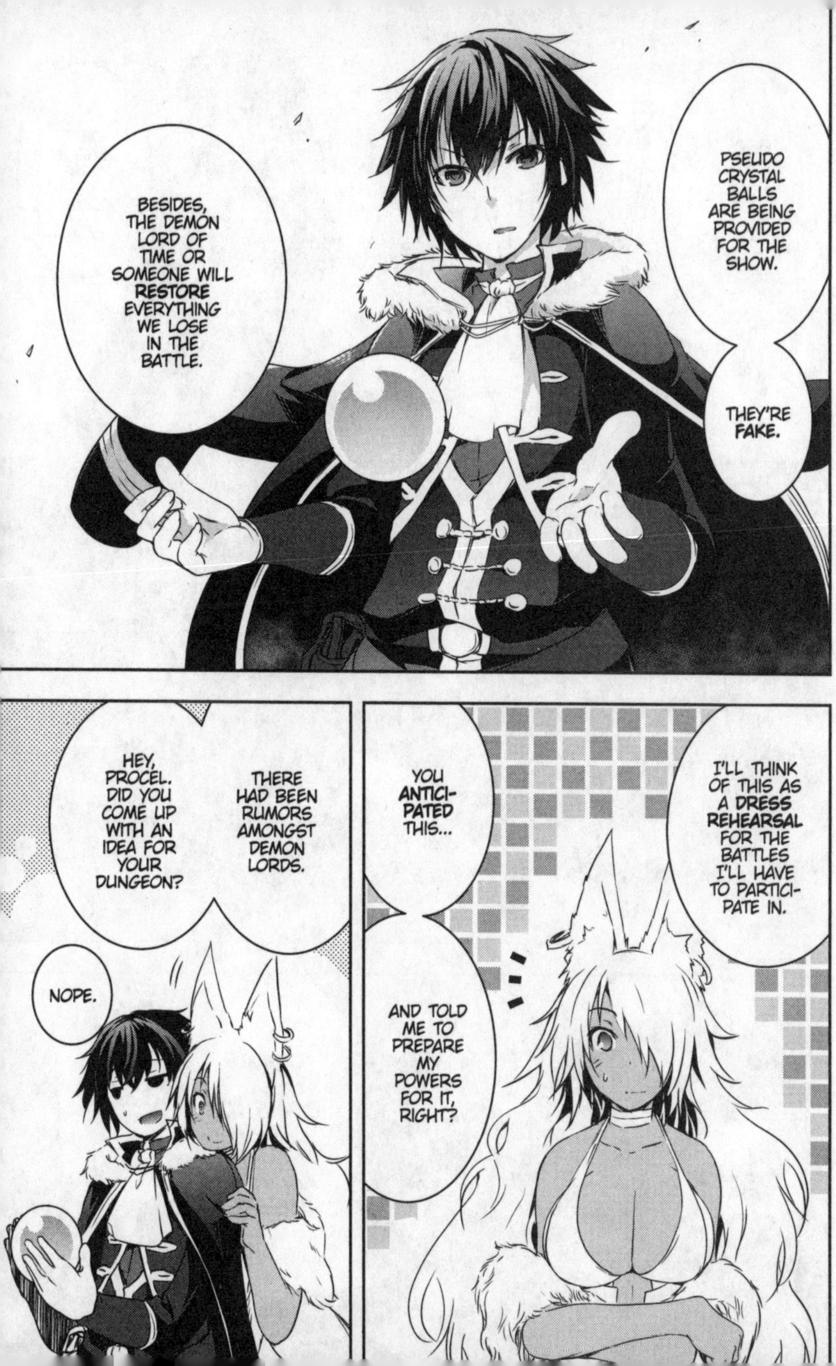
PSEUDO CRYSTAL BALLS ARE BEING PROVIDED FOR THE SHOW.
THEY'RE FAKE.
BESIDES, THE DEMON LORD OF TIME OR SOMEONE WILL RESTORE EVERYTHING WE LOSE IN THE BATTLE.
I'LL THINK OF THIS AS A DRESS REHEARSAL FOR THE BATTLES I'LL HAVE TO PARTICIPATE IN.
YOU ANTICIPATED THIS...
AND TOLD ME TO PREPARE MY POWERS FOR IT, RIGHT?
THERE HAD BEEN RUMORS AMONGST DEMON LORDS.
HEY, PROCEL. DID YOU COME UP WITH AN IDEA FOR YOUR DUNGEON?
NOPE.

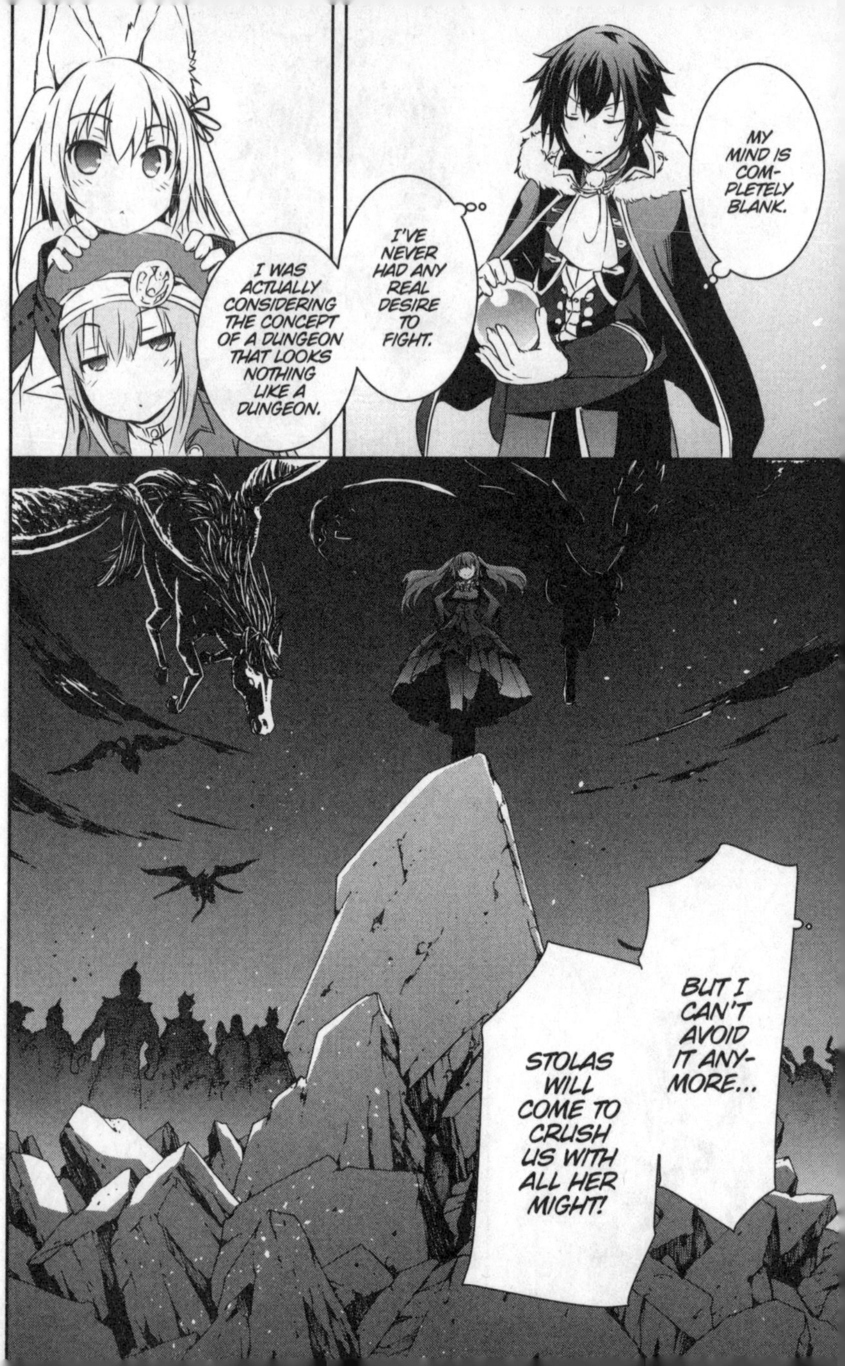
MY MIND IS COMPLETELY BLANK.
I'VE NEVER HAD ANY REAL DESIRE TO FIGHT.
I WAS ACTUALLY CONSIDERING THE CONCEPT OF A DUNGEON THAT LOOKS NOTHING LIKE A DUNGEON.
BUT I CAN'T AVOID IT ANYMORE...
STOLAS WILL COME TO CRUSH US WITH ALL HER MIGHT!

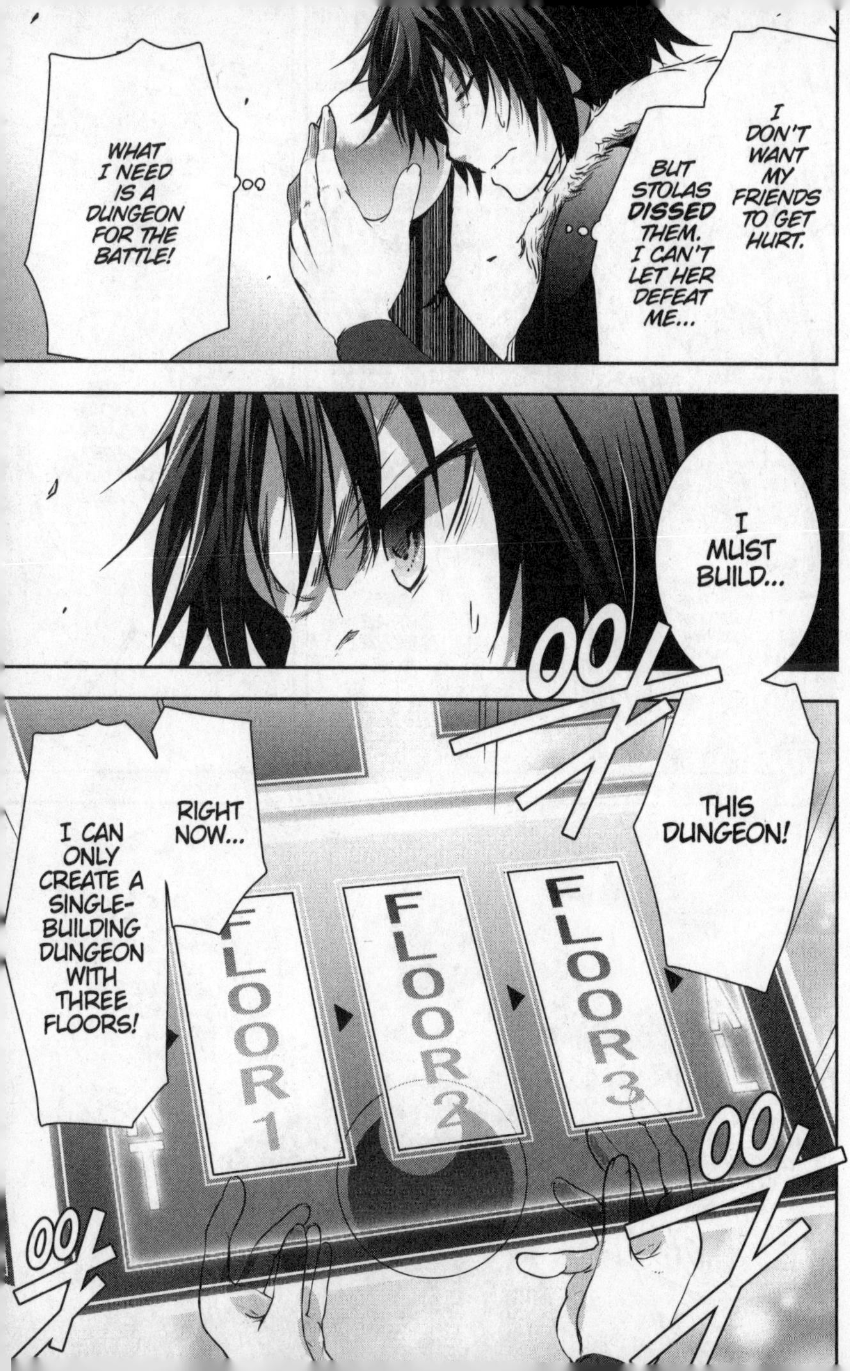
I DON'T WANT MY FRIENDS TO GET HURT.
BUT STOLAS DISSED THEM. I CAN'T LET HER DEFEAT ME...
WHAT I NEED IS A DUNGEON FOR THE BATTLE!
I MUST BUILD...
THIS DUNGEON!
RIGHT NOW...
I CAN ONLY CREATE A SINGLE-BUILDING DUNGEON WITH THREE FLOORS!
FLOOR 3
FLOOR 2
FLOOR 1

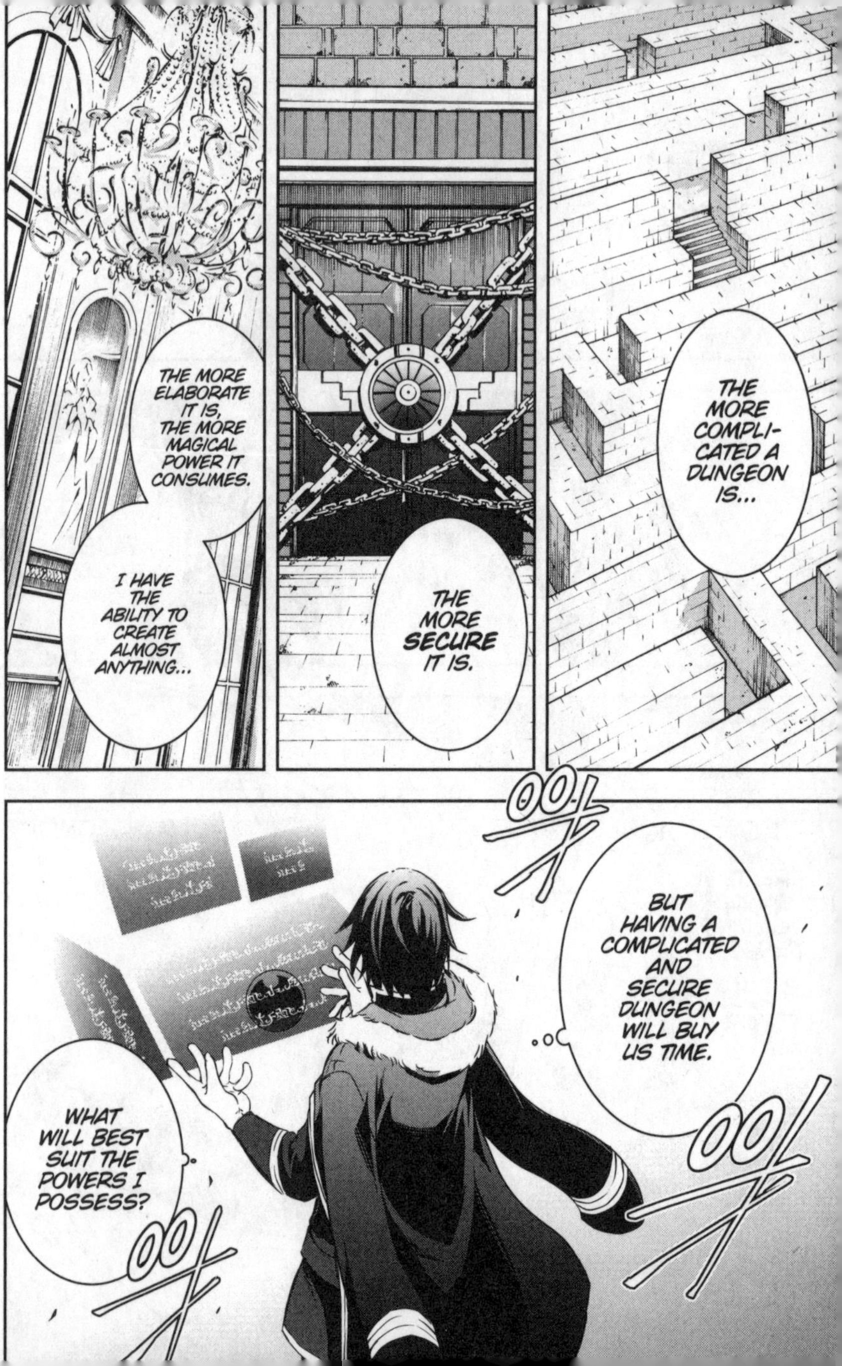
THE MORE COMPLICATED A DUNGEON IS...
THE MORE SECURE IT IS.
THE MORE ELABORATE IT IS, THE MORE MAGICAL POWER IT CONSUMES.
I HAVE THE ABILITY TO CREATE ALMOST ANYTHING...
BUT HAVING A COMPLICATED AND SECURE DUNGEON WILL BUY US TIME.
WHAT WILL BEST SUIT THE POWERS I POSSESS?

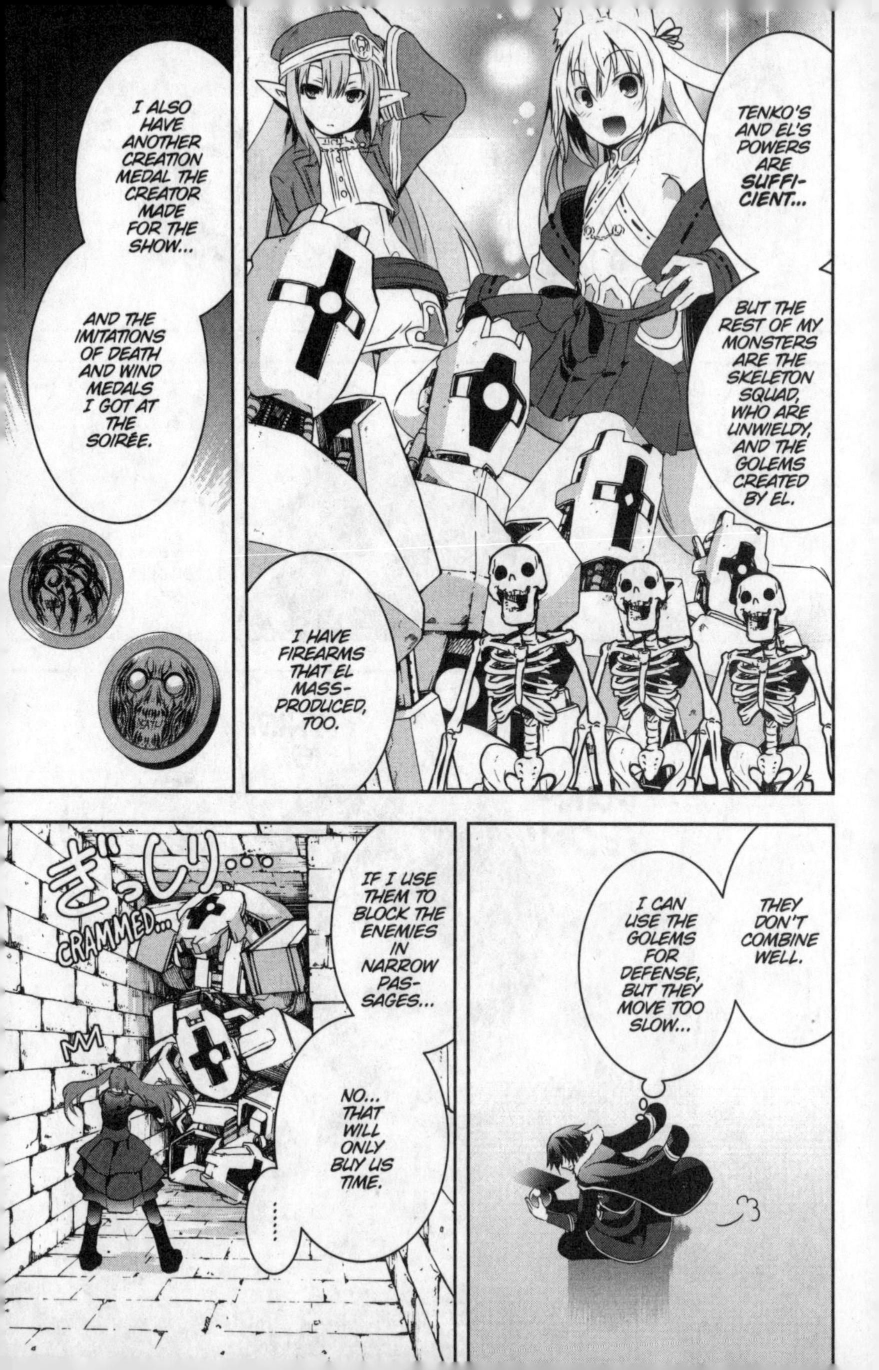
TENKO'S AND EL'S POWERS ARE SUFFICIENT...
BUT THE REST OF MY MONSTERS ARE THE SKELETON SQUAD, WHO ARE UNWIELDY, AND THE GOLEMS CREATED BY EL.
I HAVE FIREARMS THAT EL MASS-PRODUCED, TOO.
I ALSO HAVE ANOTHER CREATION MEDAL THE CREATOR MADE FOR THE SHOW...
AND THE IMITATIONS OF DEATH AND WIND MEDALS I GOT AT THE SOIRÉE.
THEY DON'T COMBINE WELL.
I CAN USE THE GOLEMS FOR DEFENSE, BUT THEY MOVE TOO SLOW...
IF I USE THEM TO BLOCK THE ENEMIES IN NARROW PASSAGES...
NO... THAT WILL ONLY BUY US TIME.
......
ぎっしり...
CRAMMED...

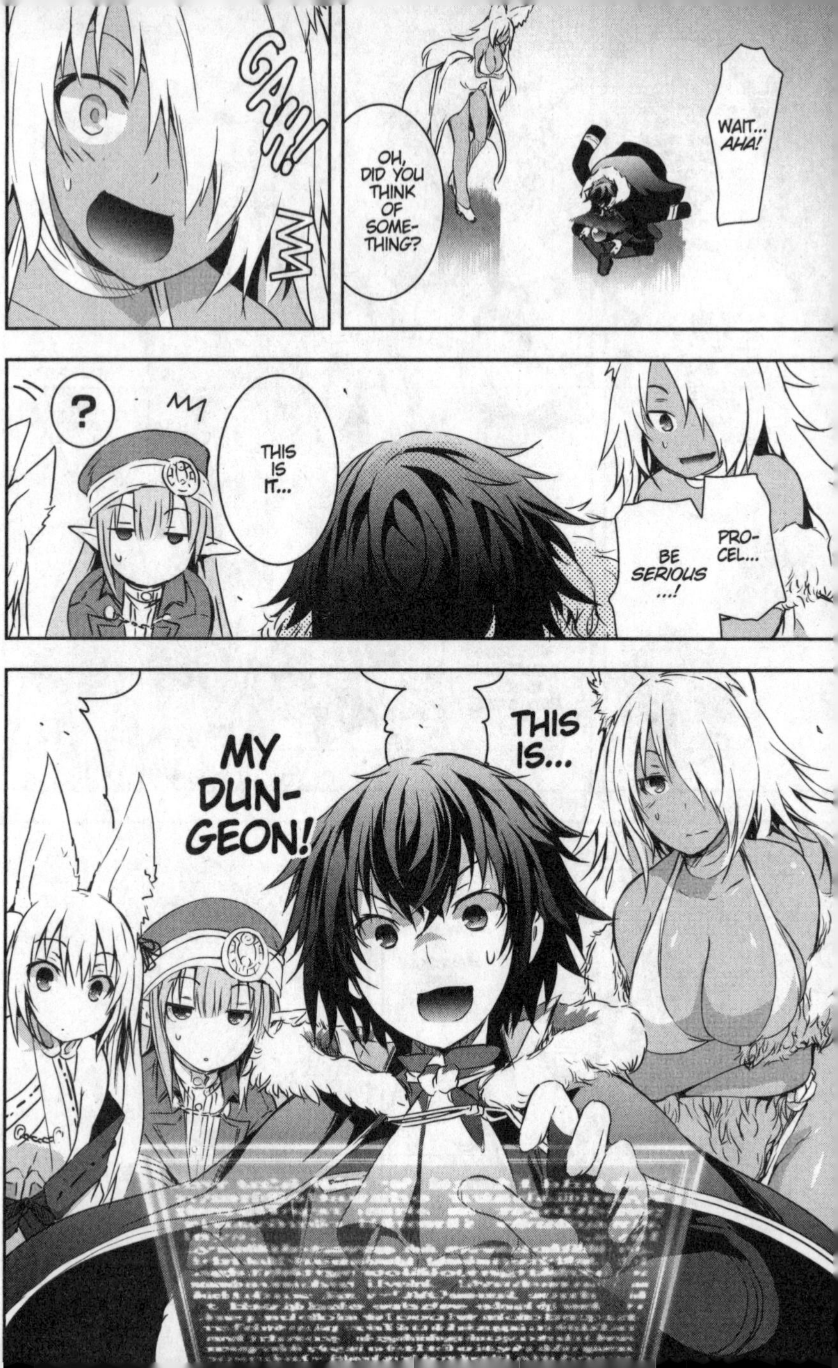
WAIT... AHA!
OH, DID YOU THINK OF SOME-THING?
GAH!
PRO-CEL... BE SERIOUS...!
THIS IS IT...
?
THIS IS...
MY DUN-GEON!

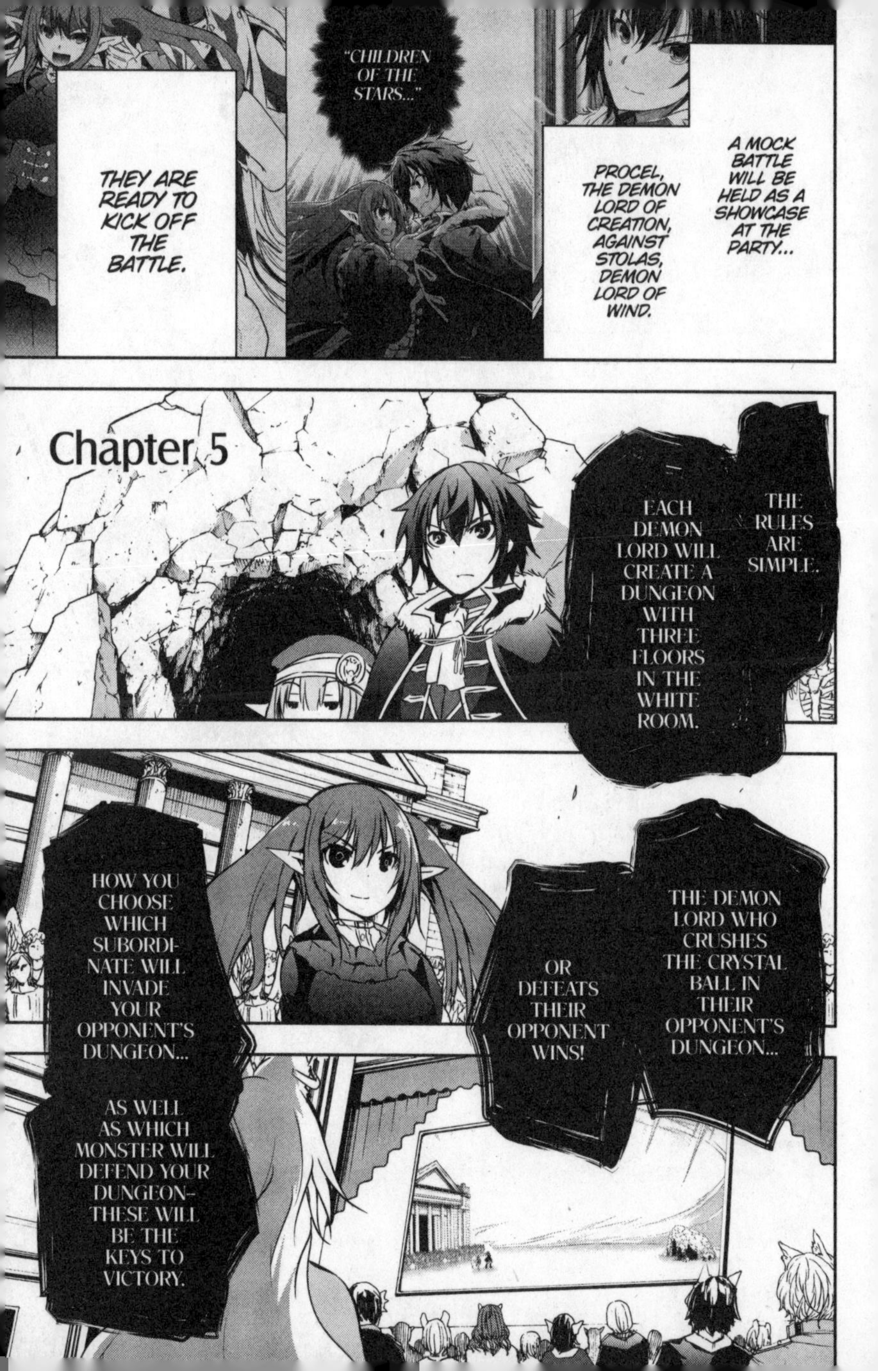
A MOCK BATTLE WILL BE HELD AS A SHOWCASE AT THE PARTY...
PROCEL, THE DEMON LORD OF CREATION, AGAINST STOLAS, DEMON LORD OF WIND.
"CHILDREN OF THE STARS..."
THEY ARE READY TO KICK OFF THE BATTLE.
Chapter 5
THE RULES ARE SIMPLE.
EACH DEMON LORD WILL CREATE A DUNGEON WITH THREE FLOORS IN THE WHITE ROOM.
THE DEMON LORD WHO CRUSHES THE CRYSTAL BALL IN THEIR OPPONENT'S DUNGEON...
OR DEFEATS THEIR OPPONENT WINS!
HOW YOU CHOOSE WHICH SUBORDI-NATE WILL INVADE YOUR OPPONENT'S DUNGEON...
AS WELL AS WHICH MONSTER WILL DEFEND YOUR DUNGEON- THESE WILL BE THE KEYS TO VICTORY.

Chapter 5: **Mithril Golem**

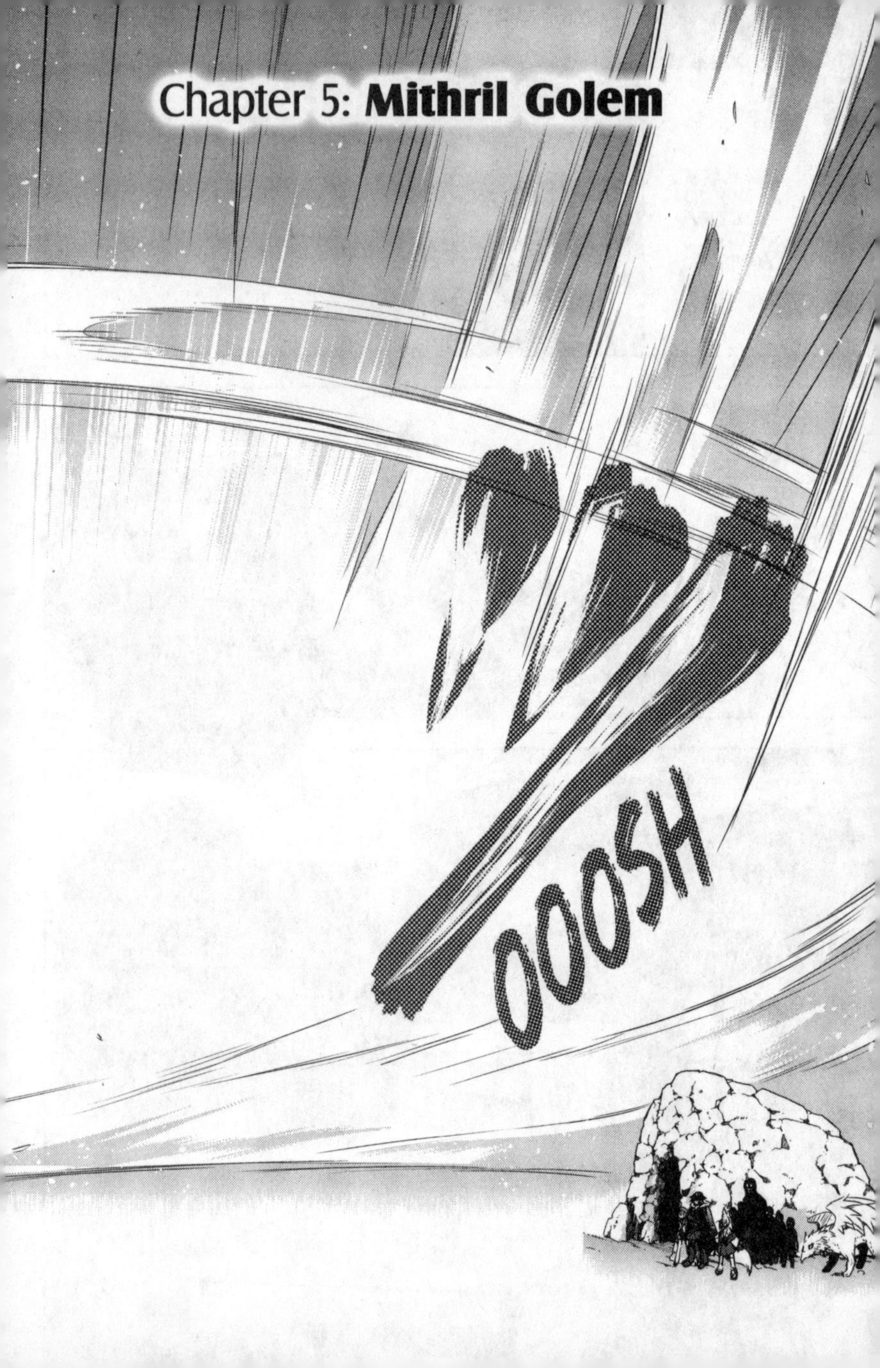
OOOSH

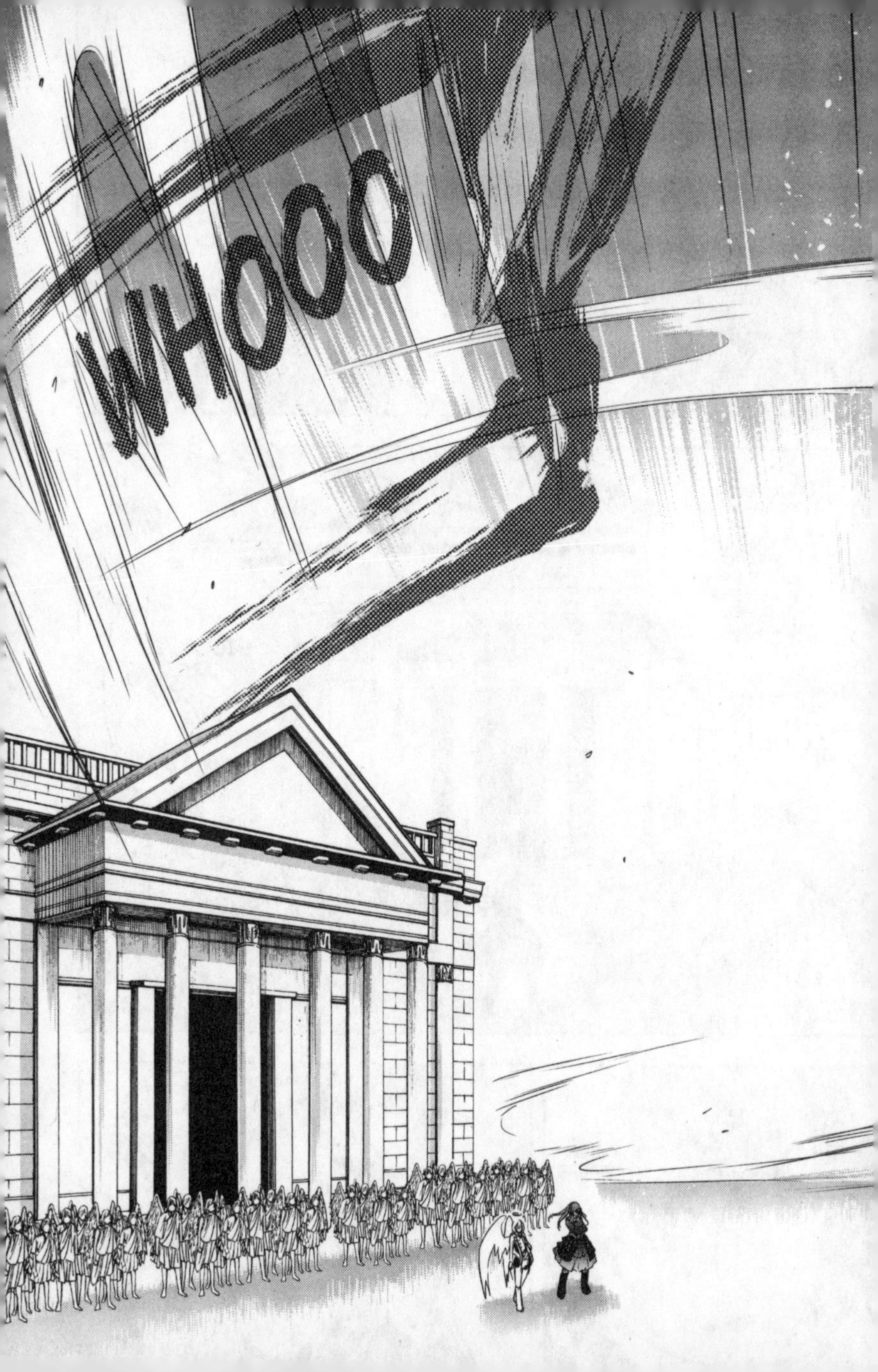
WHOOO

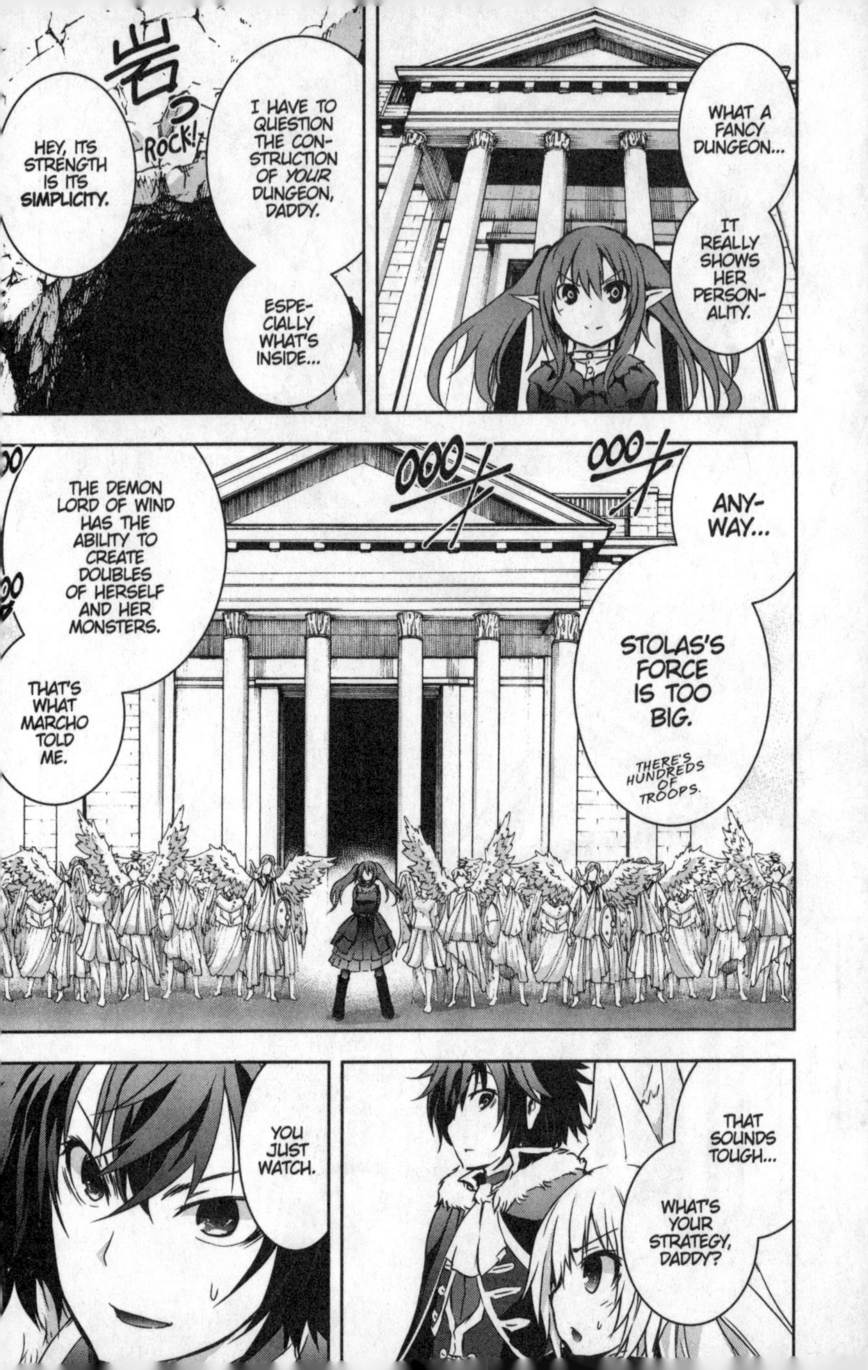
WHAT A FANCY DUNGEON...
IT REALLY SHOWS HER PERSONALITY.
I HAVE TO QUESTION THE CONSTRUCTION OF YOUR DUNGEON, DADDY.
ESPECIALLY WHAT'S INSIDE...
岩っ ROCK!
HEY, ITS STRENGTH IS ITS SIMPLICITY.
OOO
OOO
ANYWAY...
STOLAS'S FORCE IS TOO BIG.
THERE'S HUNDREDS OF TROOPS.
THE DEMON LORD OF WIND HAS THE ABILITY TO CREATE DOUBLES OF HERSELF AND HER MONSTERS.
THAT'S WHAT MARCHO TOLD ME.
THAT SOUNDS TOUGH...
WHAT'S YOUR STRATEGY, DADDY?
YOU JUST WATCH.

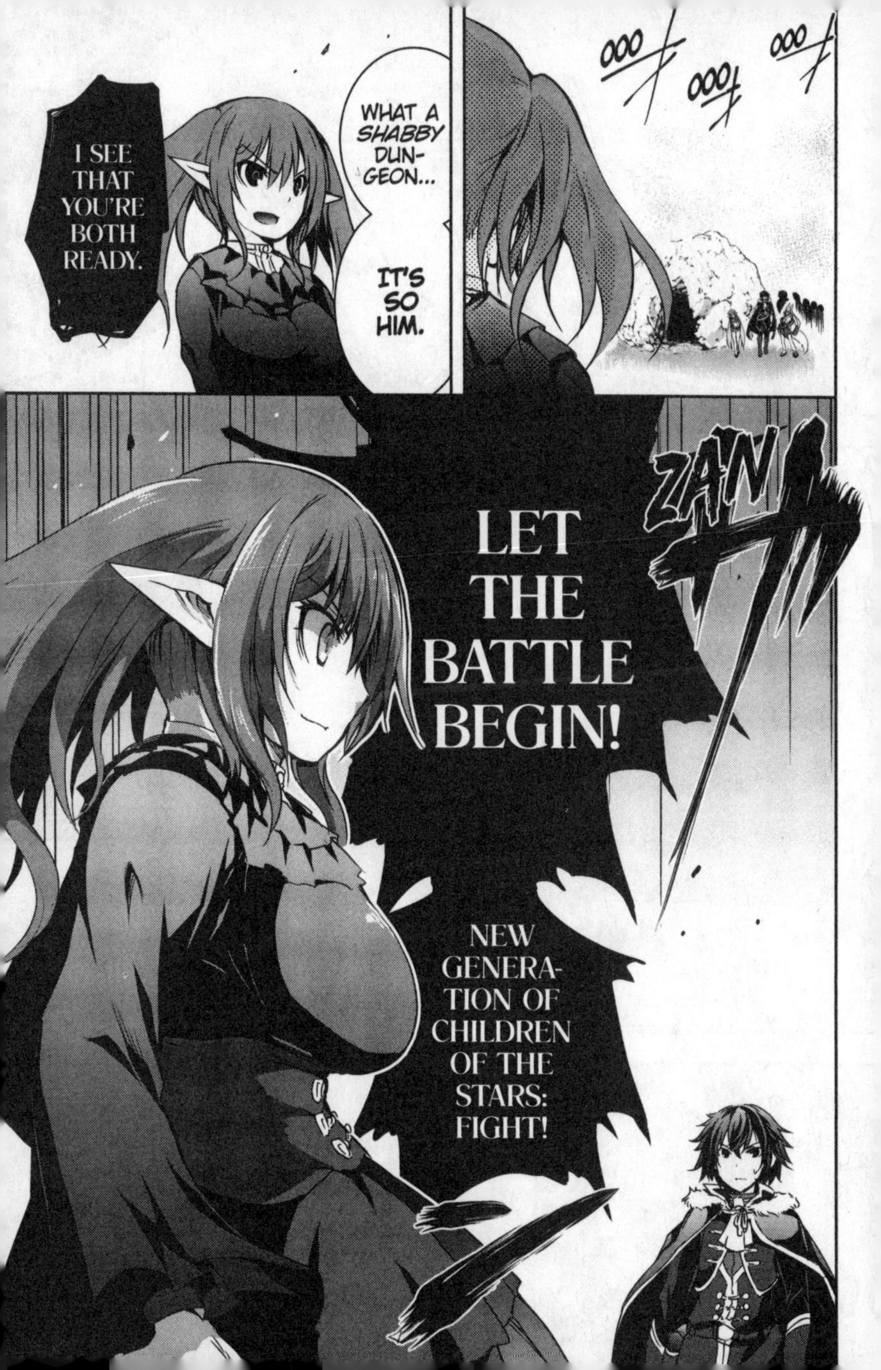
WHAT A SHABBY DUNGEON...
IT'S SO HIM.
I SEE THAT YOU'RE BOTH READY.
ZAN
LET THE BATTLE BEGIN!
NEW GENERATION OF CHILDREN OF THE STARS: FIGHT!

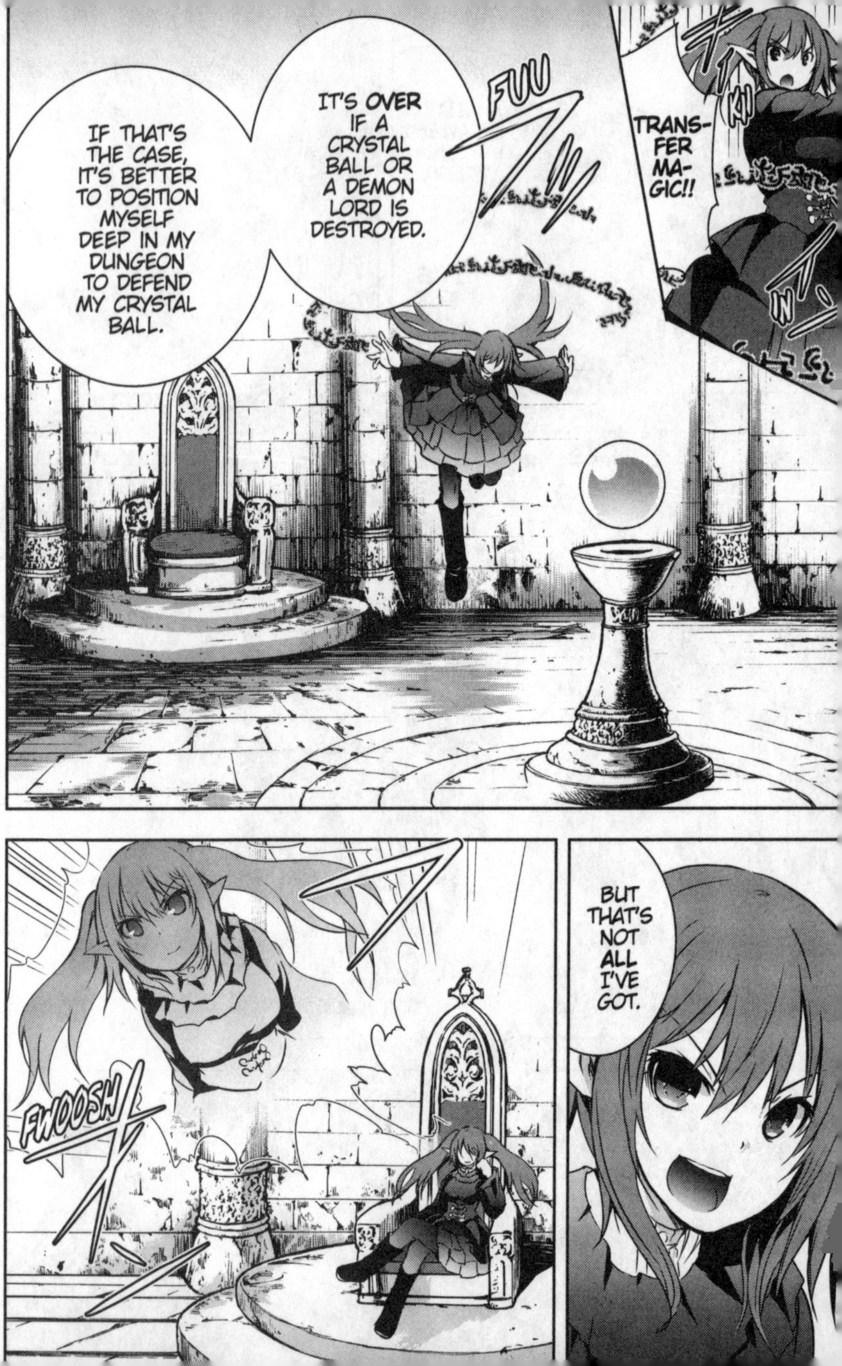
KI
TRANSFER MAGIC!!
IN
FUU
IT'S OVER IF A CRYSTAL BALL OR A DEMON LORD IS DESTROYED.
IF THAT'S THE CASE, IT'S BETTER TO POSITION MYSELF DEEP IN MY DUNGEON TO DEFEND MY CRYSTAL BALL.
BUT THAT'S NOT ALL I'VE GOT.
FWOOSH

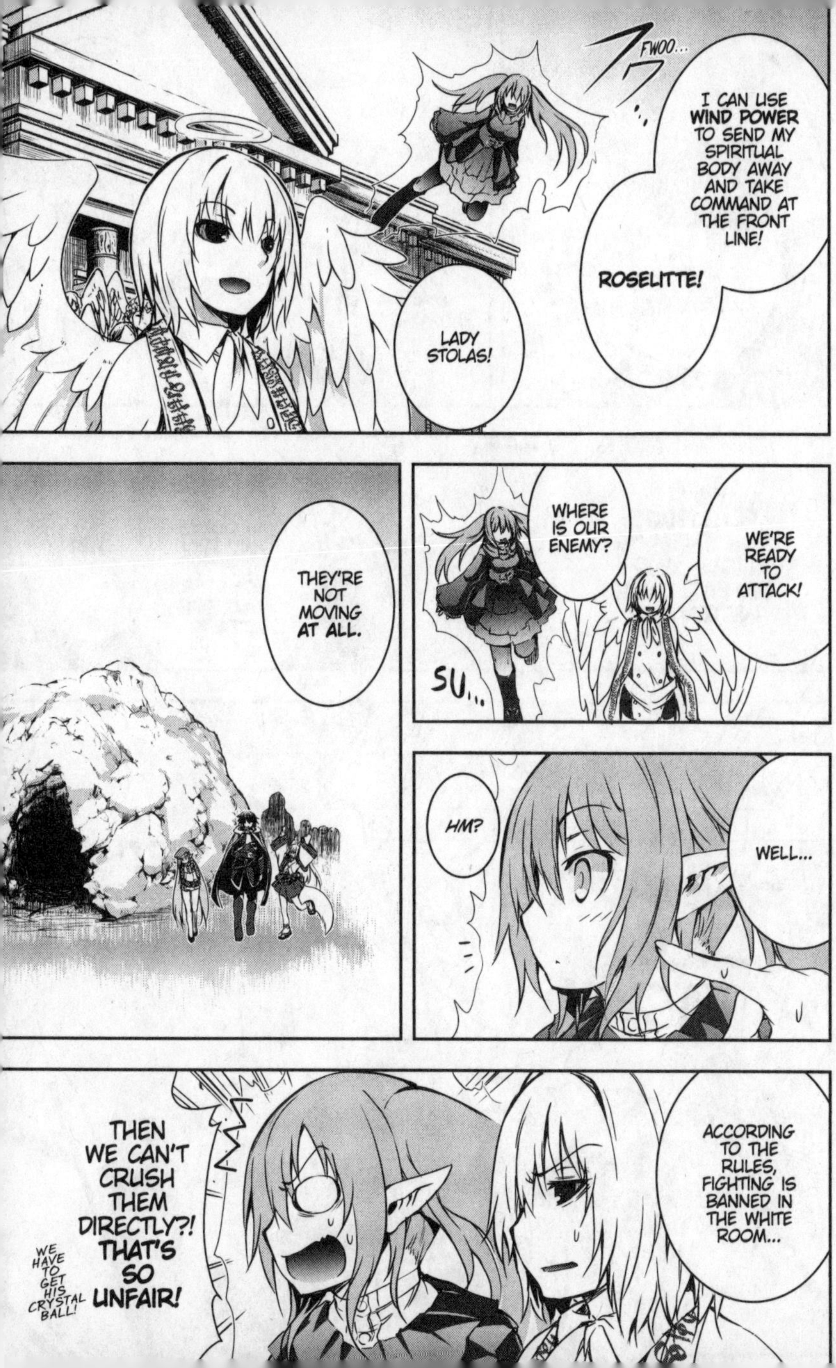
FWOO...
I CAN USE WIND POWER TO SEND MY SPIRITUAL BODY AWAY AND TAKE COMMAND AT THE FRONT LINE!
ROSELITTE!
LADY STOLAS!
WE'RE READY TO ATTACK!
WHERE IS OUR ENEMY?
SU...
WELL...
HM?
THEY'RE NOT MOVING AT ALL.
ACCORDING TO THE RULES, FIGHTING IS BANNED IN THE WHITE ROOM...
THEN WE CAN'T CRUSH THEM DIRECTLY?! THAT'S SO UNFAIR!
WE HAVE TO GET HIS CRYSTAL BALL!

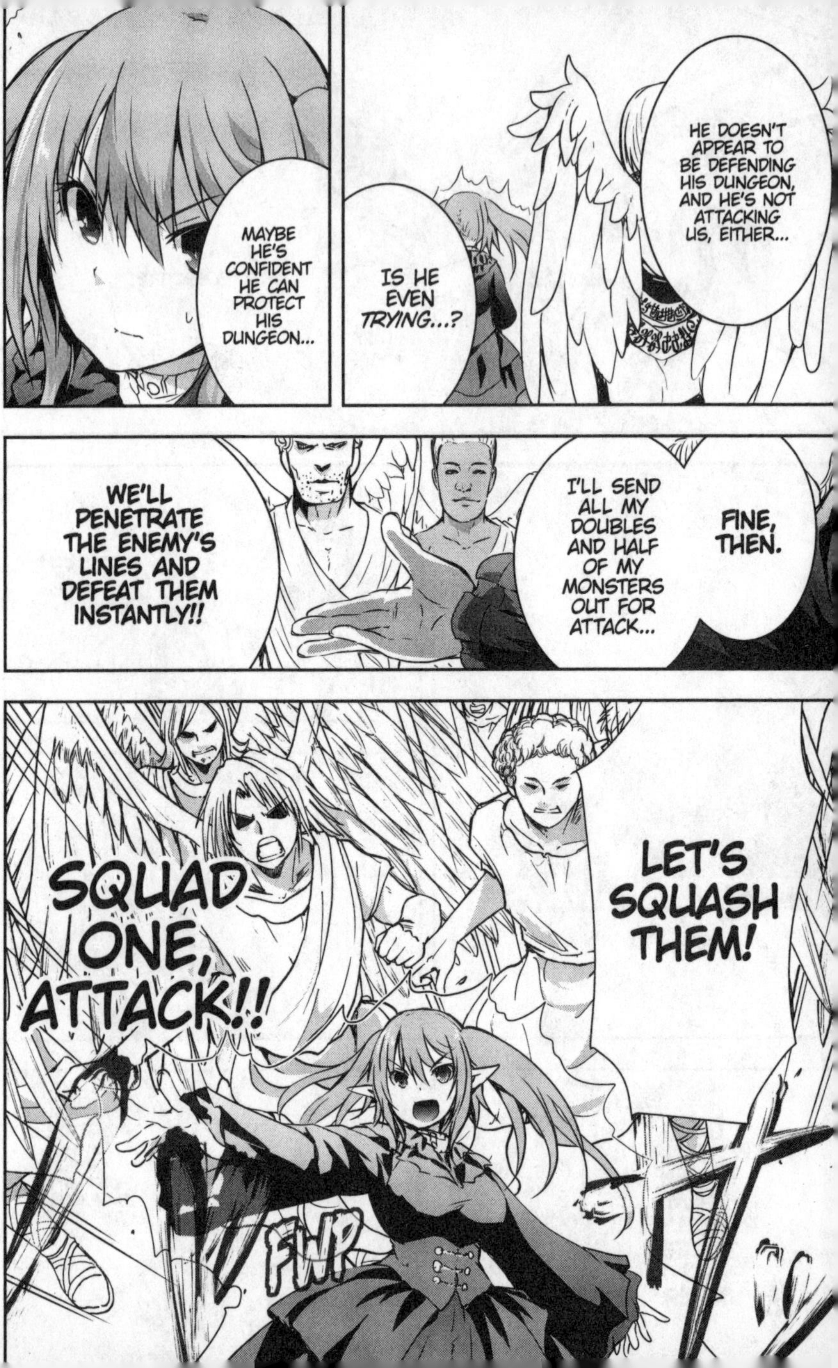
HE DOESN'T APPEAR TO BE DEFENDING HIS DUNGEON, AND HE'S NOT ATTACKING US, EITHER...
IS HE EVEN *TRYING...?*
MAYBE HE'S CONFIDENT HE CAN PROTECT HIS DUNGEON...
FINE, THEN.
I'LL SEND ALL MY DOUBLES AND HALF OF MY MONSTERS OUT FOR ATTACK...
WE'LL PENETRATE THE ENEMY'S LINES AND DEFEAT THEM INSTANTLY!!
LET'S SQUASH THEM!
SQUAD ONE, ATTACK!!
FWP

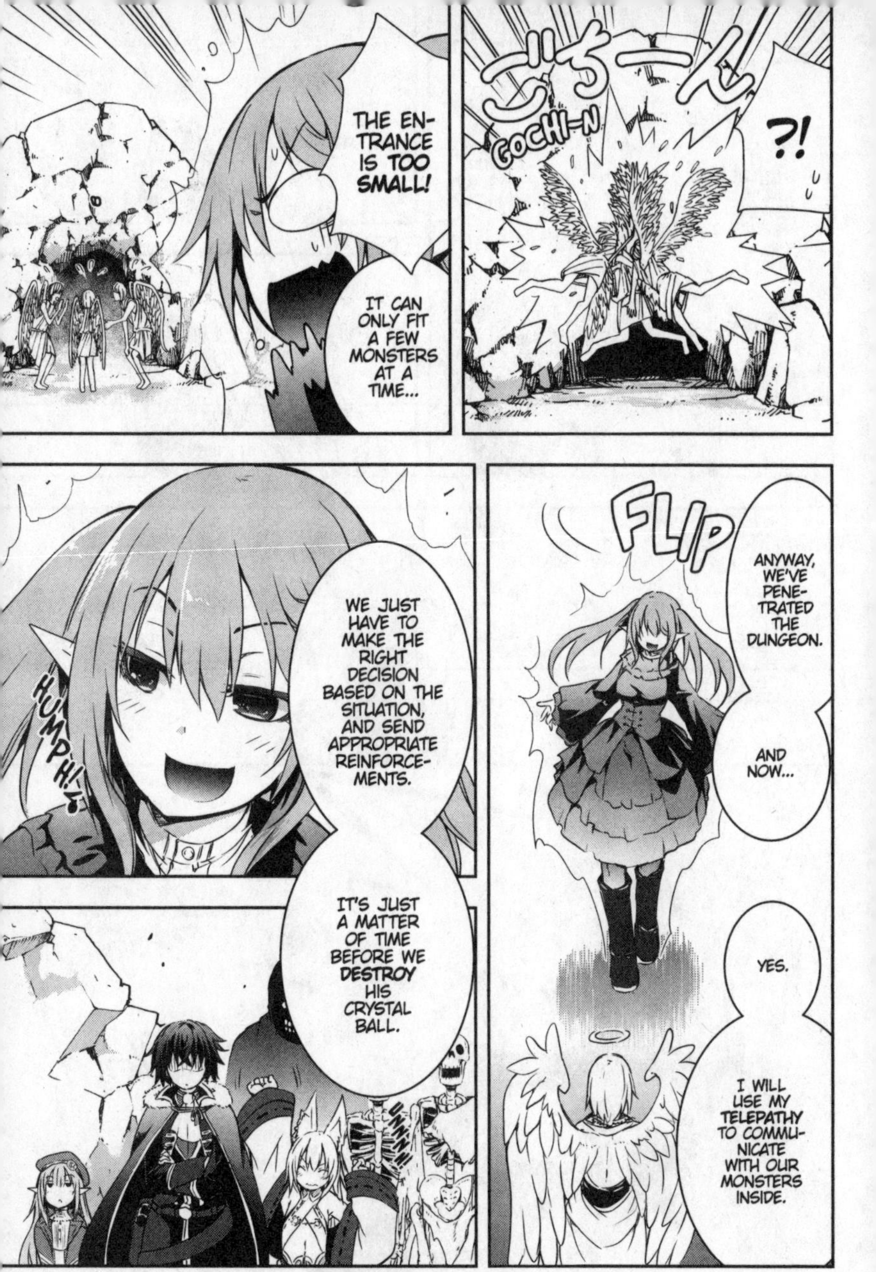

GOCHI-N
?!
THE EN-TRANCE IS TOO SMALL!
IT CAN ONLY FIT A FEW MONSTERS AT A TIME...
FLIP
ANYWAY, WE'VE PENE-TRATED THE DUNGEON.
AND NOW...
YES.
I WILL USE MY TELEPATHY TO COMMU-NICATE WITH OUR MONSTERS INSIDE.
WE JUST HAVE TO MAKE THE RIGHT DECISION BASED ON THE SITUATION, AND SEND APPROPRIATE REINFORCE-MENTS.
HUMPH!
IT'S JUST A MATTER OF TIME BEFORE WE DESTROY HIS CRYSTAL BALL.
UNNN...!

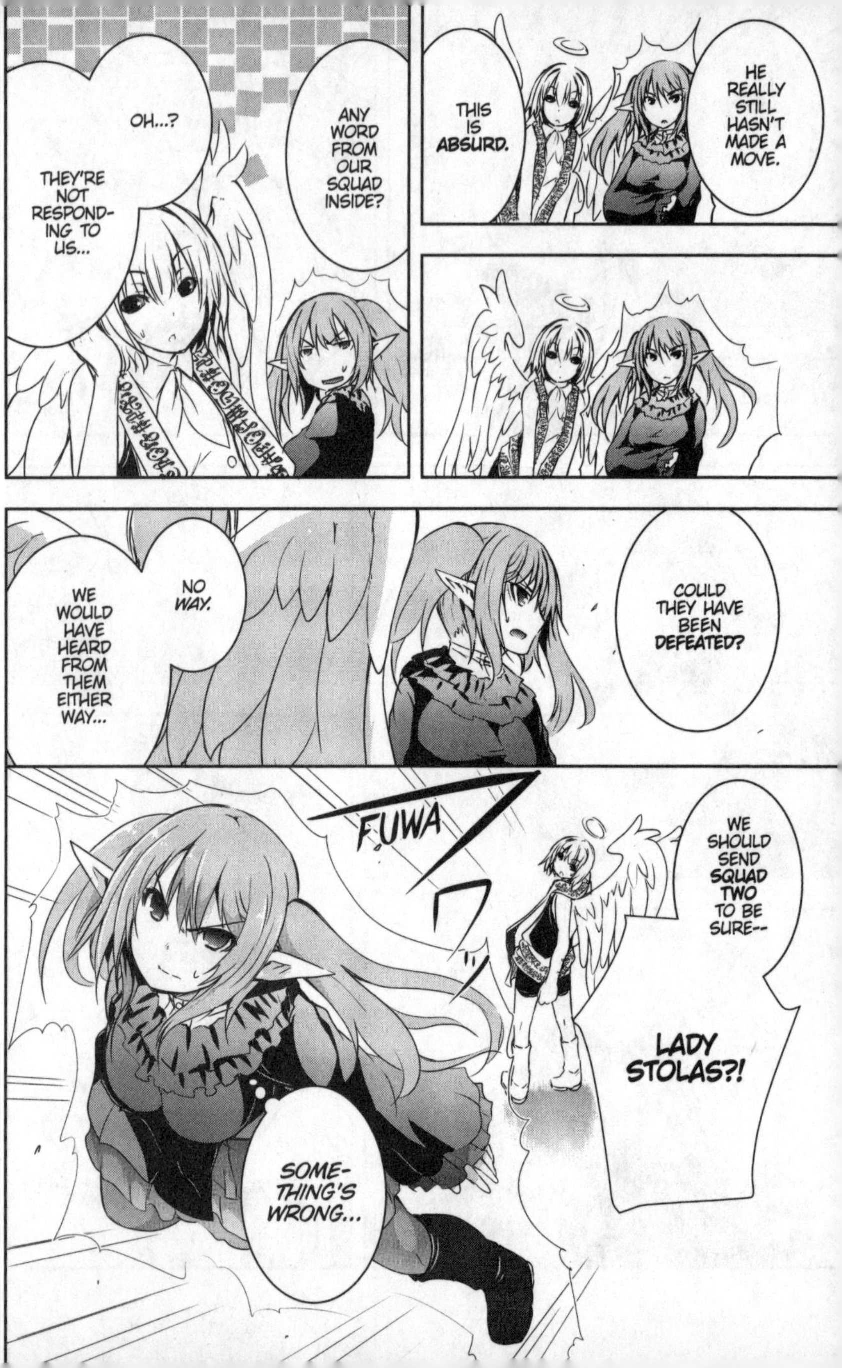
HE REALLY STILL HASN'T MADE A MOVE.
THIS IS ABSURD.
ANY WORD FROM OUR SQUAD INSIDE?
OH...?
THEY'RE NOT RESPONDING TO US...
COULD THEY HAVE BEEN DEFEATED?
NO WAY.
WE WOULD HAVE HEARD FROM THEM EITHER WAY...
WE SHOULD SEND SQUAD TWO TO BE SURE--
FUWA
LADY STOLAS?!
SOMETHING'S WRONG...

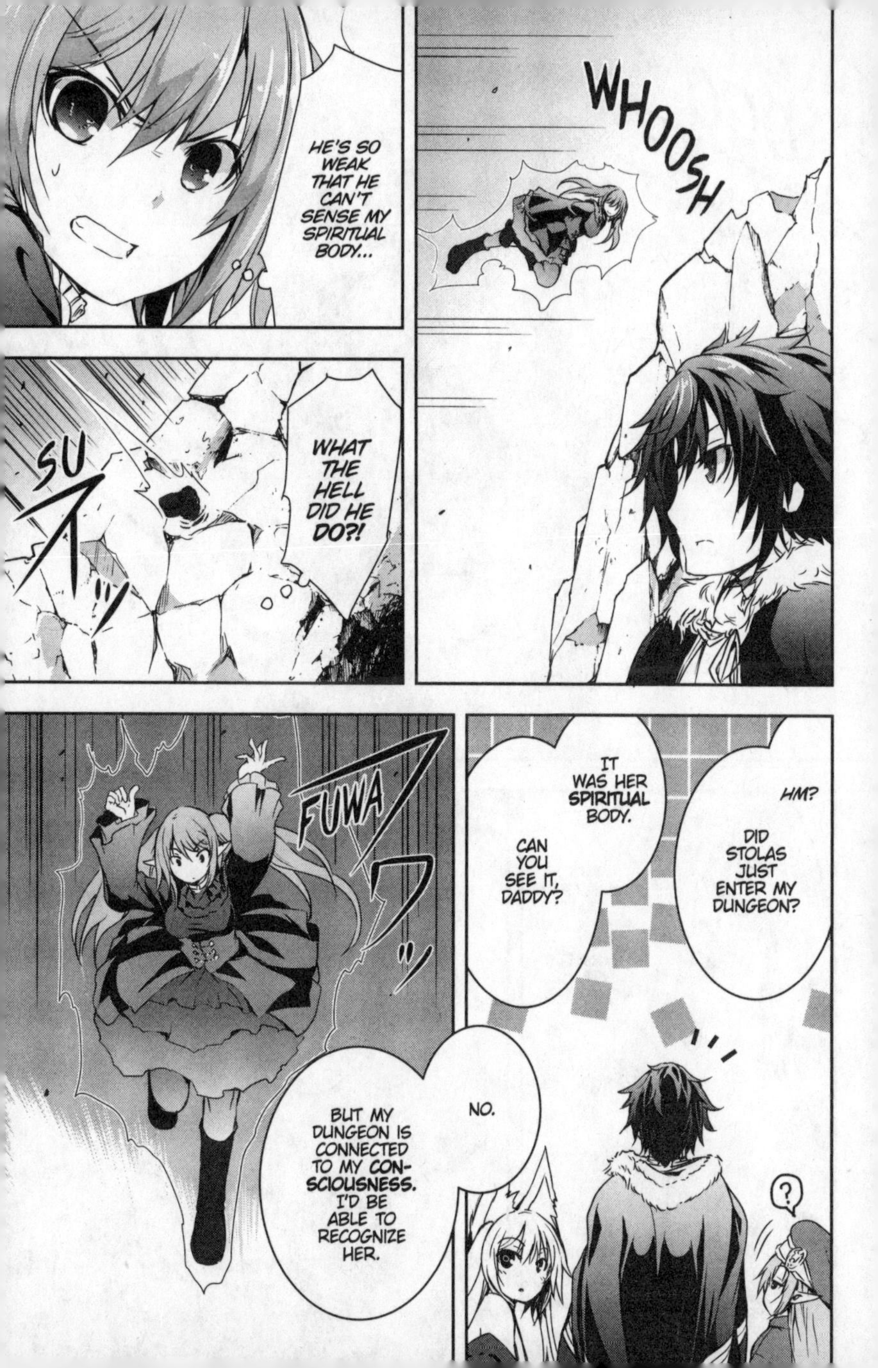
WHOOSH
HE'S SO WEAK THAT HE CAN'T SENSE MY SPIRITUAL BODY...
SU
WHAT THE HELL DID HE DO?!
HM?
DID STOLAS JUST ENTER MY DUNGEON?
IT WAS HER SPIRITUAL BODY.
CAN YOU SEE IT, DADDY?
NO.
BUT MY DUNGEON IS CONNECTED TO MY CONSCIOUSNESS. I'D BE ABLE TO RECOGNIZE HER.
?
FUWA

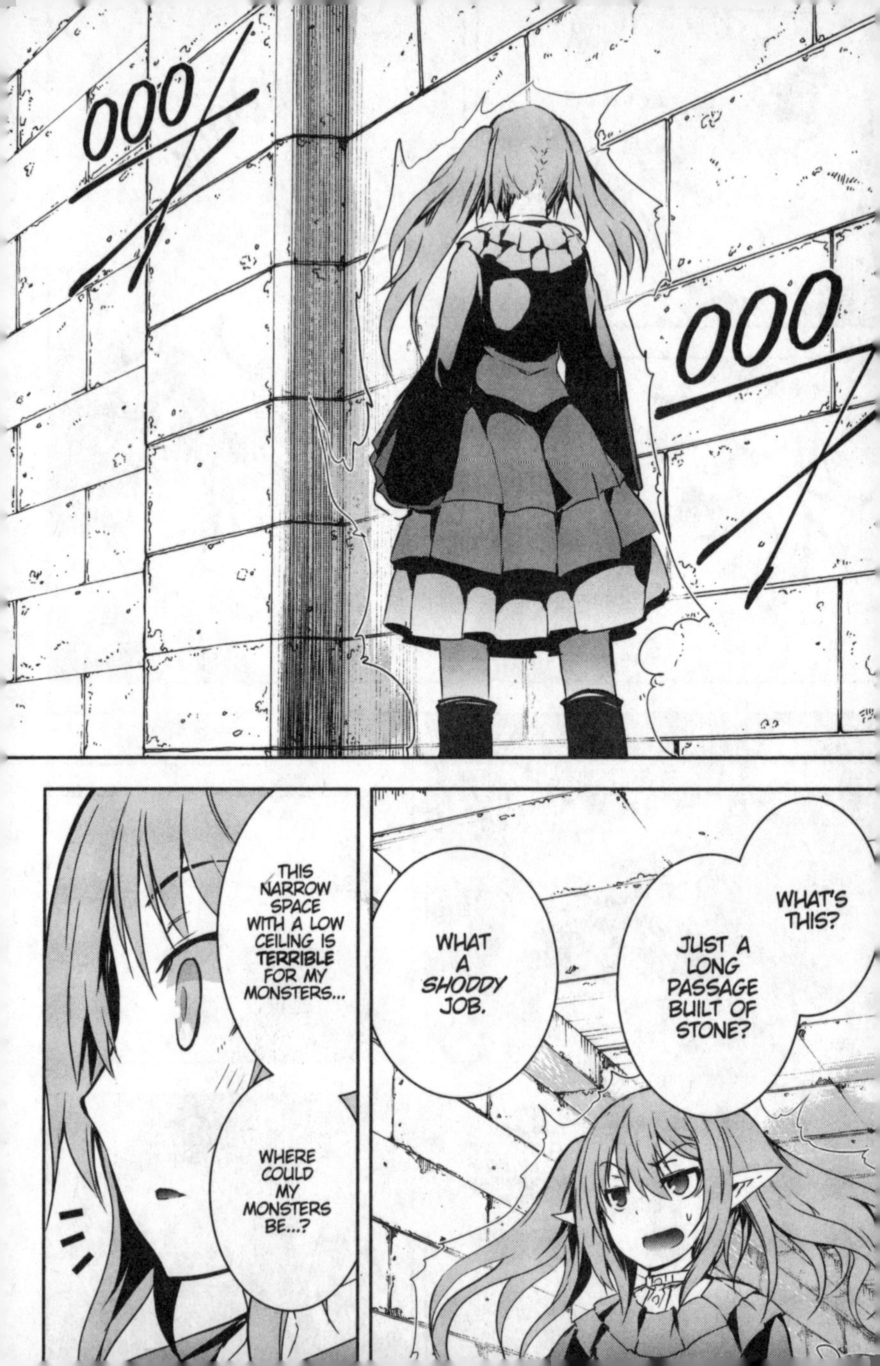
OOO
OOO
WHAT'S THIS?
JUST A LONG PASSAGE BUILT OF STONE?
WHAT A SHODDY JOB.
THIS NARROW SPACE WITH A LOW CEILING IS TERRIBLE FOR MY MONSTERS...
WHERE COULD MY MONSTERS BE...?

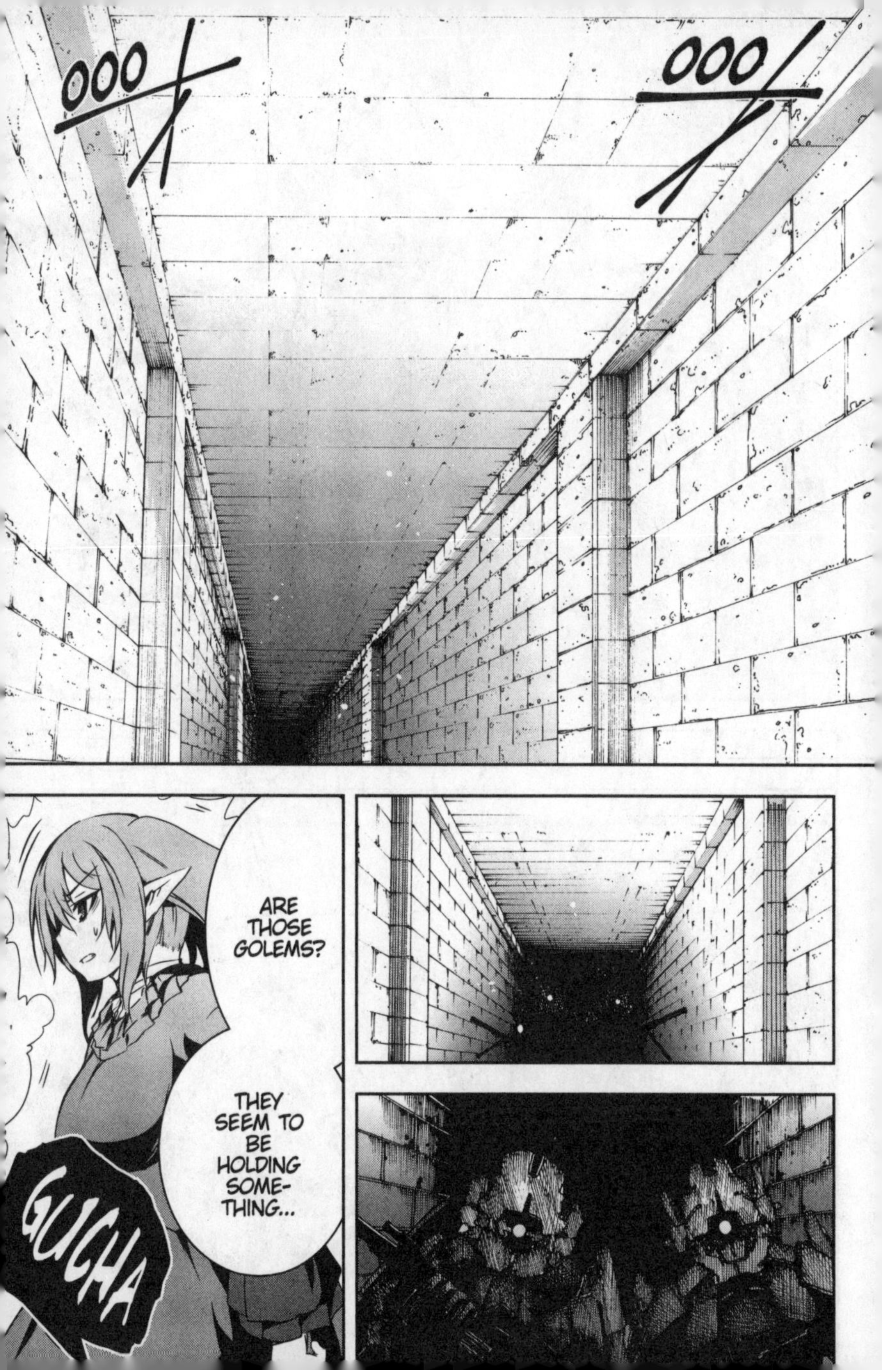
OOO
OOO
ARE THOSE GOLEMS?
THEY SEEM TO BE HOLDING SOME-THING...
GUCHA

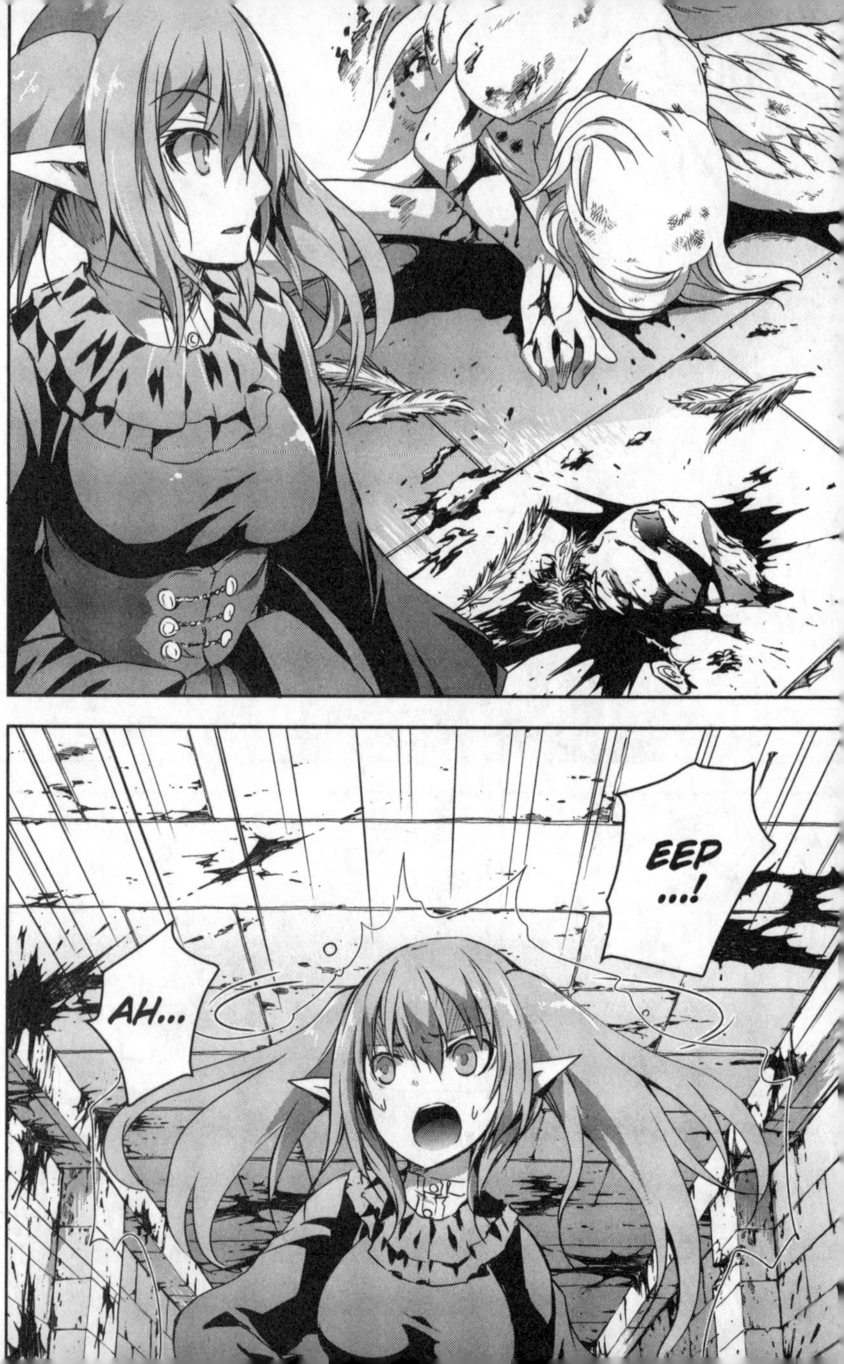
EEP ...!
AH...

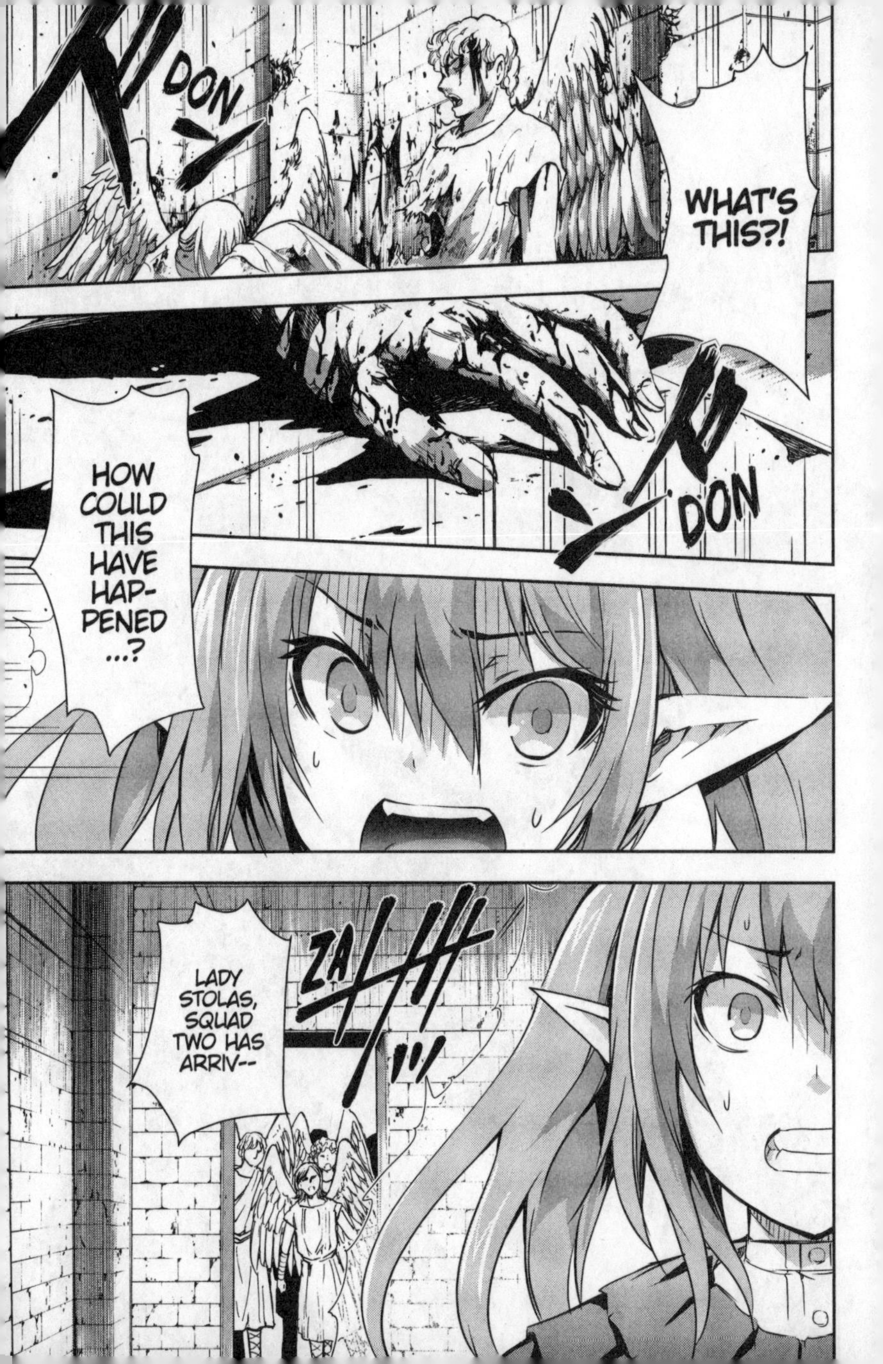
DON
WHAT'S THIS?!
DON
HOW COULD THIS HAVE HAPPENED...?
ZA
LADY STOLAS, SQUAD TWO HAS ARRIV--

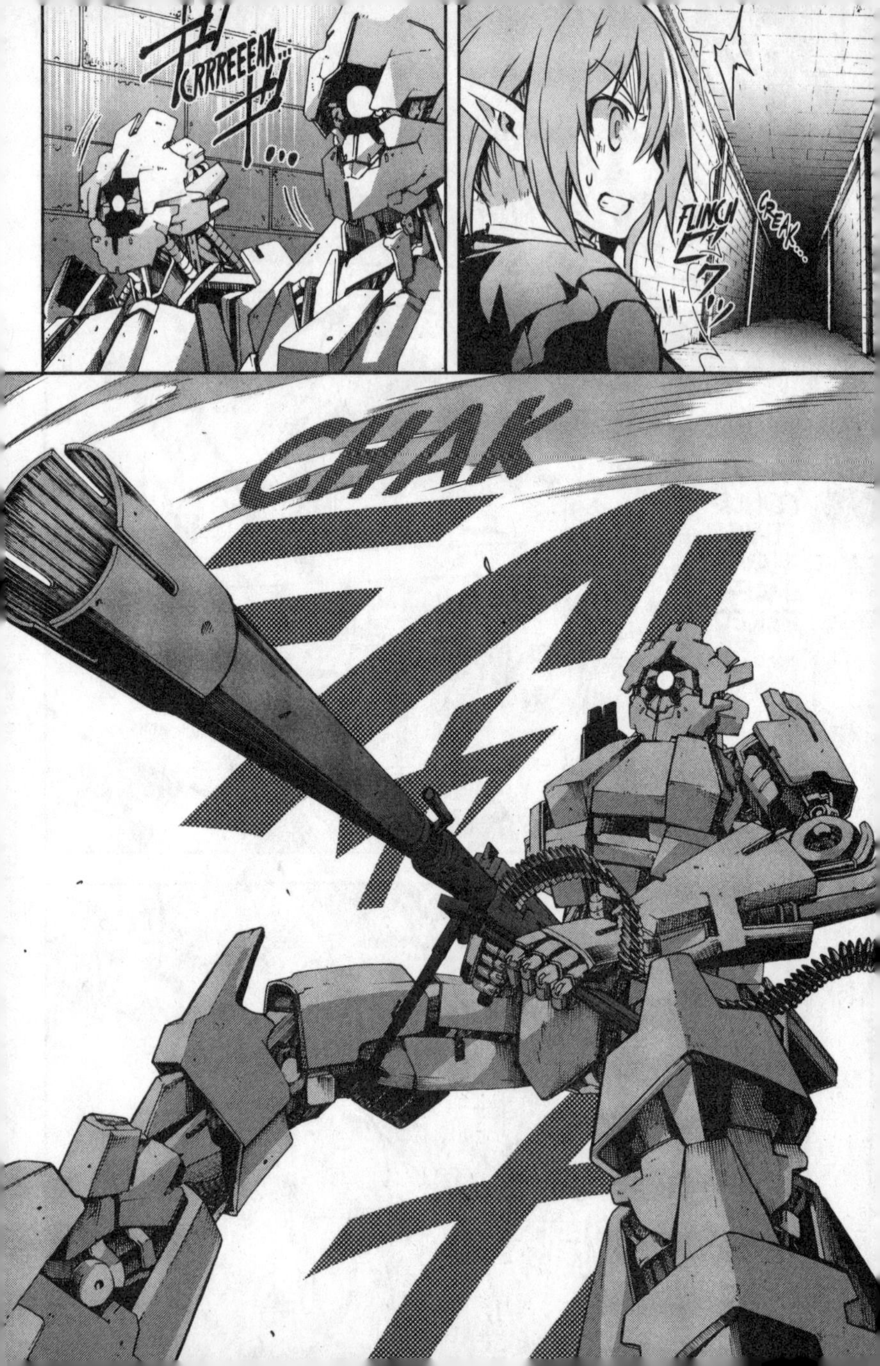
FLINCH
CREAK...
CRRREEEAK...
CHAK

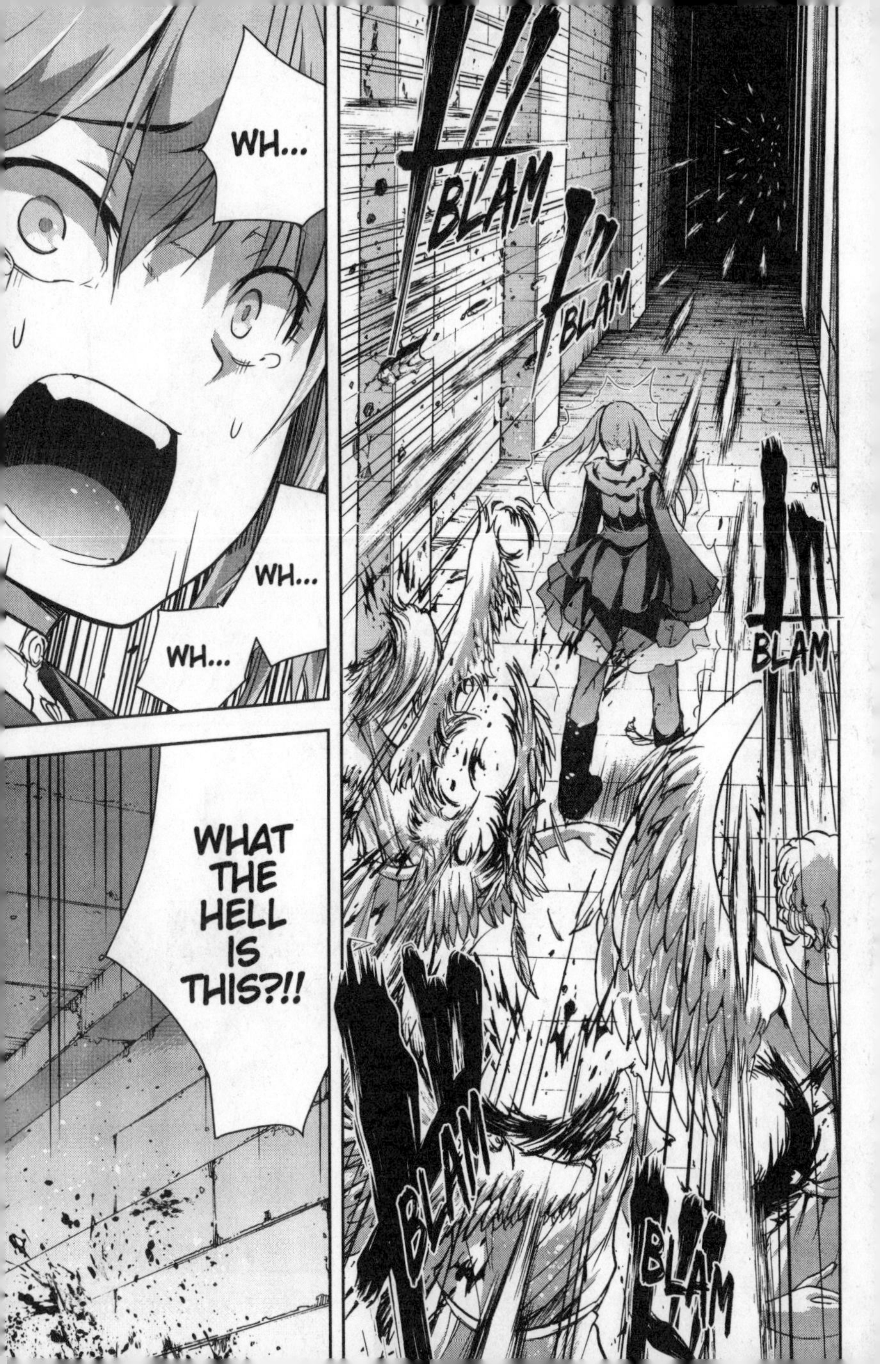
BLAM
BLAM
BLAM
BLAM
BLAM
WH...
WH...
WH...
WHAT THE HELL IS THIS?!!

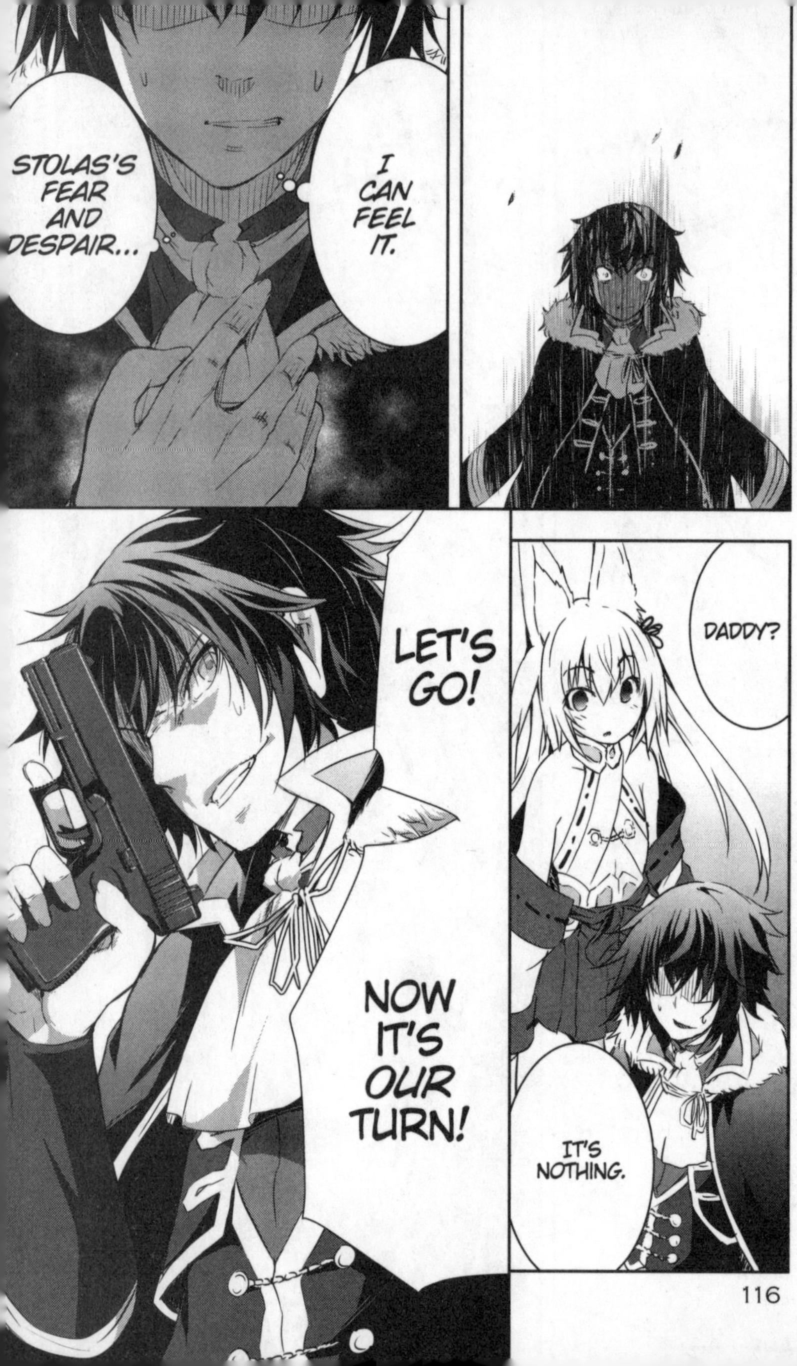
I CAN FEEL IT.
STOLAS'S FEAR AND DESPAIR...
DADDY?
IT'S NOTHING.
LET'S GO!
NOW IT'S OUR TURN!

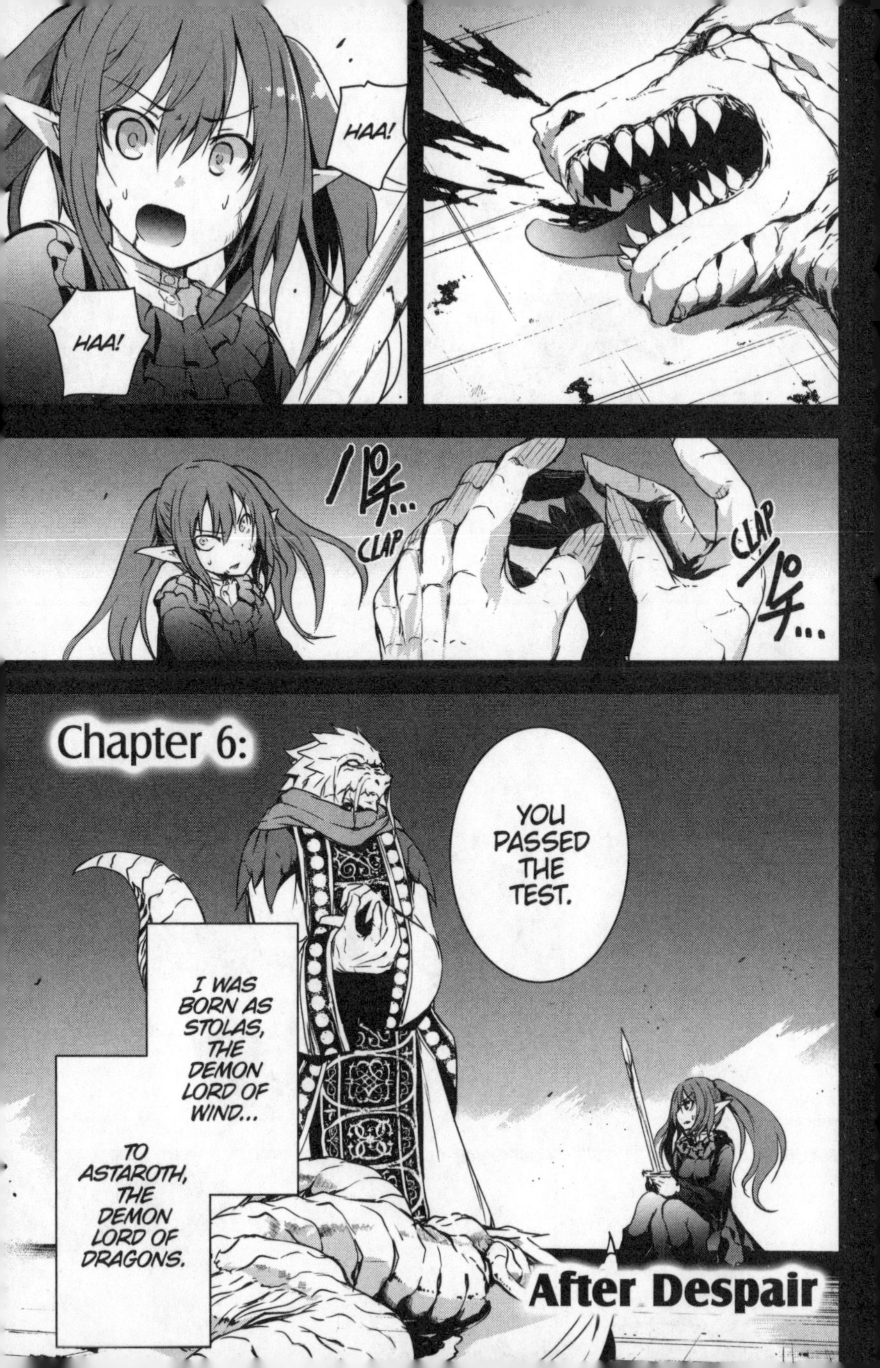
HAA!
HAA!
パチ...
CLAP
パチ...
CLAP
YOU PASSED THE TEST.
Chapter 6:
I WAS BORN AS STOLAS, THE DEMON LORD OF WIND...
TO ASTAROTH, THE DEMON LORD OF DRAGONS.
After Despair

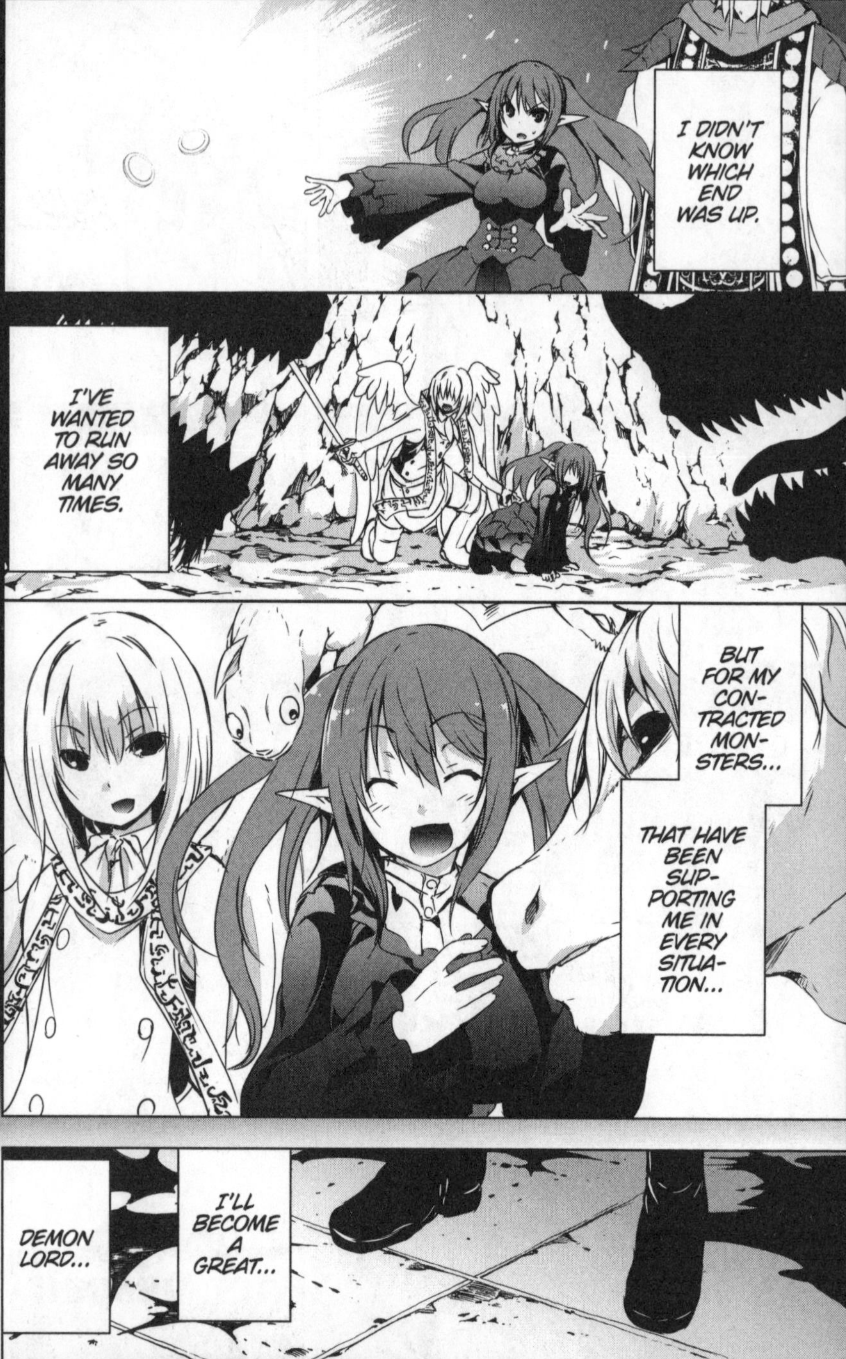

I DIDN'T KNOW WHICH END WAS UP.
I'VE WANTED TO RUN AWAY SO MANY TIMES.
BUT FOR MY CONTRACTED MONSTERS...
THAT HAVE BEEN SUPPORTING ME IN EVERY SITUATION...
I'LL BECOME A GREAT...
DEMON LORD...

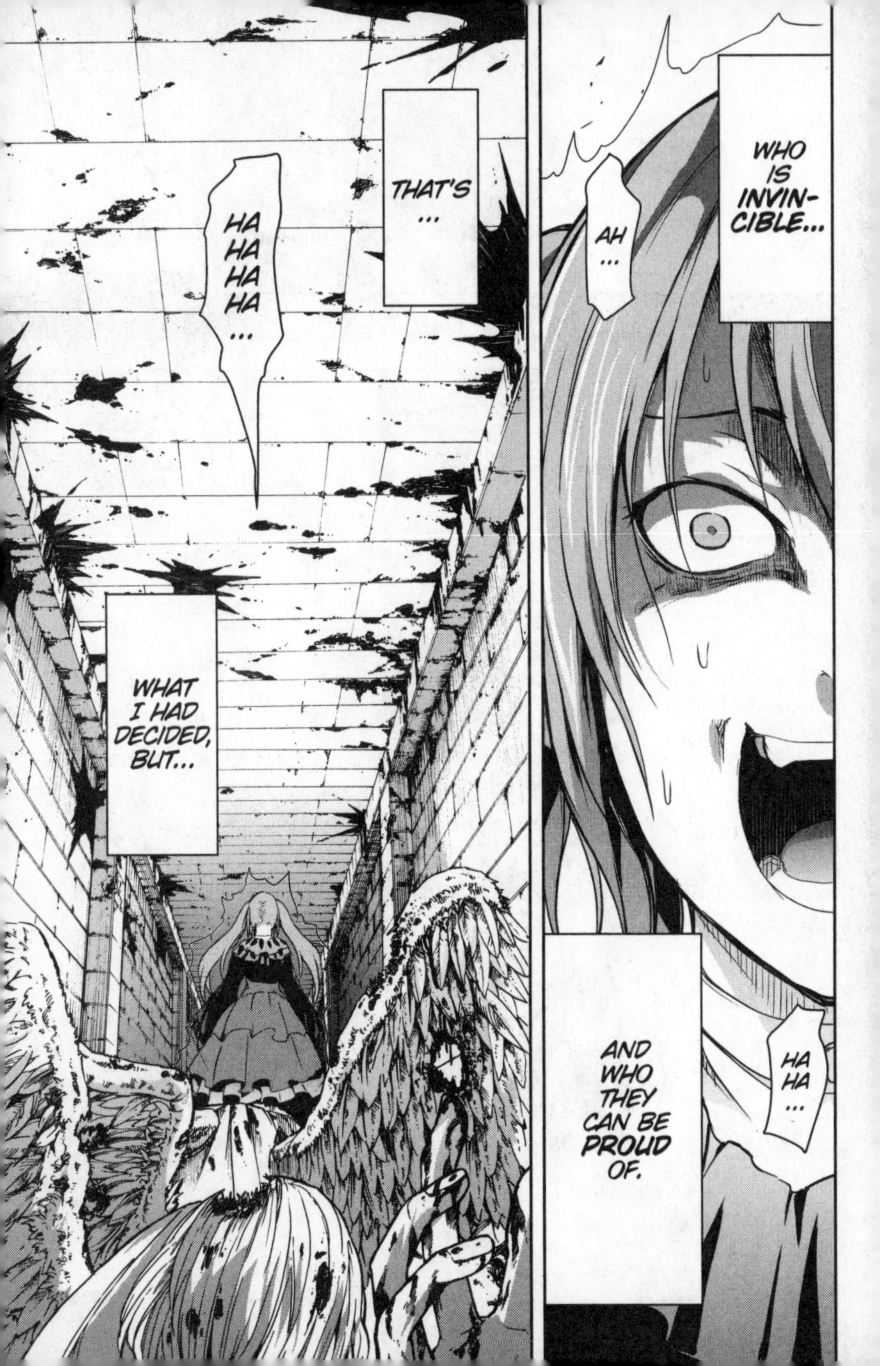
WHO IS INVINCIBLE...
AH...
AND WHO THEY CAN BE PROUD OF.
HA HA...
THAT'S...
HA HA HA HA...
WHAT I HAD DECIDED, BUT...

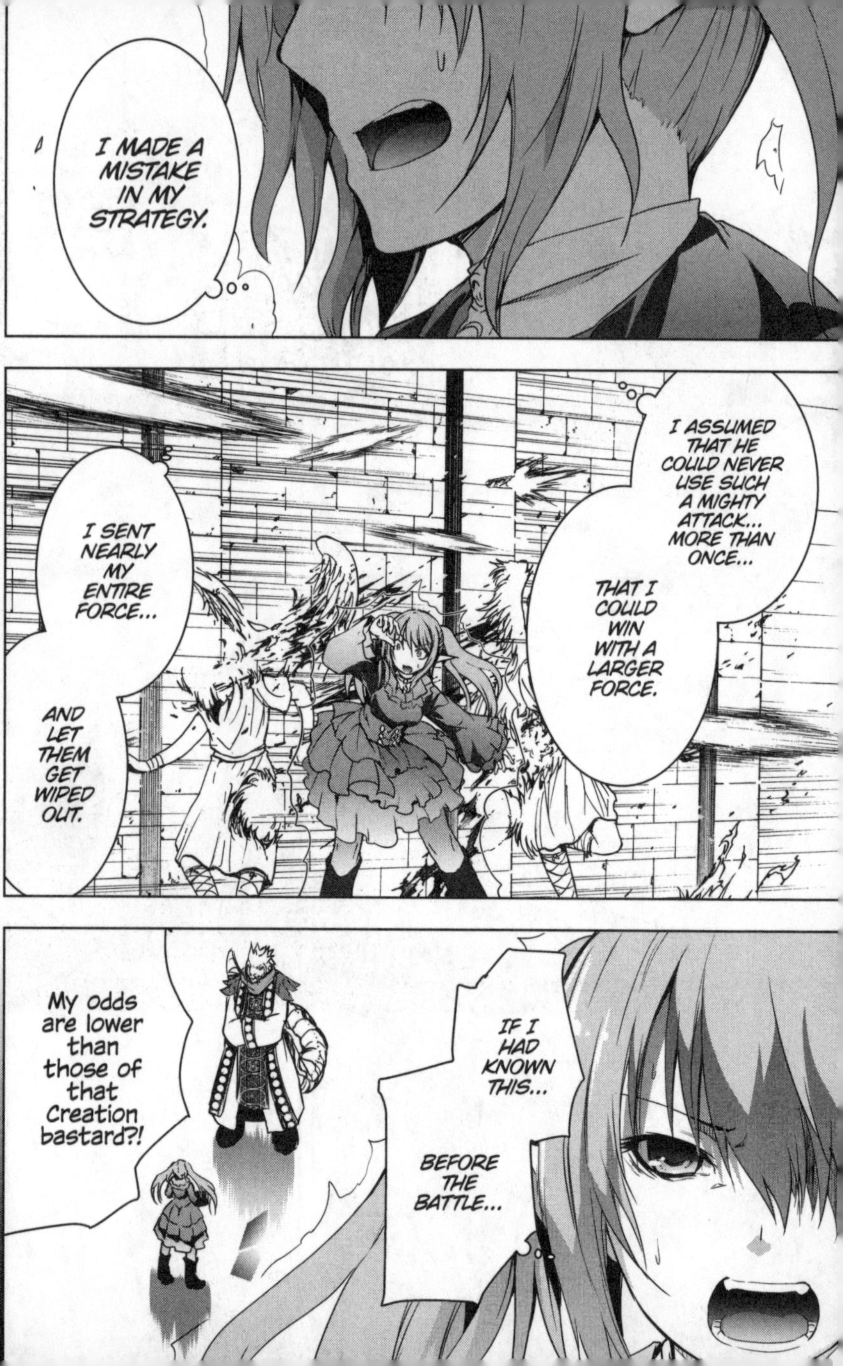
I MADE A MISTAKE IN MY STRATEGY.
I ASSUMED THAT HE COULD NEVER USE SUCH A MIGHTY ATTACK... MORE THAN ONCE...
THAT I COULD WIN WITH A LARGER FORCE.
I SENT NEARLY MY ENTIRE FORCE...
AND LET THEM GET WIPED OUT.
IF I HAD KNOWN THIS...
BEFORE THE BATTLE...
My odds are lower than those of that Creation bastard?!

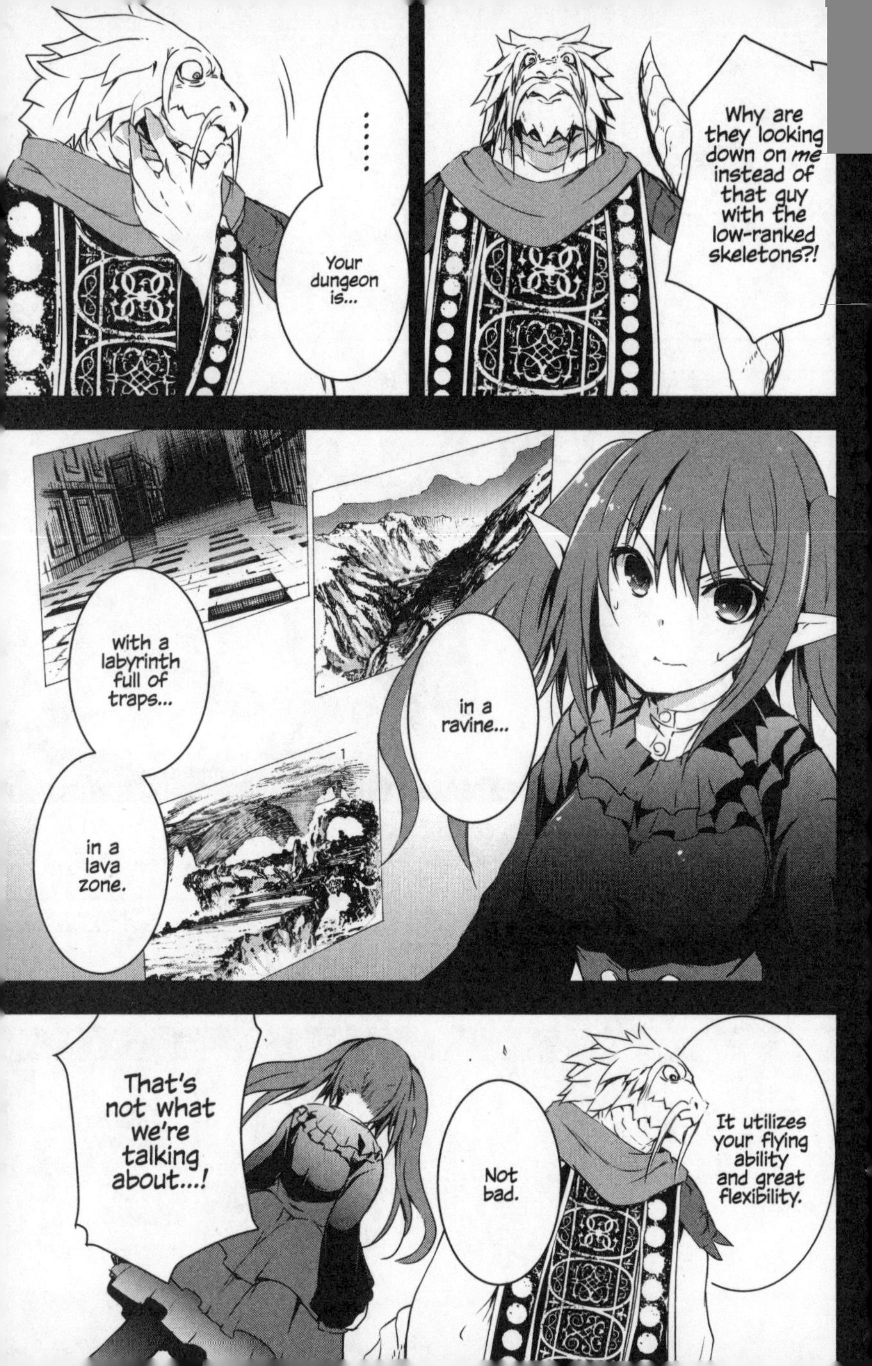
Why are they looking down on *me* instead of that guy with the low-ranked skeletons?!
......
Your dungeon is...
with a labyrinth full of traps...
in a ravine...
in a lava zone.
It utilizes your flying ability and great flexibility.
Not bad.
That's not what we're talking about...!

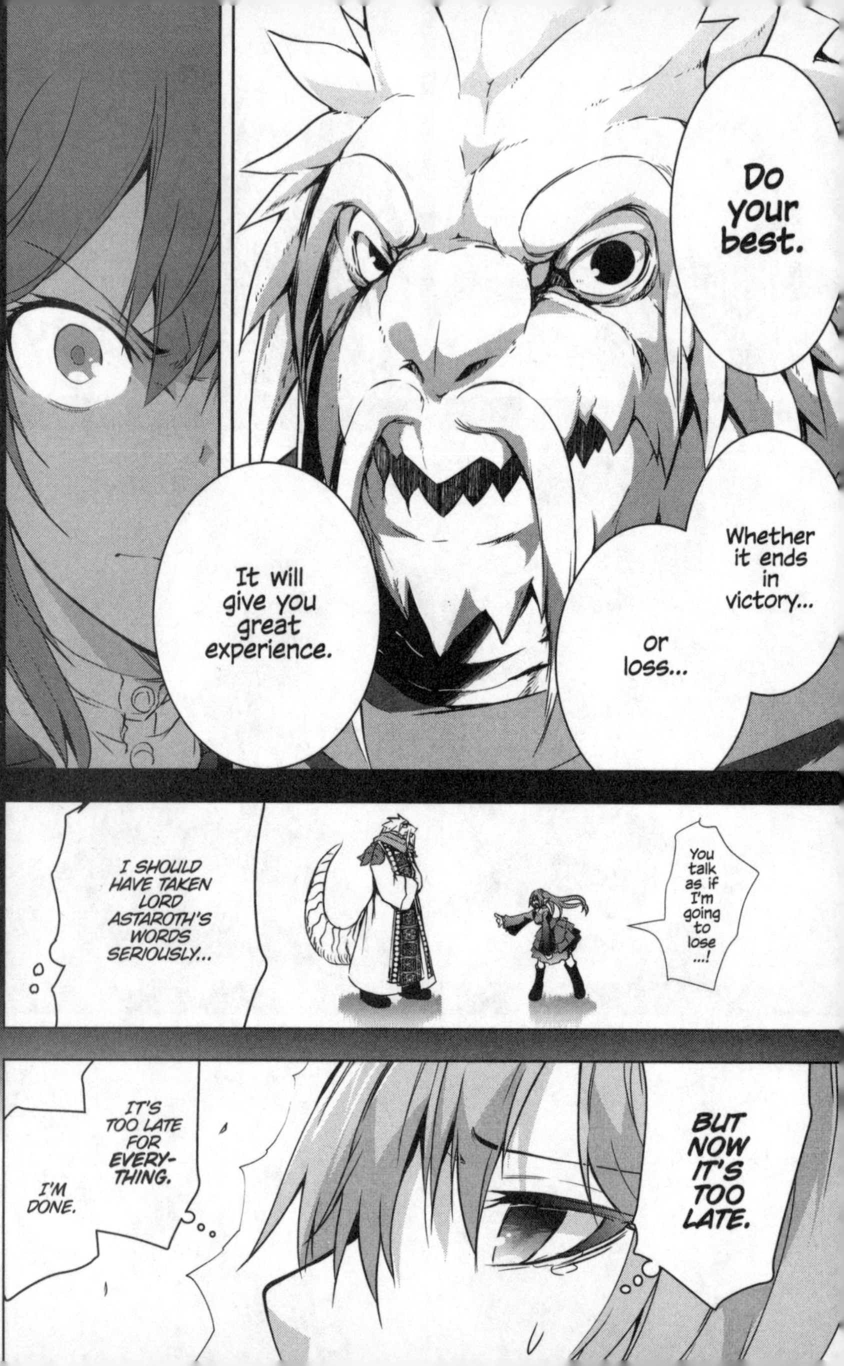
Do your best.
Whether it ends in victory...
or loss...
It will give you great experience.
You talk as if I'm going to lose ...!
I SHOULD HAVE TAKEN LORD ASTAROTH'S WORDS SERIOUSLY...
BUT NOW IT'S TOO LATE.
IT'S TOO LATE FOR EVERY-THING.
I'M DONE.

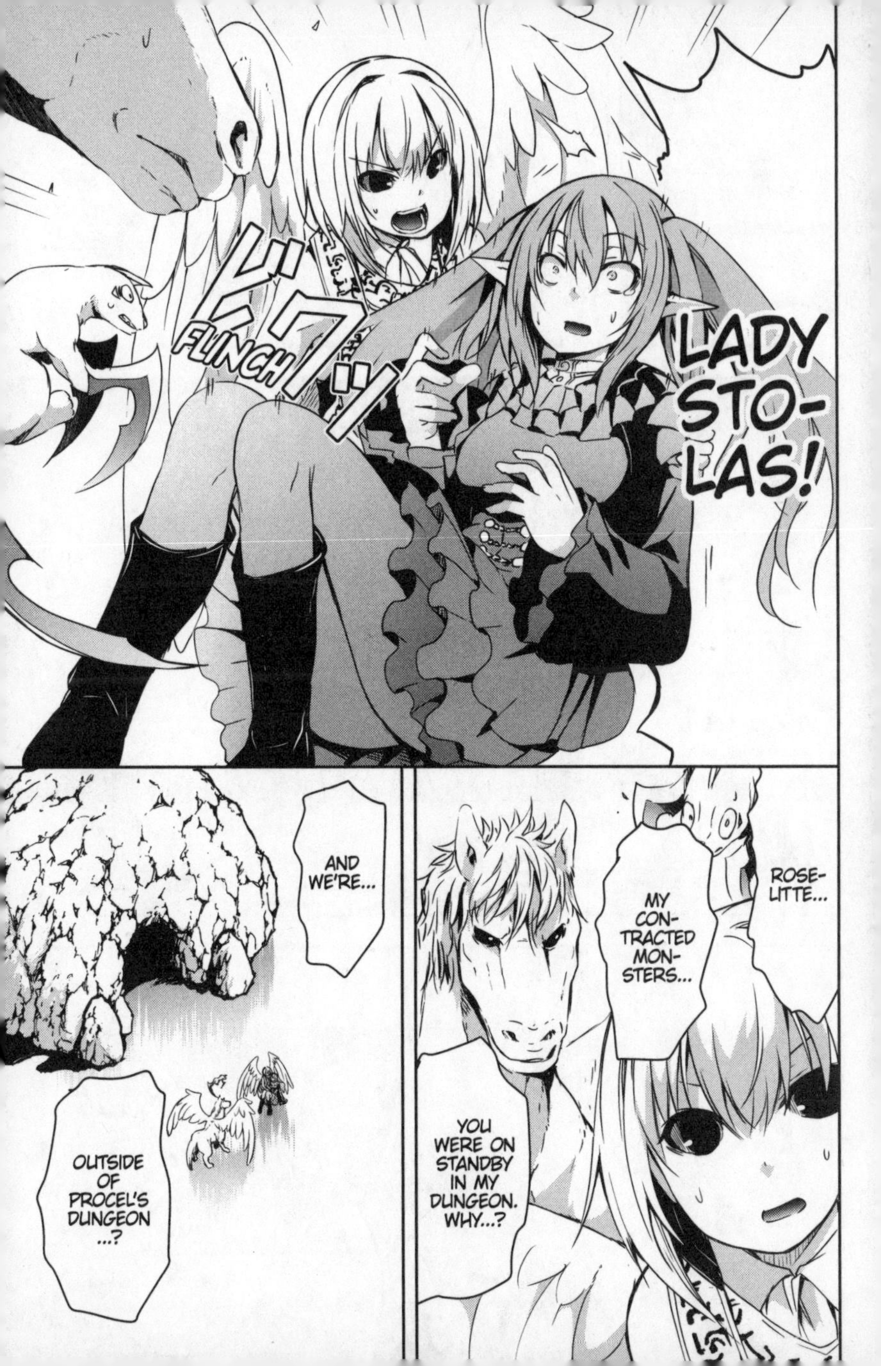
LADY STO-LAS!
FLINCH
ROSE-LITTE...
MY CON-TRACTED MON-STERS...
YOU WERE ON STANDBY IN MY DUNGEON. WHY...?
AND WE'RE...
OUTSIDE OF PROCEL'S DUNGEON ...?

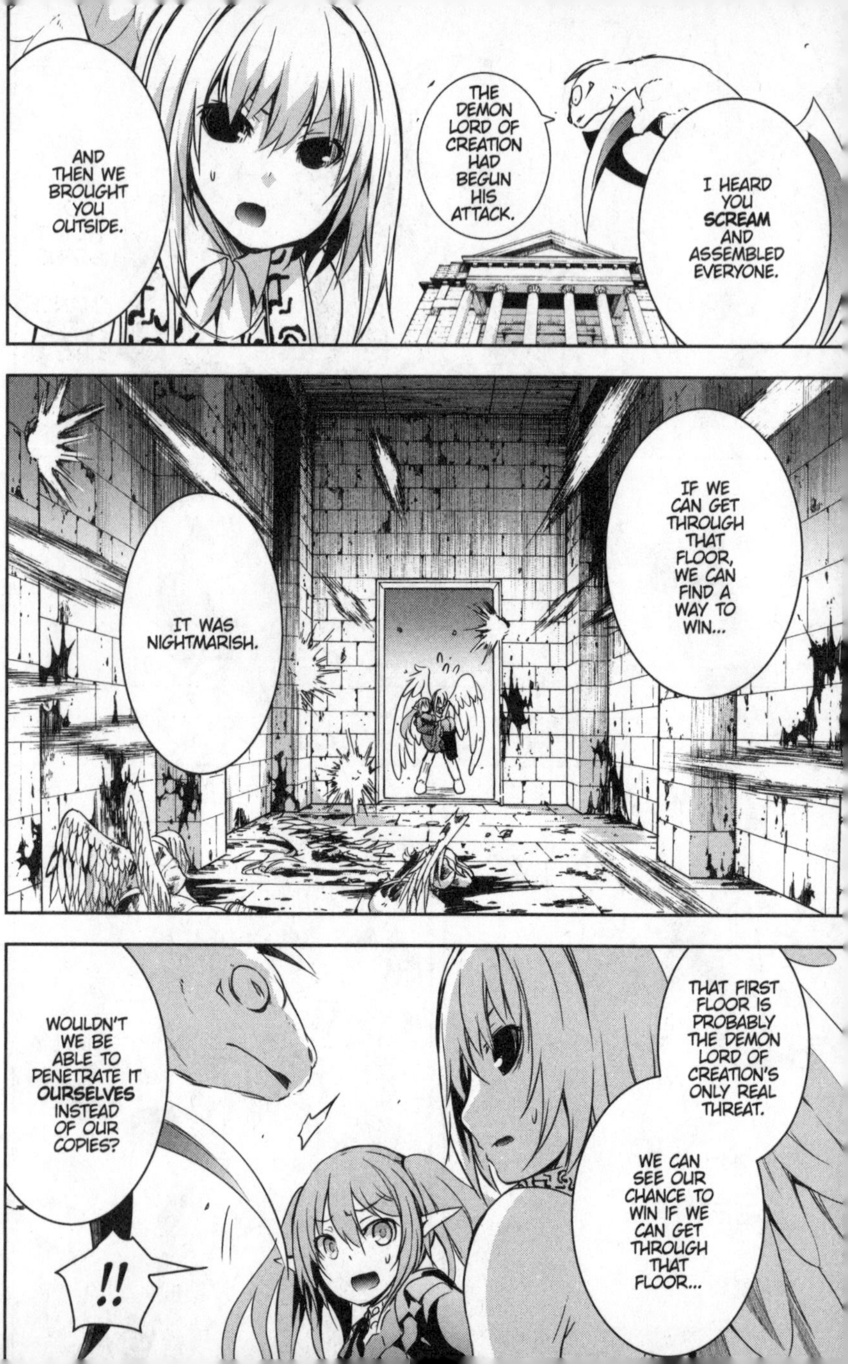

I HEARD YOU SCREAM AND ASSEMBLED EVERYONE.
THE DEMON LORD OF CREATION HAD BEGUN HIS ATTACK.
AND THEN WE BROUGHT YOU OUTSIDE.
IF WE CAN GET THROUGH THAT FLOOR, WE CAN FIND A WAY TO WIN...
IT WAS NIGHTMARISH.
THAT FIRST FLOOR IS PROBABLY THE DEMON LORD OF CREATION'S ONLY REAL THREAT.
WE CAN SEE OUR CHANCE TO WIN IF WE CAN GET THROUGH THAT FLOOR...
WOULDN'T WE BE ABLE TO PENETRATE IT OURSELVES INSTEAD OF OUR COPIES?
!!

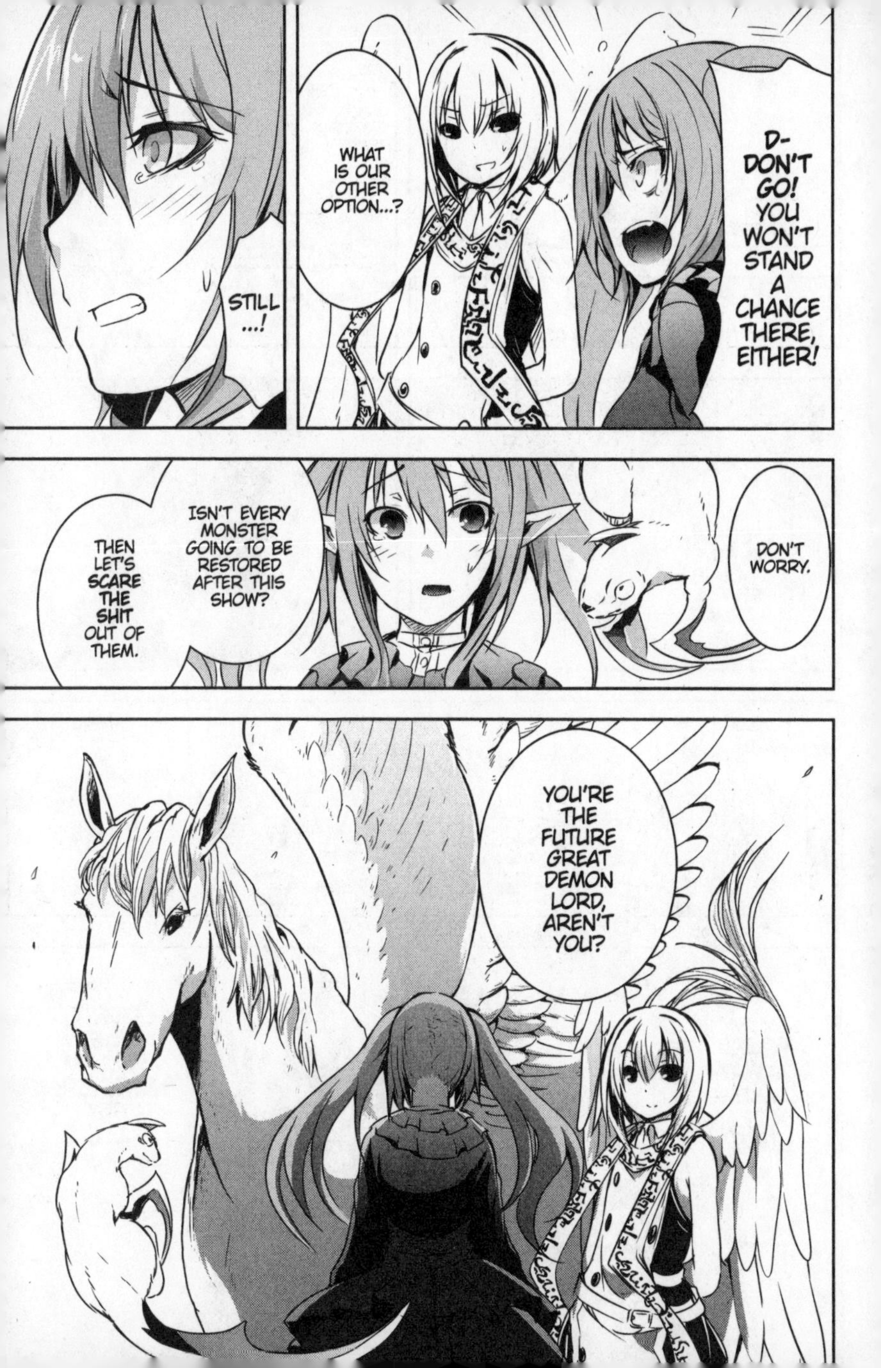

D-DON'T GO! YOU WON'T STAND A CHANCE THERE, EITHER!
WHAT IS OUR OTHER OPTION...?
STILL ...!
DON'T WORRY.
ISN'T EVERY MONSTER GOING TO BE RESTORED AFTER THIS SHOW?
THEN LET'S SCARE THE SHIT OUT OF THEM.
YOU'RE THE FUTURE GREAT DEMON LORD, AREN'T YOU?

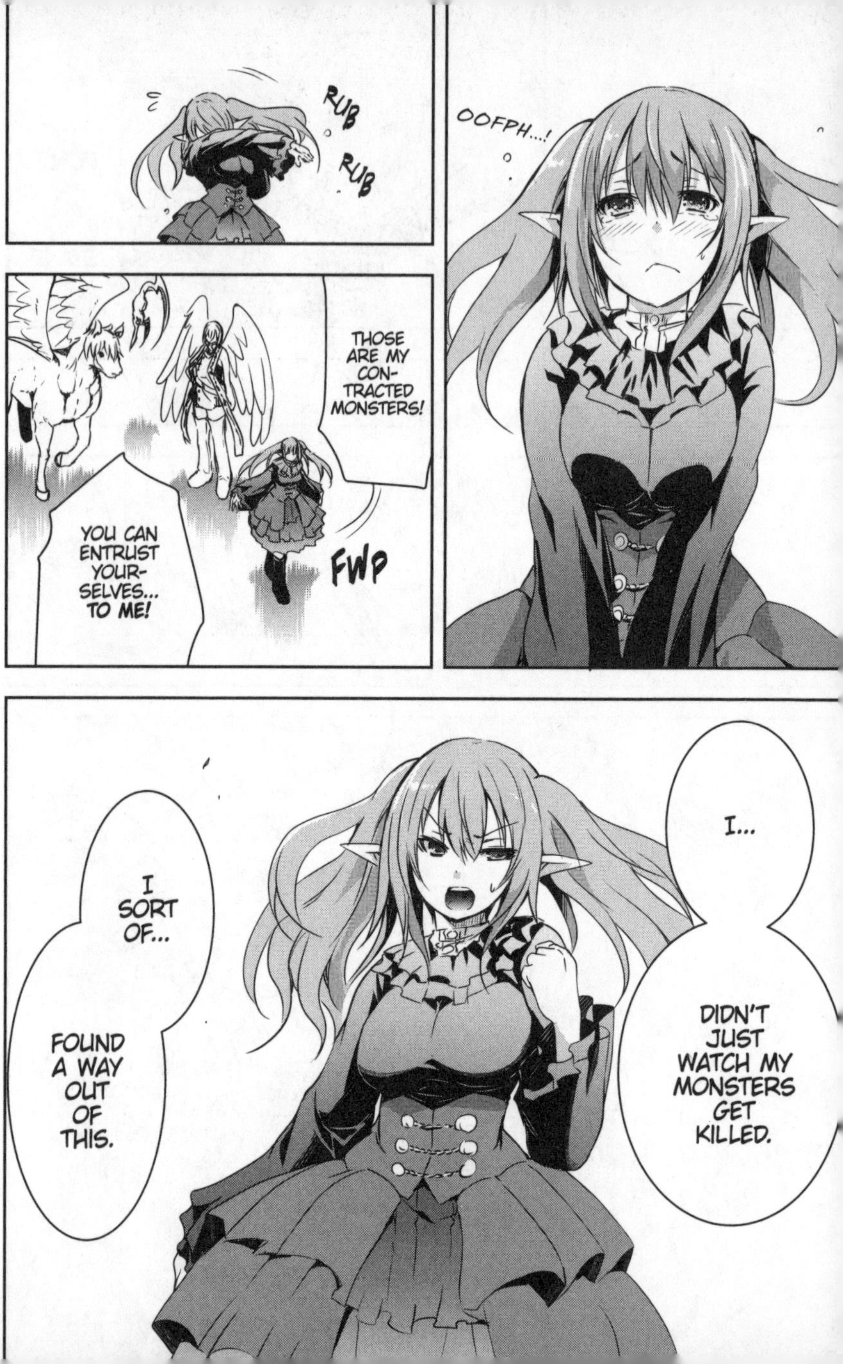
OOFPH...!
RUB RUB
THOSE ARE MY CONTRACTED MONSTERS!
YOU CAN ENTRUST YOURSELVES... TO ME!
FWP
I...
DIDN'T JUST WATCH MY MONSTERS GET KILLED.
I SORT OF...
FOUND A WAY OUT OF THIS.

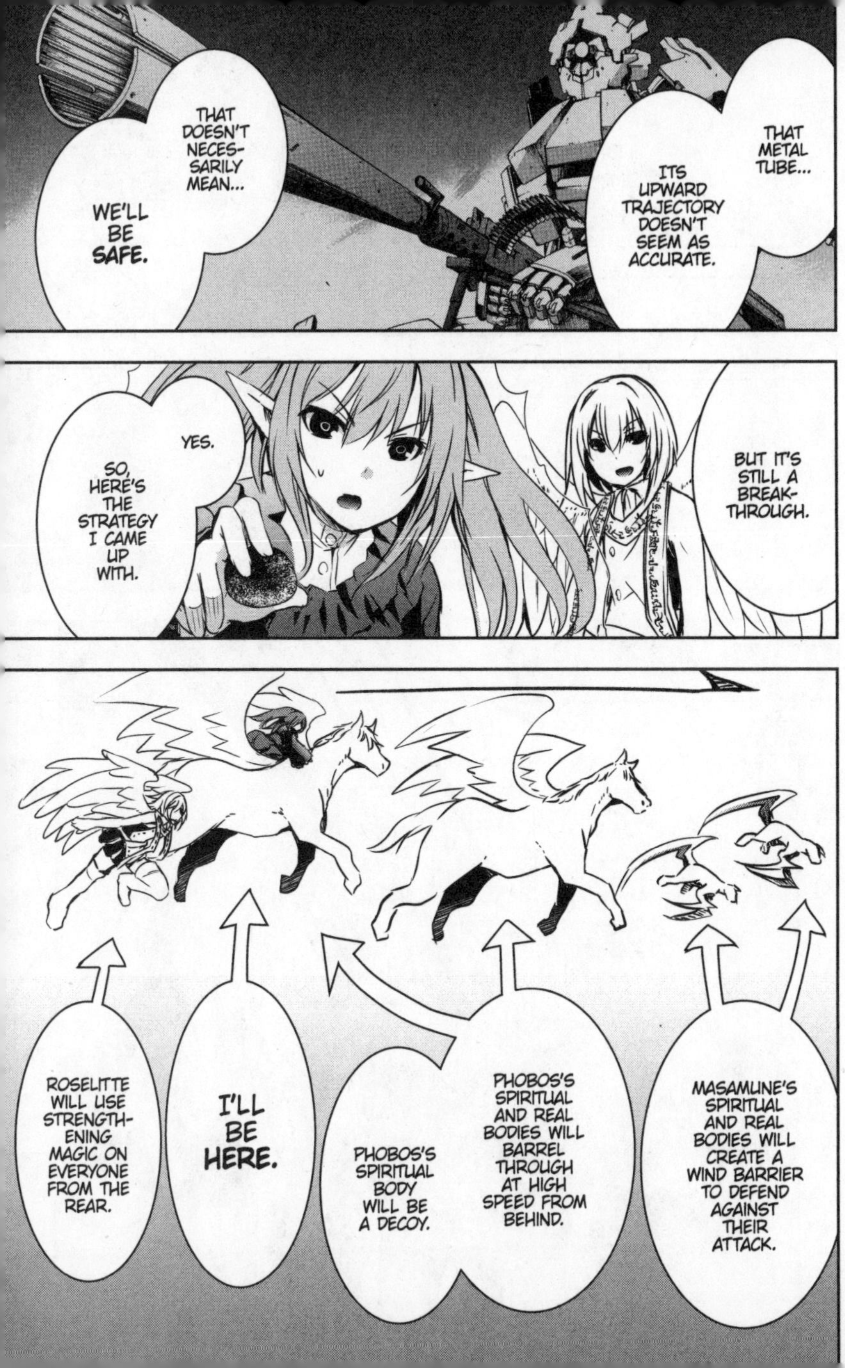
THAT METAL TUBE...
ITS UPWARD TRAJECTORY DOESN'T SEEM AS ACCURATE.
THAT DOESN'T NECES-SARILY MEAN...
WE'LL BE SAFE.
BUT IT'S STILL A BREAK-THROUGH.
YES.
SO, HERE'S THE STRATEGY I CAME UP WITH.
MASAMUNE'S SPIRITUAL AND REAL BODIES WILL CREATE A WIND BARRIER TO DEFEND AGAINST THEIR ATTACK.
PHOBOS'S SPIRITUAL AND REAL BODIES WILL BARREL THROUGH AT HIGH SPEED FROM BEHIND.
PHOBOS'S SPIRITUAL BODY WILL BE A DECOY.
I'LL BE HERE.
ROSELITTE WILL USE STRENGTH-ENING MAGIC ON EVERYONE FROM THE REAR.

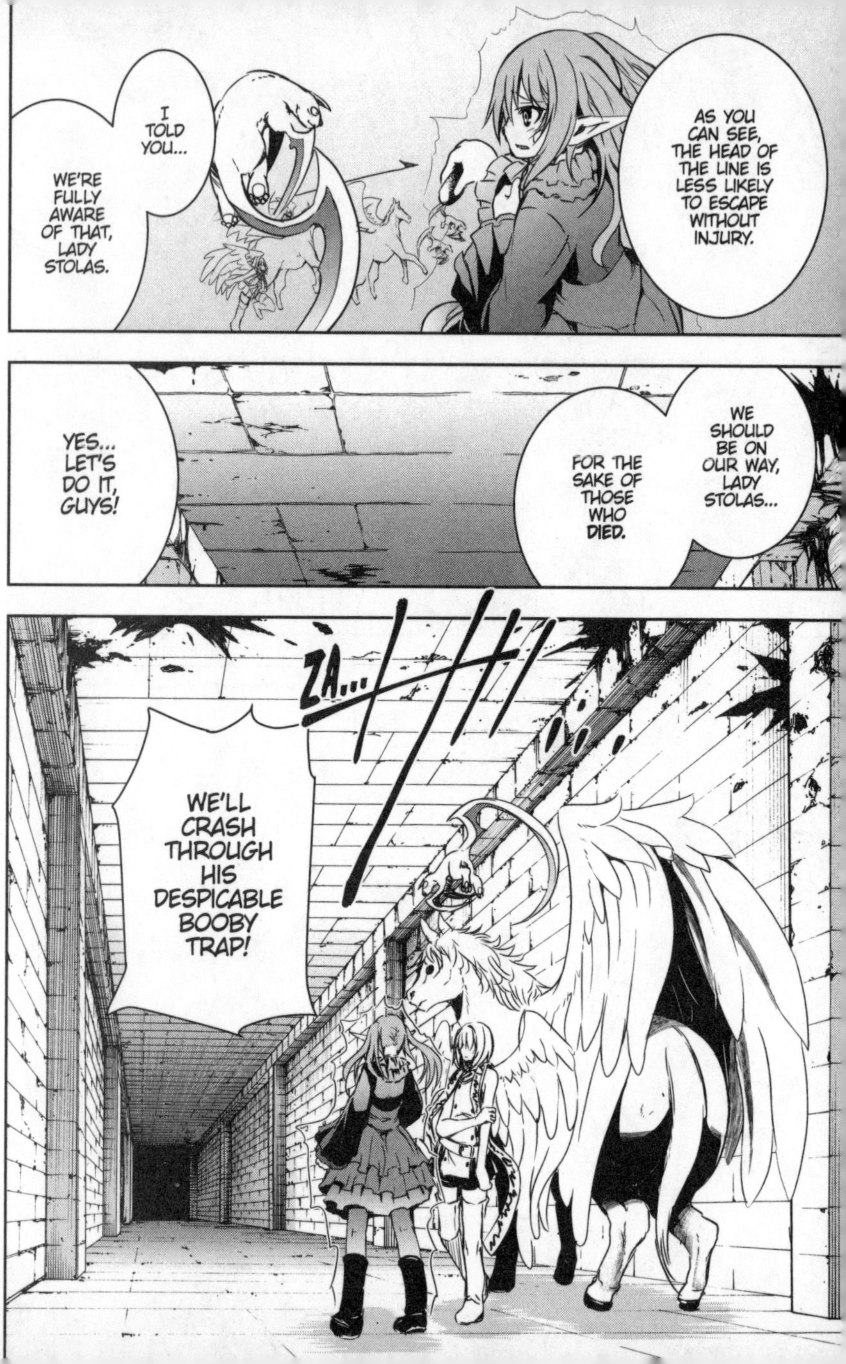
AS YOU CAN SEE, THE HEAD OF THE LINE IS LESS LIKELY TO ESCAPE WITHOUT INJURY.
I TOLD YOU...
WE'RE FULLY AWARE OF THAT, LADY STOLAS.
WE SHOULD BE ON OUR WAY, LADY STOLAS...
FOR THE SAKE OF THOSE WHO DIED.
YES... LET'S DO IT, GUYS!
ZA...
WE'LL CRASH THROUGH HIS DESPICABLE BOOBY TRAP!

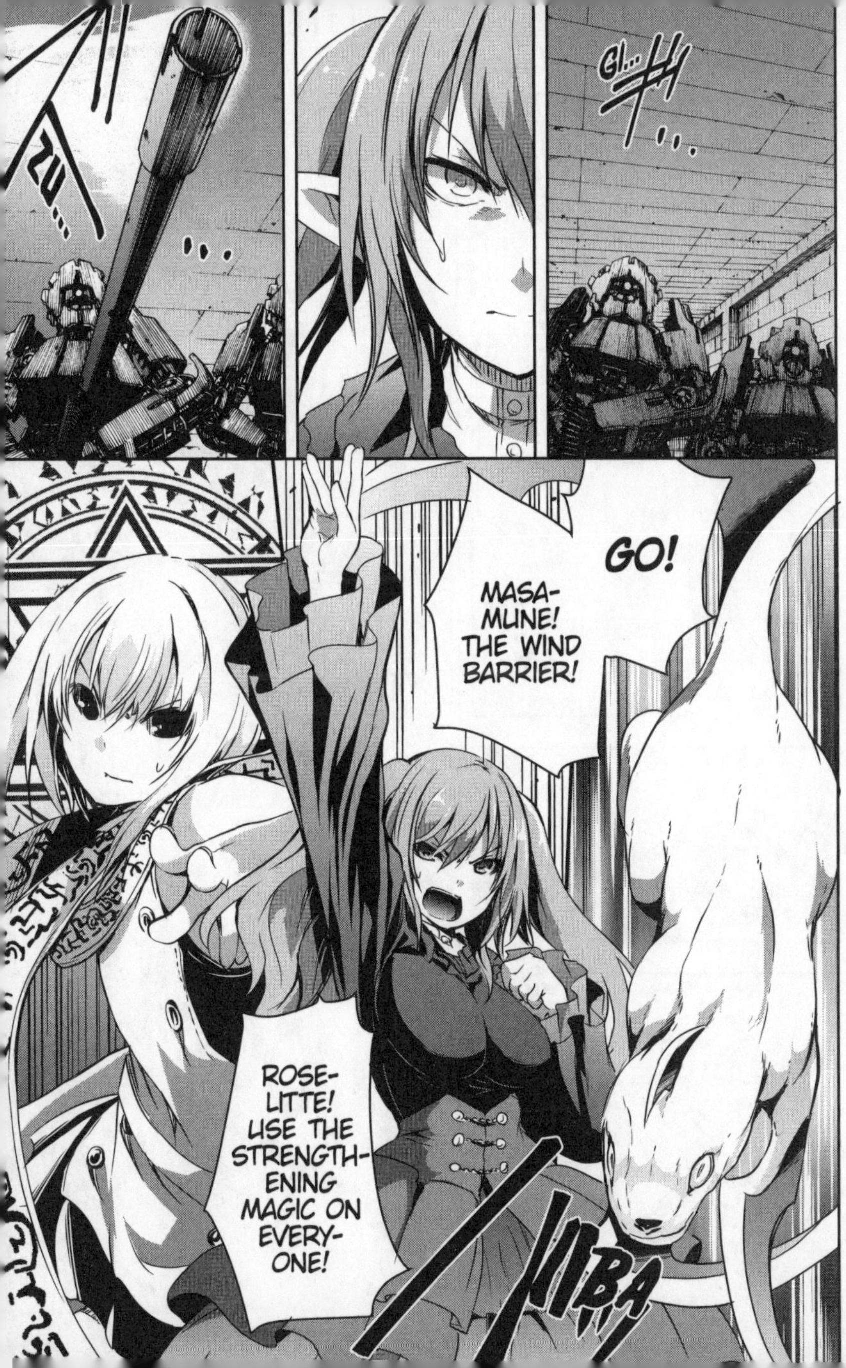
GI...
...
ZU...
...
MASA-MUNE! THE WIND BARRIER! GO!
ROSE-LITTE! USE THE STRENGTH-ENING MAGIC ON EVERY-ONE!
BA

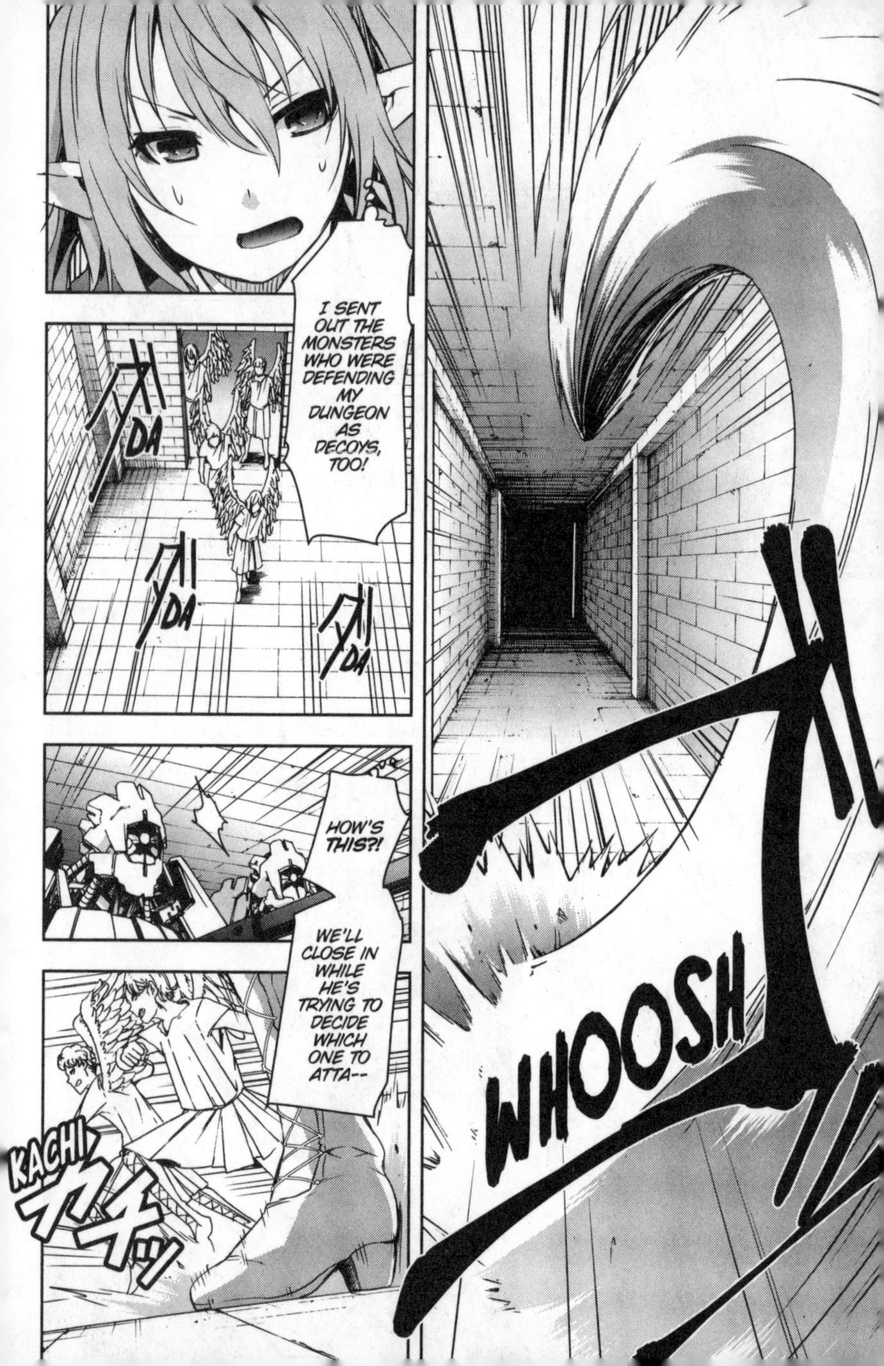
WHOOSH
I SENT OUT THE MONSTERS WHO WERE DEFENDING MY DUNGEON AS DECOYS, TOO!
DA
DA
DA
HOW'S THIS?!
WE'LL CLOSE IN WHILE HE'S TRYING TO DECIDE WHICH ONE TO ATTA--
KACHI

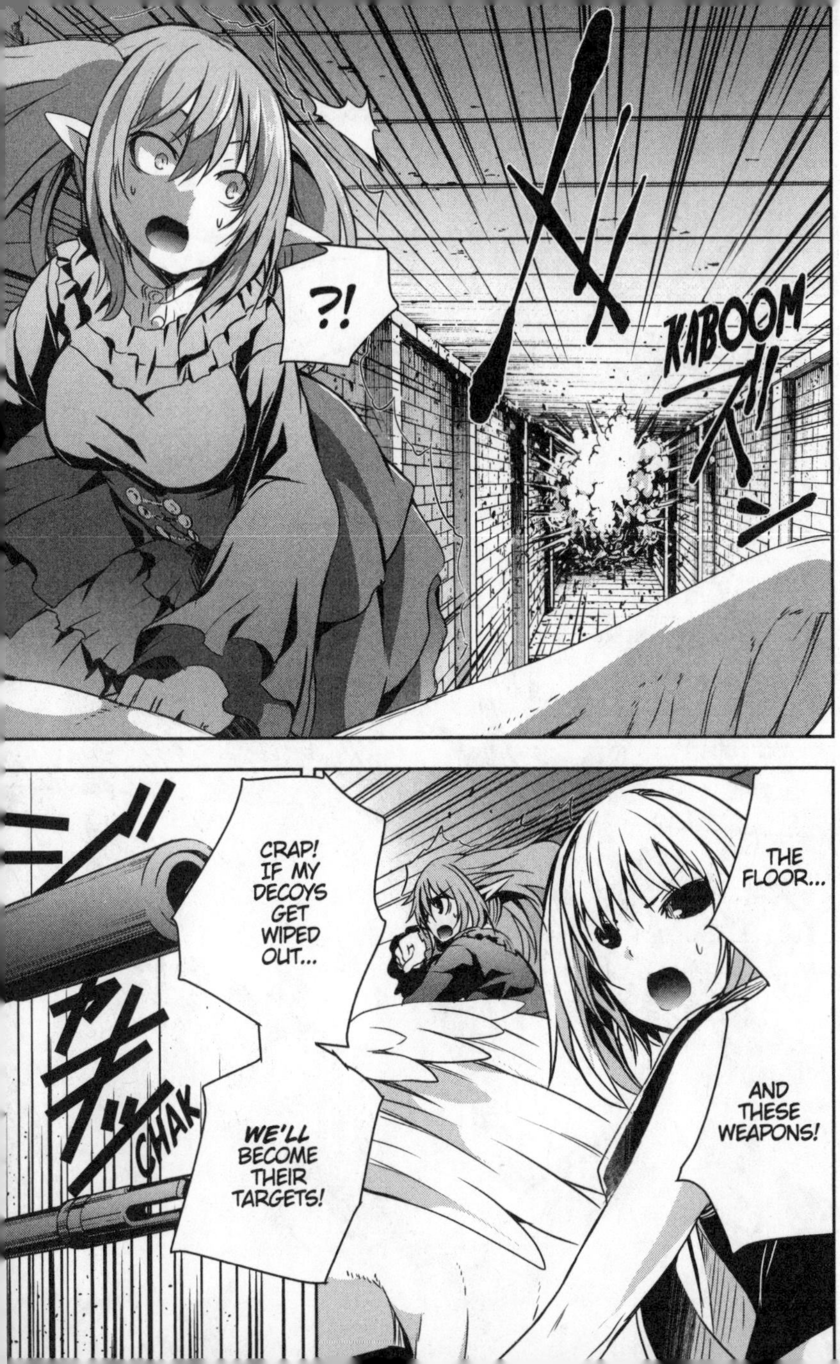
KABOOM
?!
THE FLOOR...
AND THESE WEAPONS!
CRAP! IF MY DECOYS GET WIPED OUT...
WE'LL BECOME THEIR TARGETS!
CHAK

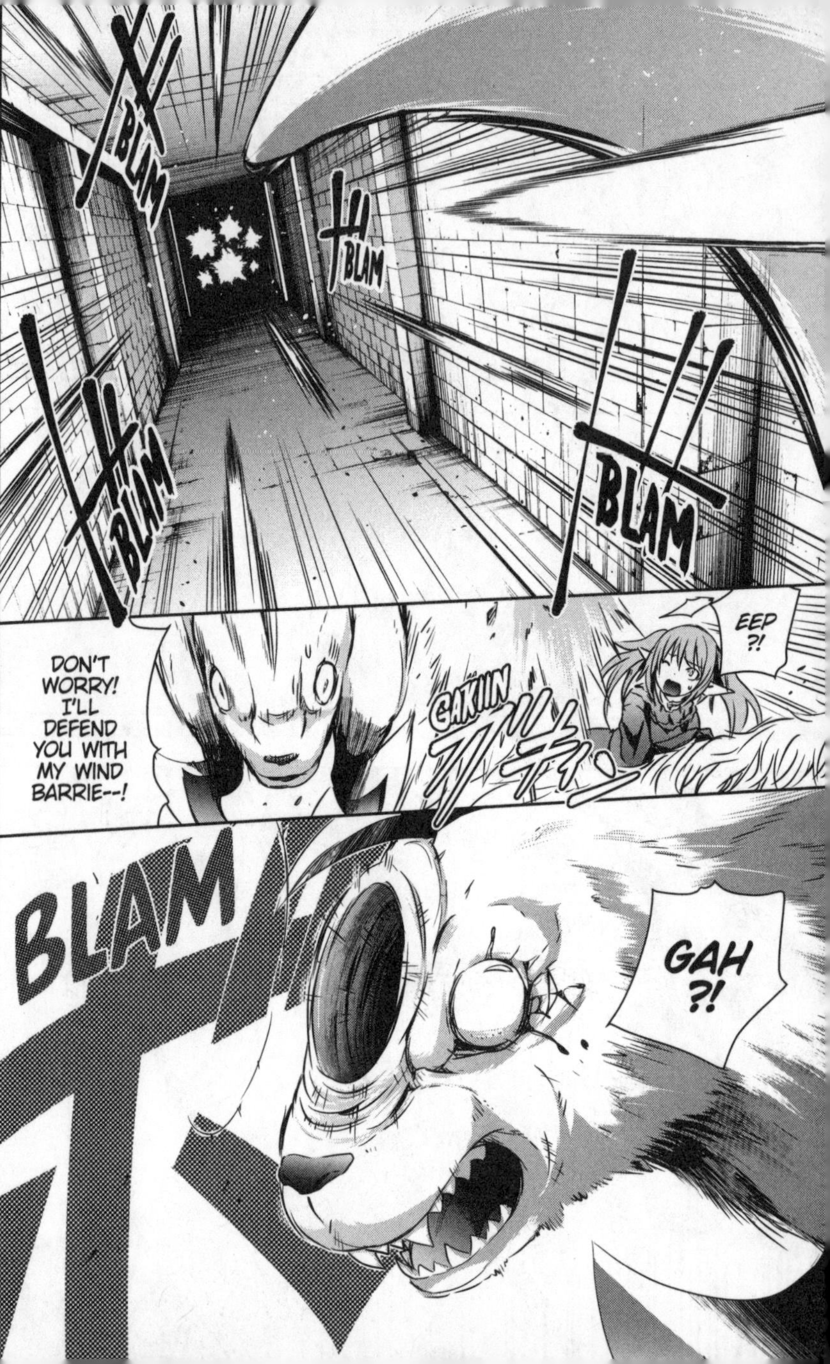
BLAM
BLAM
BLAM
BLAM
EEP ?!
GAKIIN
DON'T WORRY! I'LL DEFEND YOU WITH MY WIND BARRIE--!
GAH ?!
BLAM

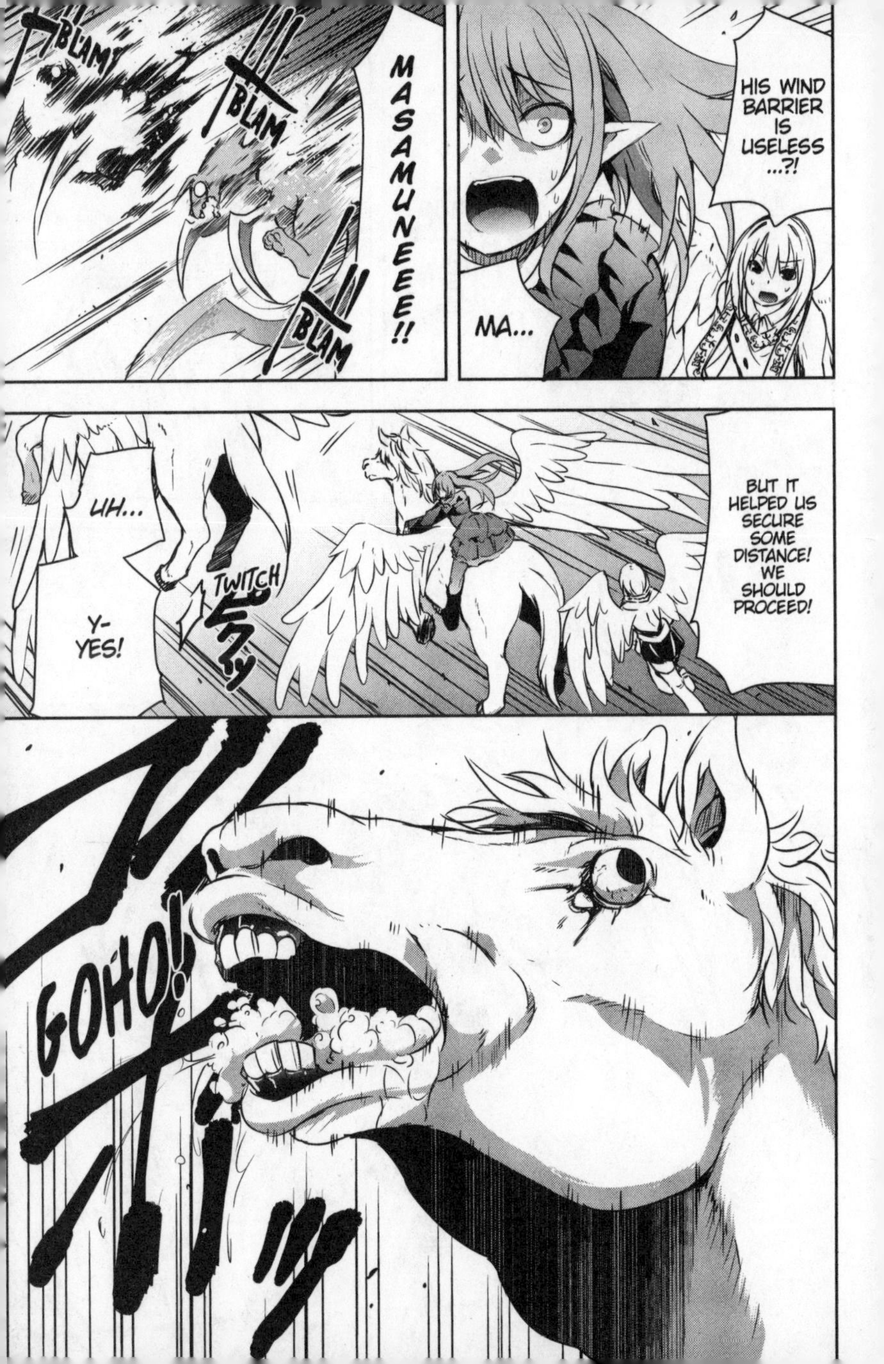
HIS WIND BARRIER IS USELESS ...?!
MA...
MASAMUNEEEE!!
BLAM
BLAM
BLAM
BUT IT HELPED US SECURE SOME DISTANCE! WE SHOULD PROCEED!
TWITCH
UH...
Y-YES!
GOHO!

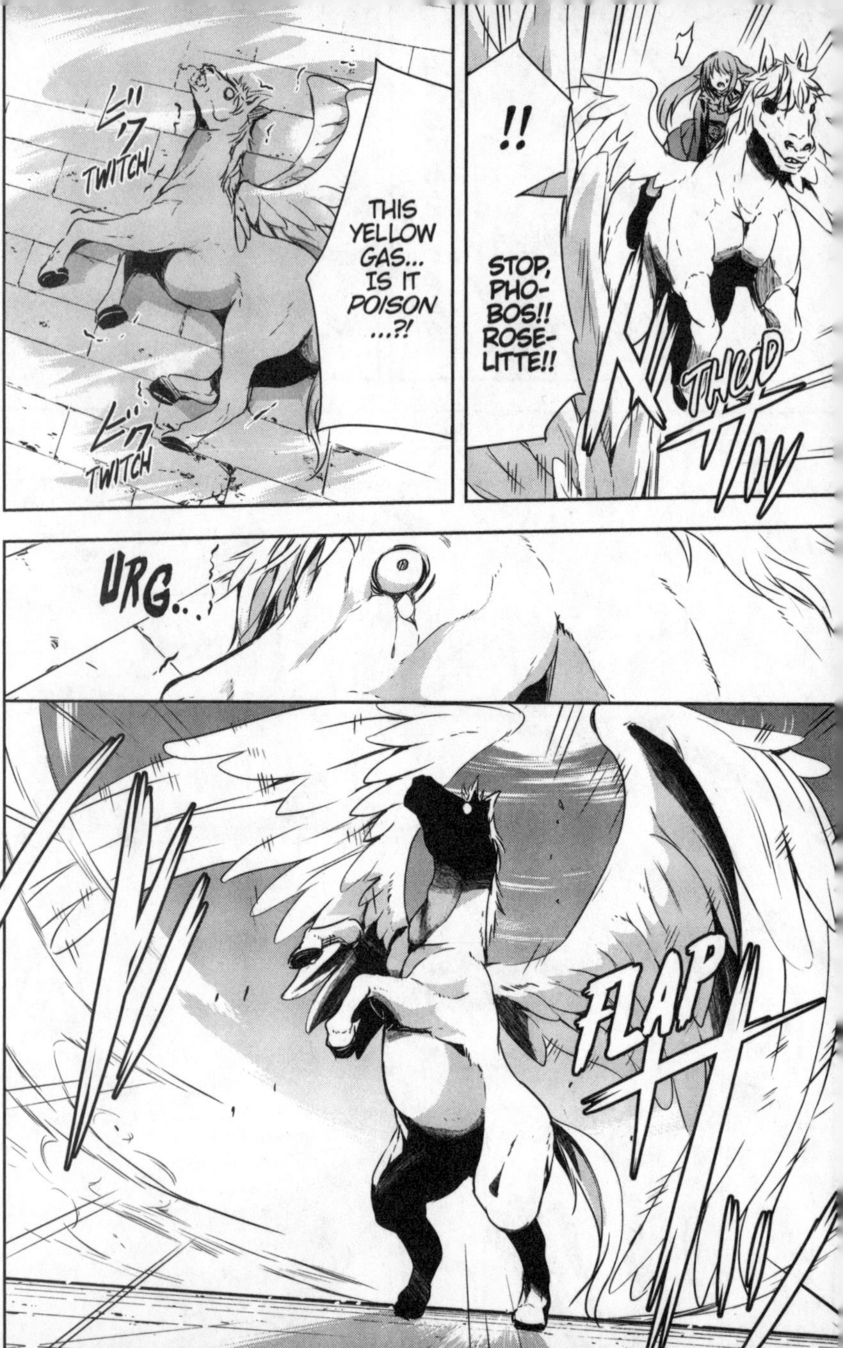
!!
STOP, PHOBOS!! ROSELITTE!!
THUD
TWITCH
THIS YELLOW GAS... IS IT POISON...?!
TWITCH
URG...
FLAP

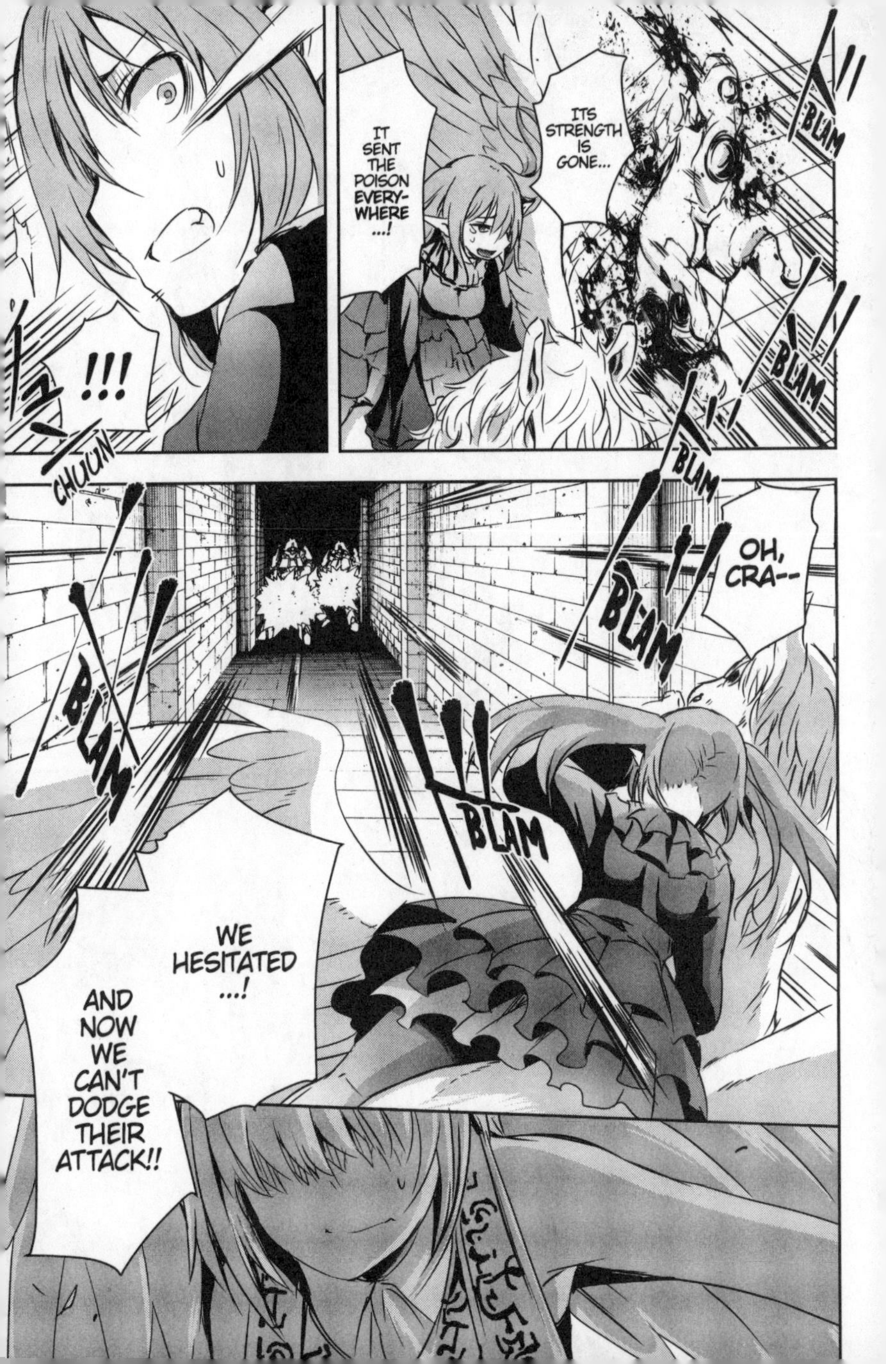

BLAM
ITS STRENGTH IS GONE...
IT SENT THE POISON EVERY-WHERE...!
BLAM
!!!
CHUUN
BLAM
OH, CRA--
BLAM
BLAM
BLAM
WE HESITATED...!
AND NOW WE CAN'T DODGE THEIR ATTACK!!

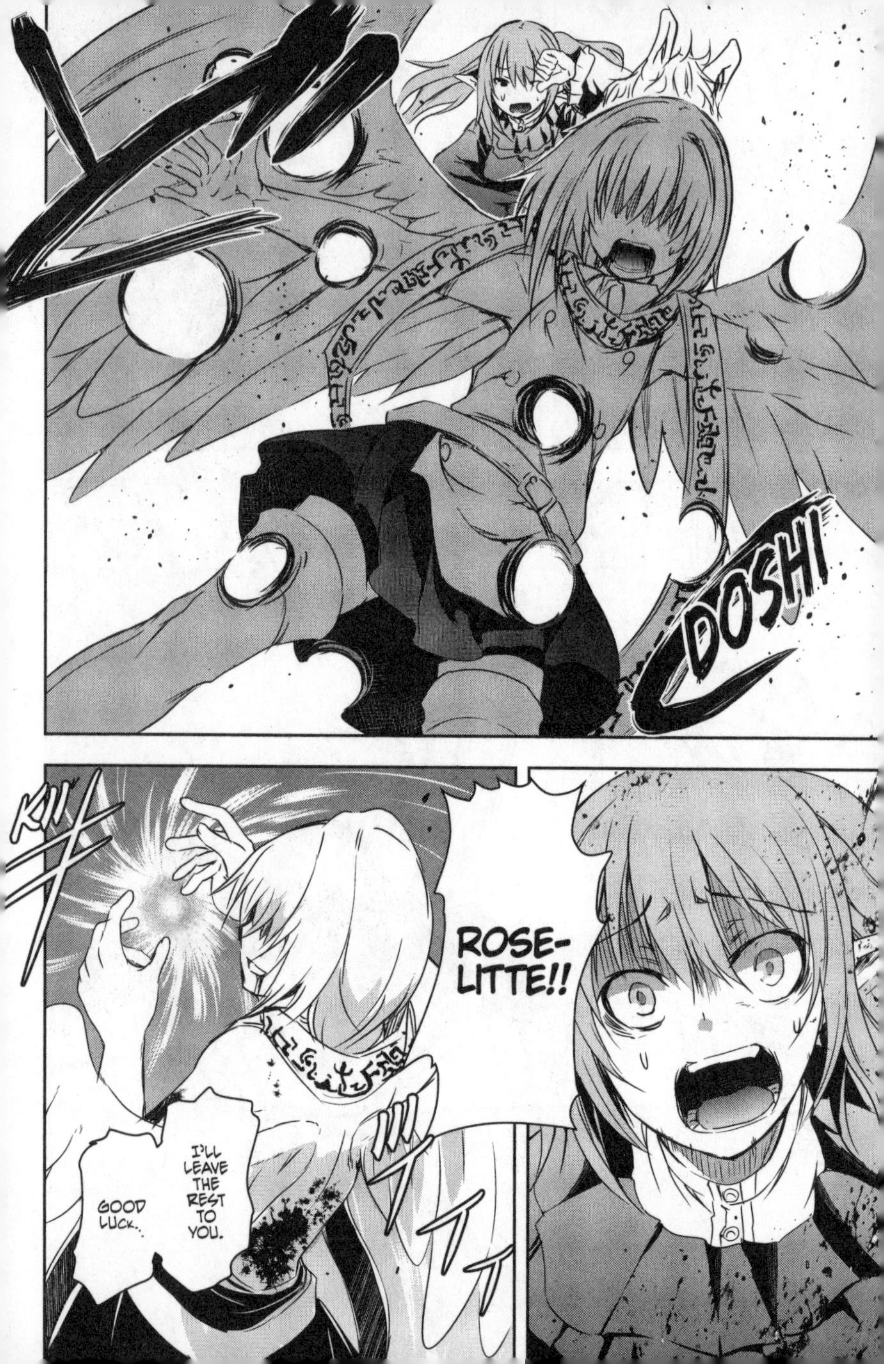
DOSHI
ROSE-LITTE!!
KII
I'LL LEAVE THE REST TO YOU.
GOOD LUCK..

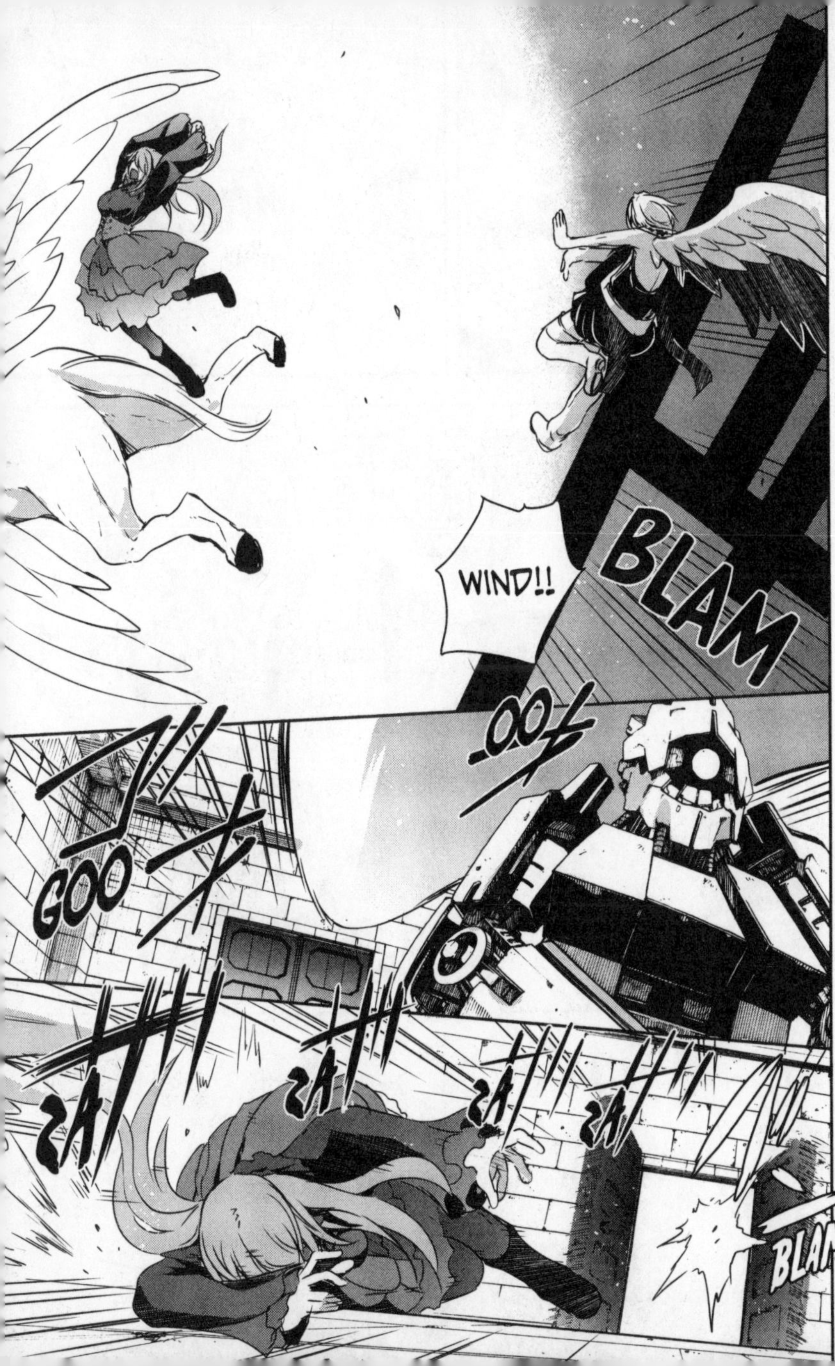
WIND!!
BLAM
BLAM
ZA
ZA
ZA
ZA
GOO

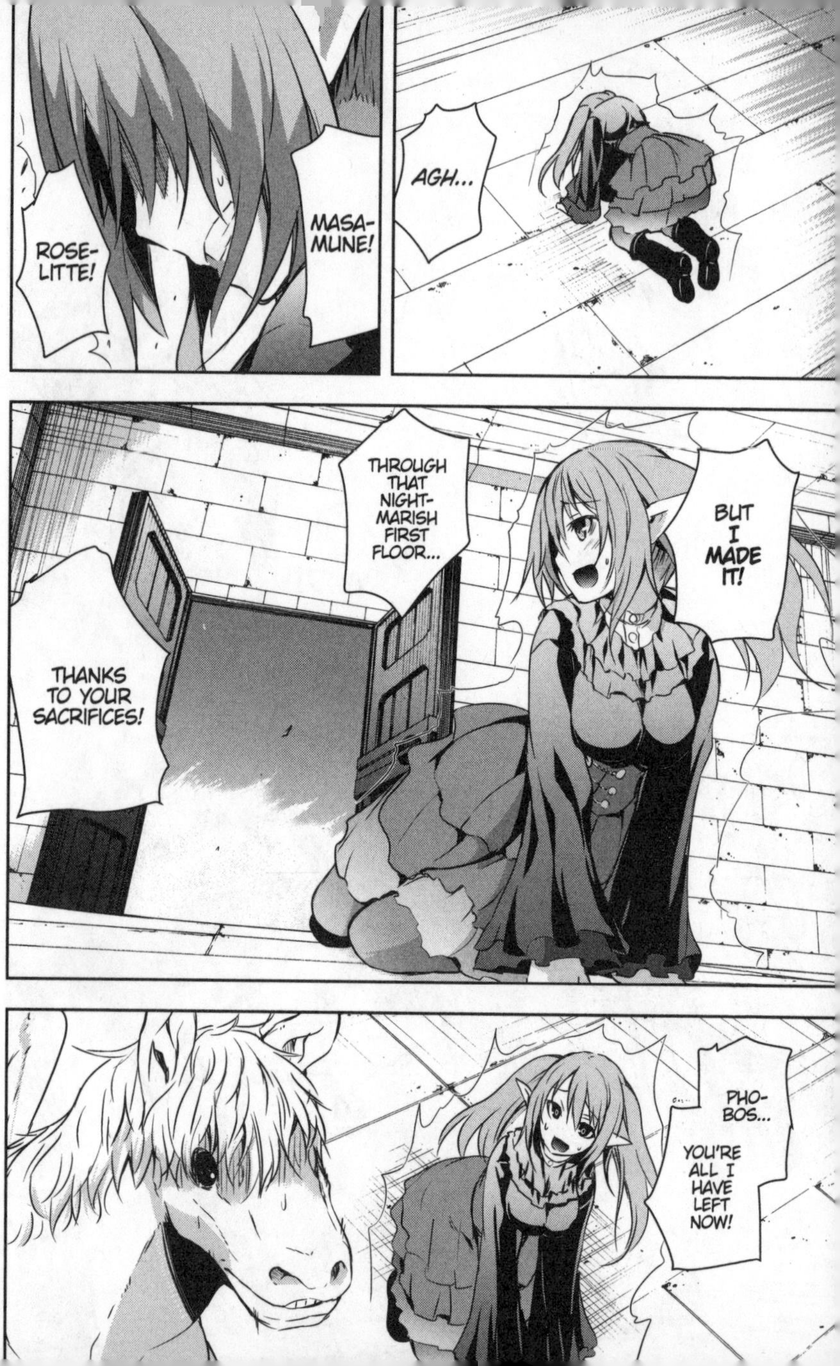
AGH...
MASA-MUNE!
ROSE-LITTE!
BUT I MADE IT!
THROUGH THAT NIGHT-MARISH FIRST FLOOR...
THANKS TO YOUR SACRIFICES!
PHO-BOS...
YOU'RE ALL I HAVE LEFT NOW!

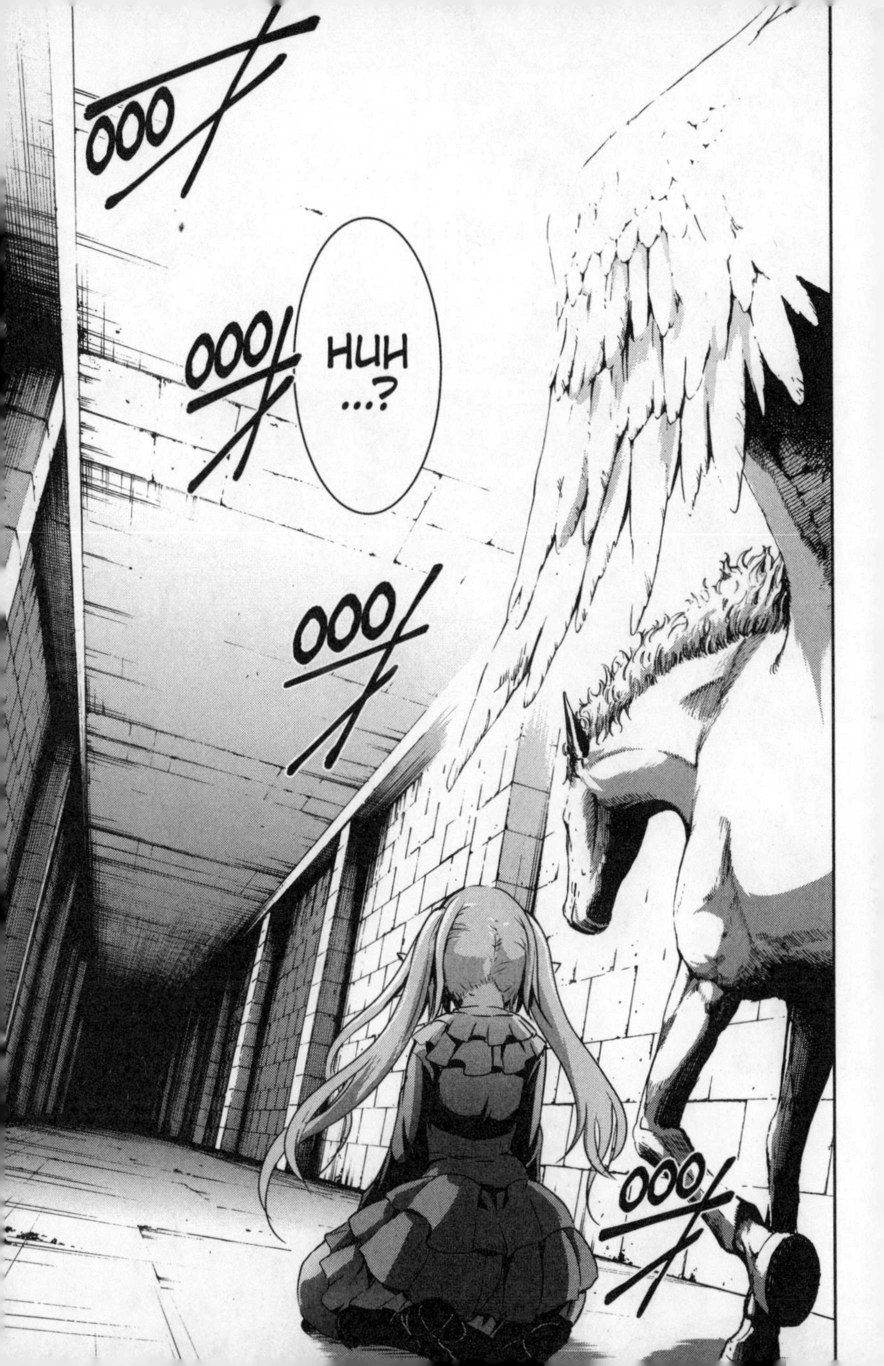
OOO
HUH ...?
OOO
OOO
OOO

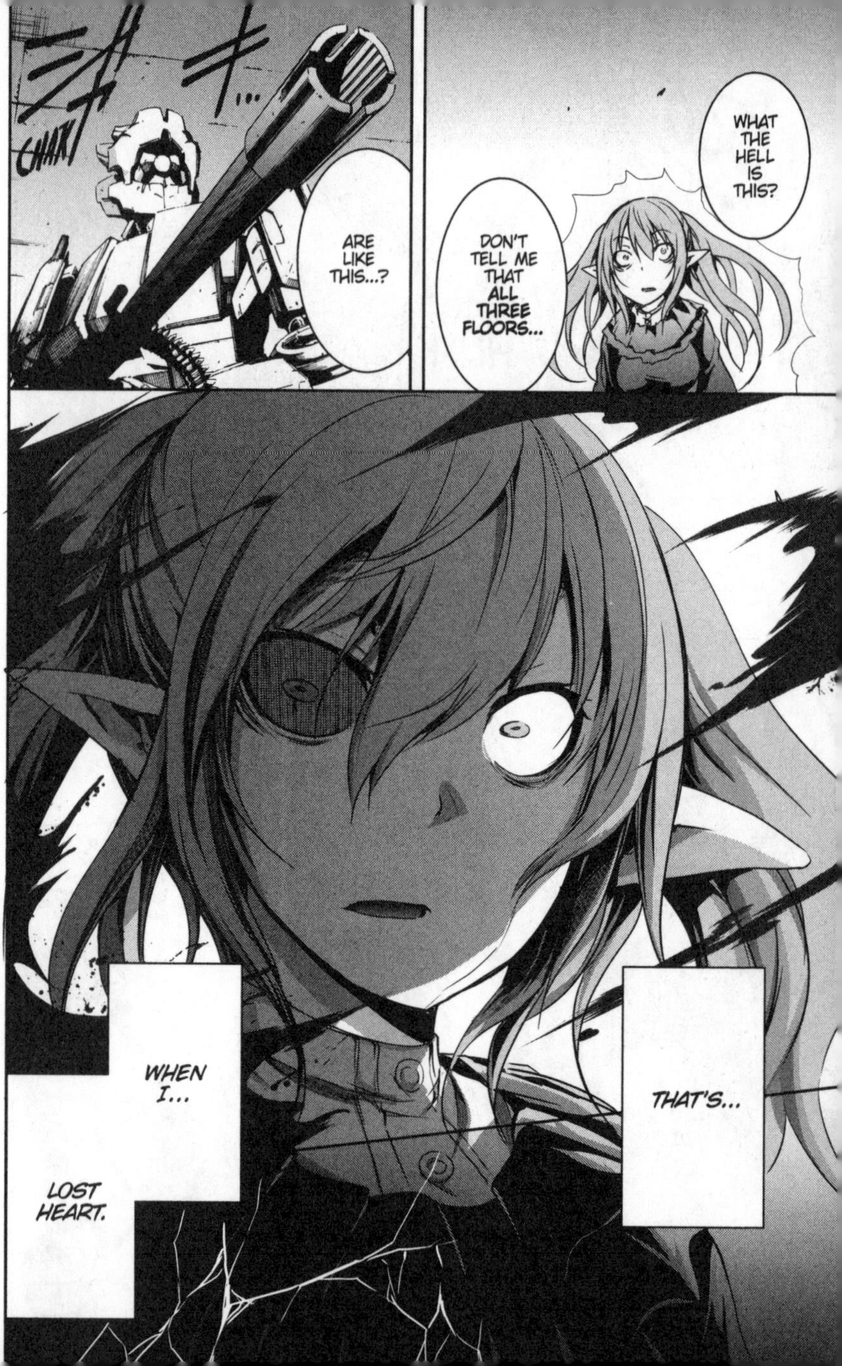
WHAT THE HELL IS THIS?
DON'T TELL ME THAT ALL THREE FLOORS...
CHAK!
ARE LIKE THIS...?
THAT'S...
WHEN I...
LOST HEART.

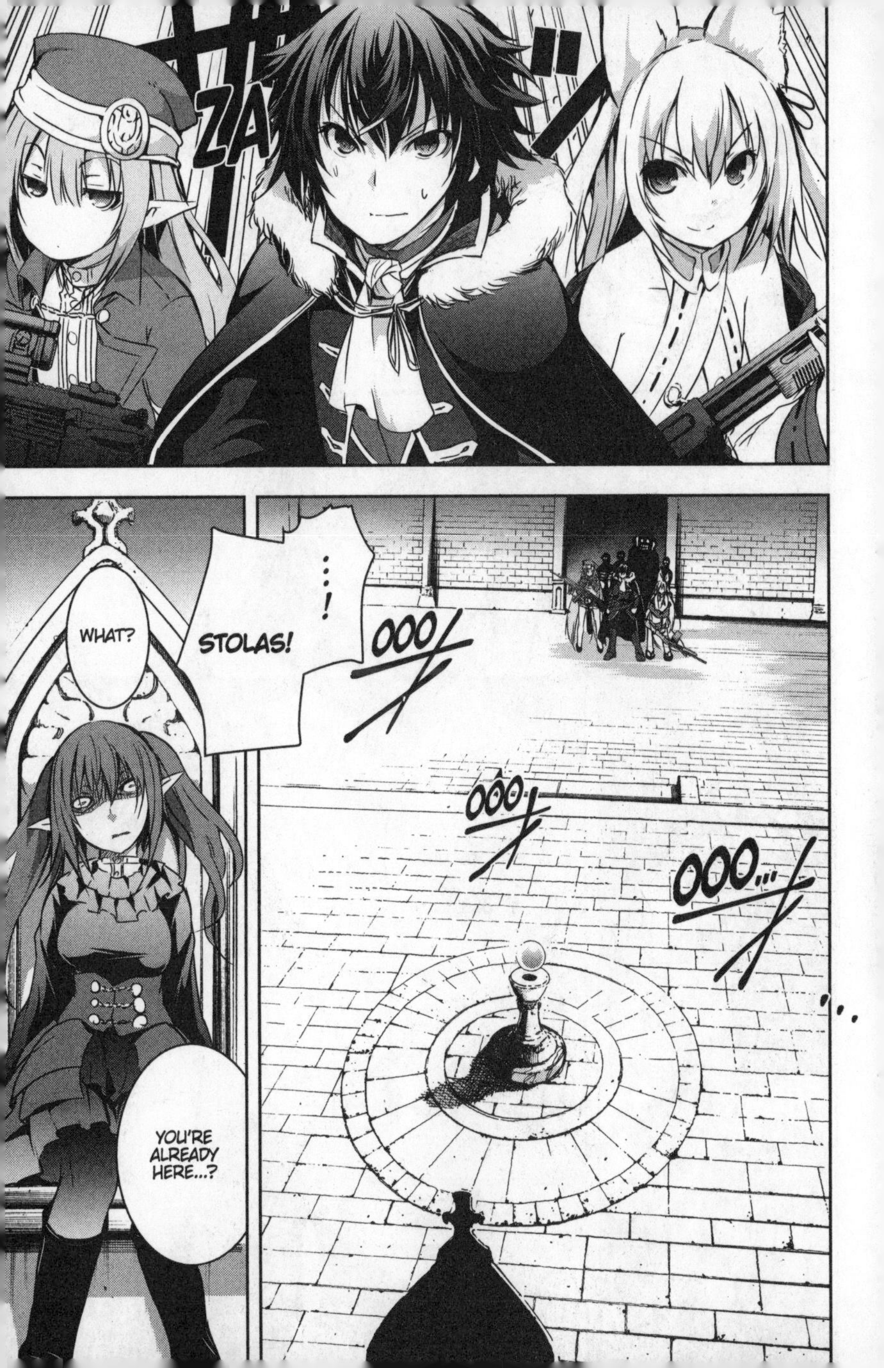
ZA
...!
STOLAS!
OOO
OOO
OOO...
...
WHAT?
YOU'RE ALREADY HERE...?

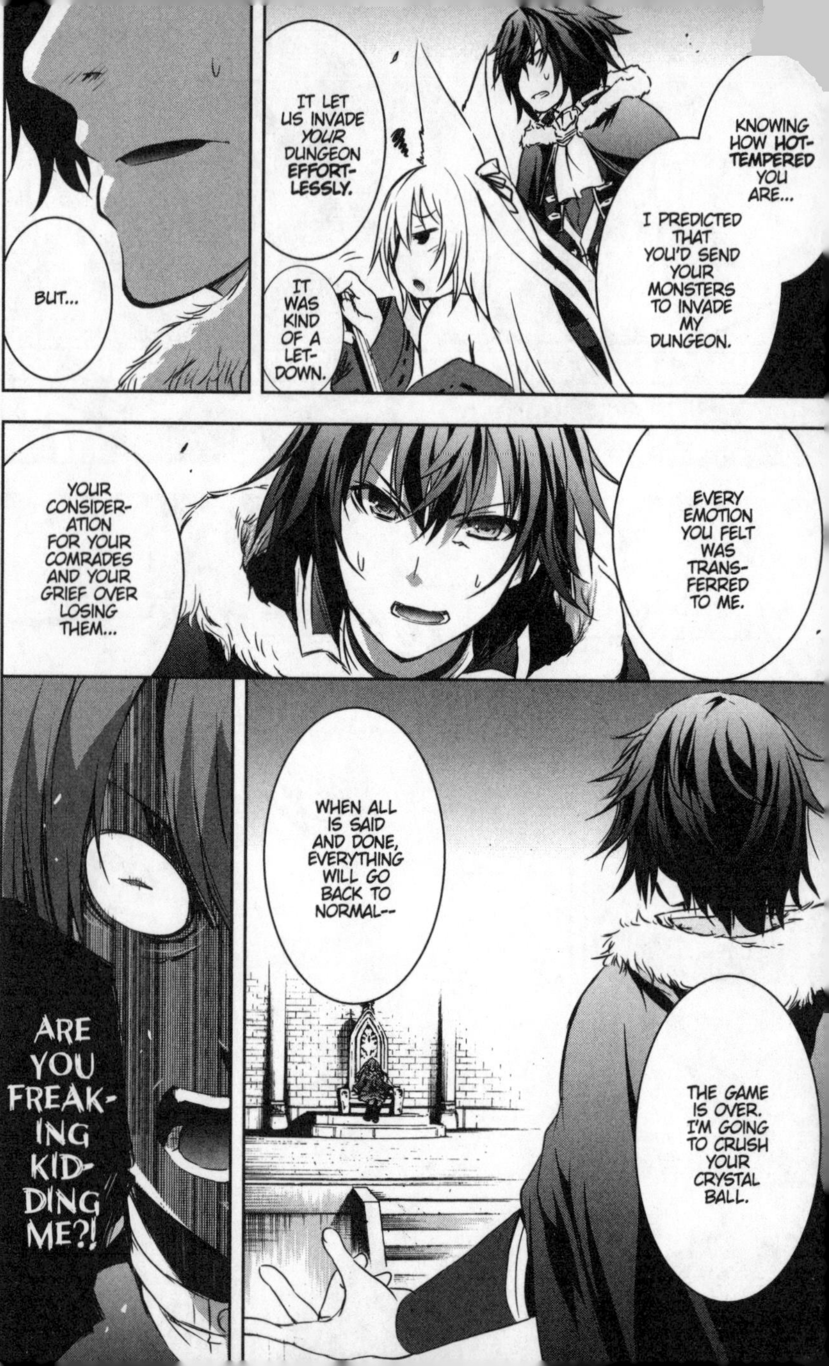
KNOWING HOW HOT-TEMPERED YOU ARE...
I PREDICTED THAT YOU'D SEND YOUR MONSTERS TO INVADE MY DUNGEON.
IT LET US INVADE *YOUR* DUNGEON EFFORTLESSLY.
IT WAS KIND OF A LET-DOWN.
BUT...
EVERY EMOTION YOU FELT WAS TRANSFERRED TO ME.
YOUR CONSIDERATION FOR YOUR COMRADES AND YOUR GRIEF OVER LOSING THEM...
THE GAME IS OVER. I'M GOING TO CRUSH YOUR CRYSTAL BALL.
WHEN ALL IS SAID AND DONE, EVERYTHING WILL GO BACK TO NORMAL--
ARE YOU FREAKING KIDDING ME?!

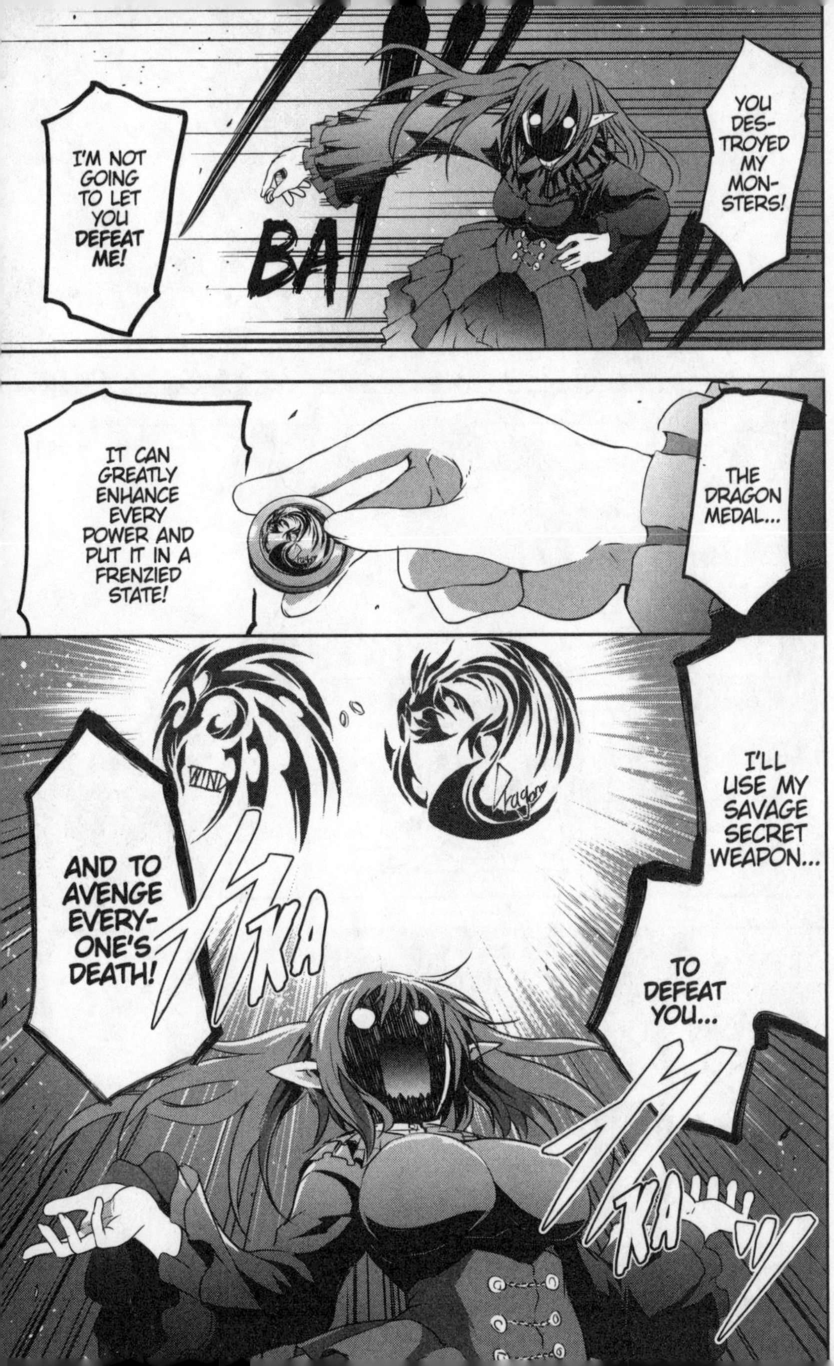
YOU DES-TROYED MY MON-STERS!
BA
I'M NOT GOING TO LET YOU DEFEAT ME!
THE DRAGON MEDAL...
IT CAN GREATLY ENHANCE EVERY POWER AND PUT IT IN A FRENZIED STATE!
WIND
I'LL USE MY SAVAGE SECRET WEAPON...
TO DEFEAT YOU...
AND TO AVENGE EVERY-ONE'S DEATH!
KA
KA

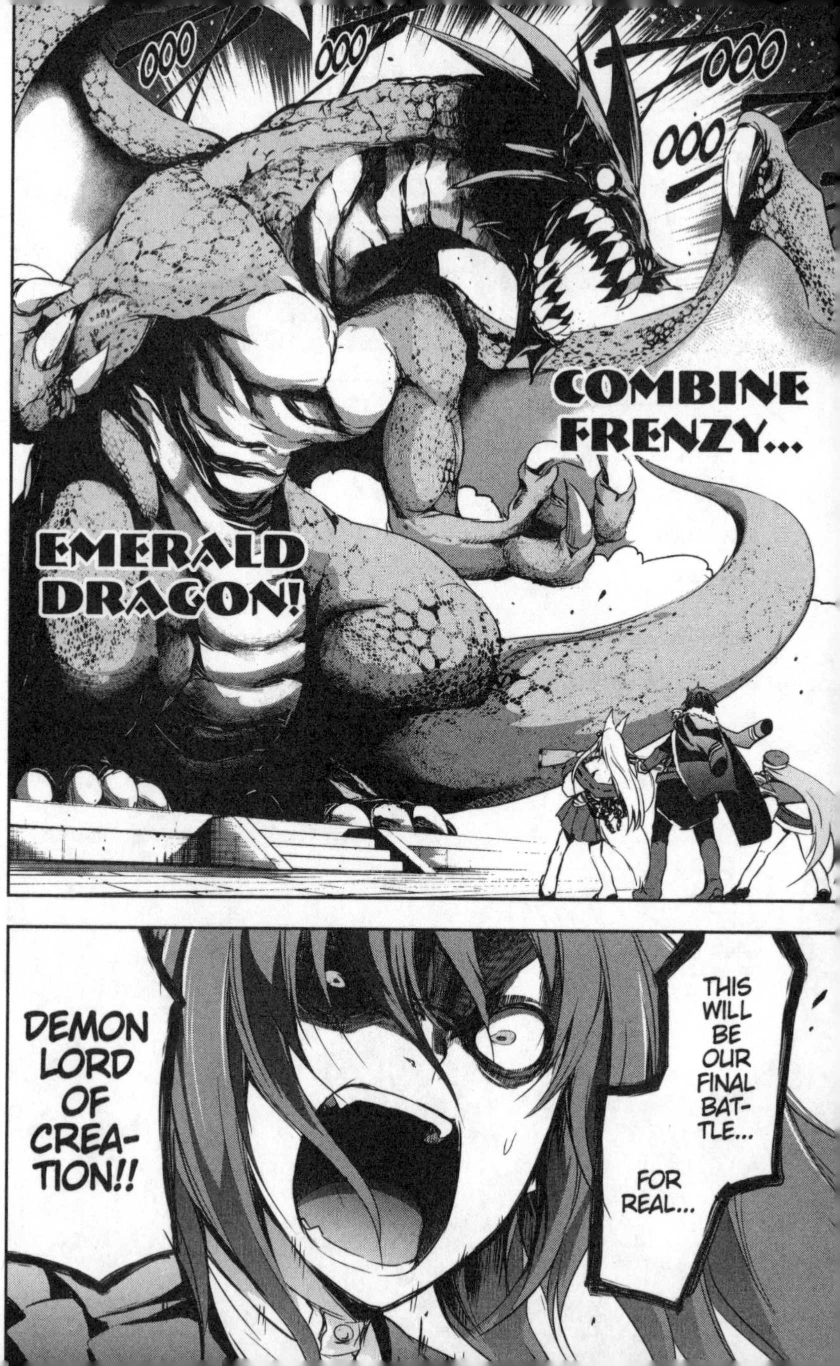
OOO
OOO
OOO
OOO
COMBINE FRENZY...
EMERALD DRAGON!
THIS WILL BE OUR FINAL BAT-TLE...
FOR REAL...
DEMON LORD OF CREA-TION!!

DUNGEON BUILDER:
THE DEMON KING'S
LABYRINTH IS A
MODERN CITY!

Bonus Short Story: **Stolas the Rookie Demon Lord**

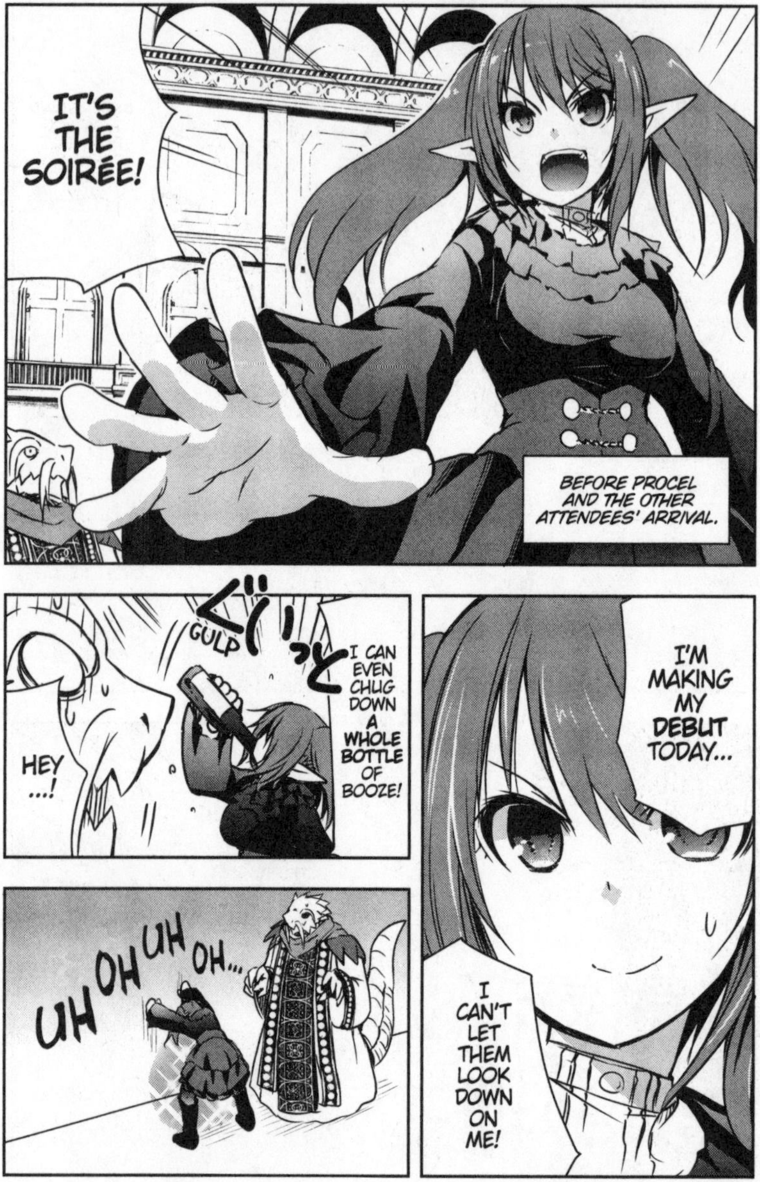
IT'S THE SOIRÉE!
BEFORE PROCEL AND THE OTHER ATTENDEES' ARRIVAL.
I'M MAKING MY DEBUT TODAY...
I CAN'T LET THEM LOOK DOWN ON ME!
ぐいっと
GULP
I CAN EVEN CHUG DOWN A WHOLE BOTTLE OF BOOZE!
HEY ...!
UH OH UH OH...

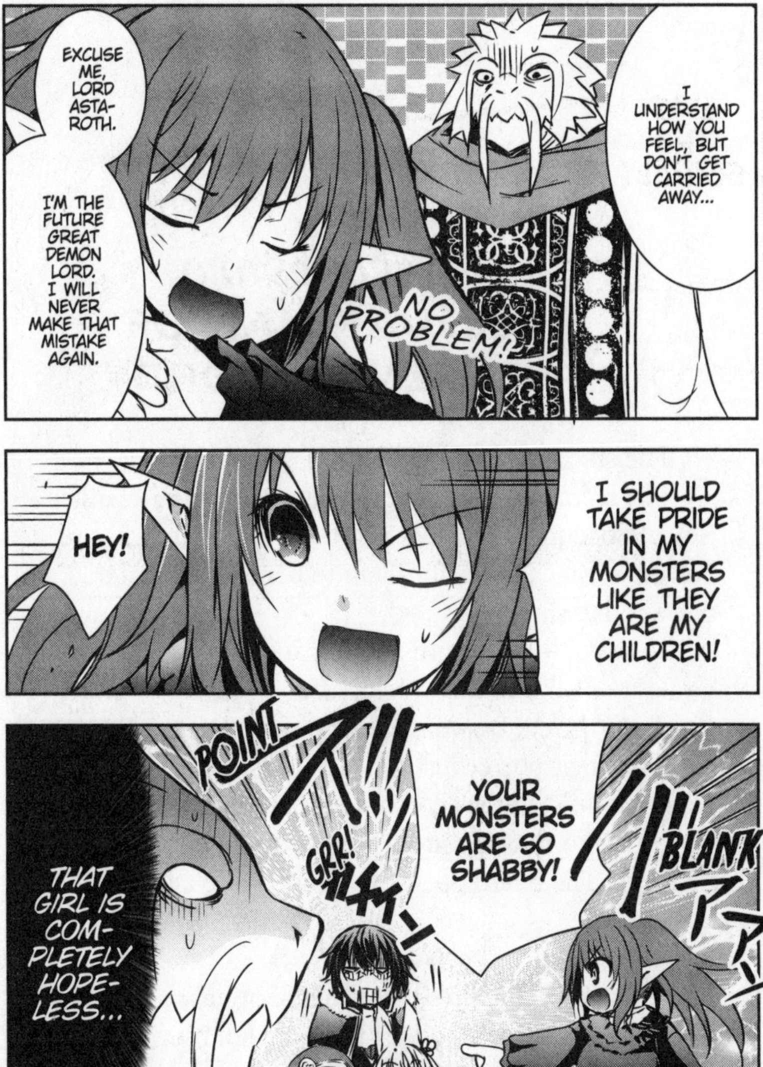
I UNDERSTAND HOW YOU FEEL, BUT DON'T GET CARRIED AWAY...
NO PROBLEM!
EXCUSE ME, LORD ASTA-ROTH.
I'M THE FUTURE GREAT DEMON LORD. I WILL NEVER MAKE THAT MISTAKE AGAIN.
I SHOULD TAKE PRIDE IN MY MONSTERS LIKE THEY ARE MY CHILDREN!
HEY!
BLANK
YOUR MONSTERS ARE SO SHABBY!
POINT
GRR!
THAT GIRL IS COM-PLETELY HOPE-LESS...
Rank: S

BONUS SHORT STORY:
THE GUARDIAN OF THE DEMON LORD

The soirée is about to begin.

The soirée is where every Demon Lord will gather. Since it occurs in the year when new demon lords are born, it's also a place for them to become acquainted with one another.

To make things more complicated, the Creator, who brought us all into this world, often holds an event to check out a new Demon Lord's power. Demon Lords build up their power just for the occasion.

Even now, in the scorching dungeon of the Crimson Cove, Tenko runs toward a large lizard that is walking on two legs. The lizard opens its mouth wide and blows fire at her.

"Too slow!"

She dodges the fire, points her shotgun at the lizard, and shoots it at close range. The gunshot blows off the lizard's upper body.

An ordinary shotgun wouldn't do this, but in this world, a monster's power amplifies its attack.

The shooter is a very pretty girl in her early teens with fox ears and a tail. Looks can be deceiving, however—she is actually an S-ranked monster, a Tenko, with a power that defies imagination.

The shotgun Tenko carries doesn't look ordinary, either.

"Good work today. You've earned some experience and Dungeon Points. Now, it's getting late, so let's call it a day."

"Mrr... Daddy, I'm tired of this dungeon. We keep doing the same old thing every single day!" Tenko whines as she puffs out her cheeks.

"I hear you, but there isn't any other dungeon where we can level up. We can't earn medals and Dungeon Points that quickly, either. We just have to work our way up in this dungeon."

Tenko's fluffy tail droops. She seems to understand, but she is unable to work up any enthusiasm.

"I understand what Tenko is saying. Doing the same thing over and over won't give me any new data, either. I'd rather be doing research at my studio," the reliable Elder Dwarf adds unexpectedly.

The Elder Dwarf is a pretty, silver-haired girl. She looks like a regular girl, but she is actually a dwarf of the highest rank, and a brilliant monster.

"Elder Dwarf needs to raise her level more than Tenko," I say. "She'll have more magical power to use and it'll strengthen her muscles. Wouldn't it be helpful in her smithcraft?"

"I agree. Look, more enemies are coming," says the Elder Dwarf as she fires her assault rifle in full-automatic mode and takes down fiery bats.

Her assault rifle is a weapon I made with my Creation power, and the Elder Dwarf enhanced it with her technique and skills. Every one of its abilities has been improved until now it can riddle a powerful monster with bullets. It isn't as powerful as Tenko's shotgun, but it's easy to use.

Being able to defeat monsters this easily explains her calm demeanor.

"I have a great idea! It's boring to beat weak monsters like this—we should come up with a special move! It could make us stronger and it would be a nice change of pace."

"Can it be done that easily? Isn't it too risky? It'll make us do awkward moves during battle."

"N-no it won't. *Um,* you don't have to have Tenko do something awesome. Just make Tenko's *weapon* awesome. The shotgun El made... It's super-powerful and it goes bang, but Tenko wants one that goes BOOM. A bigger shell made it more powerful, so we can make that even bigger!" Tenko is babbling.

The bigger the bullet, the more powerful it will be. It increases the explosion.

Tenko's remodeled shotgun, however, is of nonstandard caliber and it's designed to be utilized by Tenko alone, whose muscle strength surpasses that of any human. If I were to use it, the recoil would knock me off my feet each time I fired.

Making the gun any more powerful than this would make it difficult for Tenko to use. It's already reached maximum strength. Enlarging the entire gun and making it sturdier will give it more power, but will also make it heavier and harder to control.

"I can make it go boom even louder. It's just that it'll have a completely different function from a shotgun. Come to think of it, I have tons of steel lying around. I haven't used all of it because I've been using mithril to enhance power while securing the strength of our weapons. I might as well use all that steel on this. Yeah, I've got the gist of it. It's not that difficult to create... It's possible. I'll make something that goes boom even louder than Tenko's shotgun."

"I knew you could, El! I can't wait to go hunting tomorrow."

"Me too. It'll give me better data." Tenko and the Elder Dwarf are excited.

It's nice to see my monsters so happy, but I have an uneasy feeling about this.

That day, we returned to our house that Marchosias, the Demon Lord of Beasts, had provided us, and had dinner. Normally I would chat with the other monsters, but tonight it was just Tenko and me. The Elder Dwarf had holed herself up inside a studio attached to the mansion.

"I can't wait to see what El comes up with!" Tenko remarks as she climbs into my lap, while I'm sitting in a chair, and leans into me.

"Yeah, it'll definitely be exciting."

Tenko is such a baby and she enjoys doing this. I don't mind. Tenko is cute and smells nice, and best of all, she's fluffy. I will never get tired of petting her fox tail.

"Hey, Daddy. Let's go peek into El's studio!"

"Let's *not* do that. She already warned us against it."

Every once in a while, we would check out El's studio to see the work of the world's highest-ranked dwarf, but after dinner, she told us flatly, "No peeking until tomorrow morning. If you do...well, never you mind."

Curiosity killed the cat. If the Elder Dwarf is making us something great, we should wait patiently until she finishes.

"That makes me want to peek even more! *Mrr*...this is torture." Tenko is like a bundle of curiosity, itching to go. Her fox ears perk up and her tail puffs out.

"You can try it, but she won't go easy on you. She probably won't let you use the new weapon."

"Ack, I don't want that. I can't miss the one that really goes boom, even louder than the amazing shotgun." Tenko becomes disheartened. She shakes her head several times and clings to me again.

As I laugh nervously, I toss some dried fruit snacks into Tenko's mouth. Tenko munches and smiles radiantly. She seems to have sorted herself out. I'm just as curious about El's work, but I can wait until tomorrow. I'll just relax and hang out with Tenko today.

The Elder Dwarf never came home that day. It's not

unusual for her to be immersed in research and smithing, so I'm not worried about her.

As I'm making breakfast, the door opens.

"I don't approve of you staying out all night," I scold.

"Well, I went a bit crazy, but it turned out great. I'm more than satisfied." The Elder Dwarf smiles at her accomplishment as she rubs her sleepy eyes and gives a thumbs-up.

"I see. I can't wait to go hunting today."

"No! I wanna see it go boom *now!*" Tenko, who has been anxious since the day before, comes out of her room with her eyes twinkling. She was in such a hurry her clothes were disheveled, so I fixed them for her. Sometimes I wish she would be a bit more demure.

"Yeah, you're going to love it. You can make it go boom all you want."

"El, you're awesome!"

"Anyway, let's have breakfast. After that, shouldn't you take a quick nap, Elder Dwarf?"

"No, I don't need to. Being up all night is part of a metalsmith's life."

"Okay, we'll go practice right after breakfast."

El *is* a higher-ranked monster. Losing sleep for a day or two won't kill her. The Elder Dwarf seems more anxious to show us her finished product than anything, so we should respect her wishes.

We head out to the studio. When we get there, instead of a door, we find walls sliding open on both sides for us.

"Was this here before?"

"Uh-uh, it wasn't, so I made it. A door would be too hard to get that thing through," the Elder Dwarf says matter-of-factly.

And then, with a low-pitched sound, the object appears on rotating tank treads. This lump of steel, this big gun, is nothing like Tenko's shotgun or the Elder Dwarf's assault rifle. This is basically a tank, and it's huge.

"Wow, it has a gun big enough to fit my hand inside! I bet it can let out a real loud bang."

"Of course. It's a 160-mm caliber. It's ten times larger than my assault rifle and ten times more powerful, so nothing can stand up against it. It'll beat any monster, hands down."

Of course it can. It's on a whole other level from any other firearms.

"How does this work?"

"It's driven by the Golem Core. Normally it's used in a humanoid form, but I assembled a drive system and converted it into torque. It's a perpetual motion machine."

"Did you build this in one day?"

"Mm-hm. I'm an Elder Dwarf—the world's best dwarf. I can handle it. Besides, I just added the Golem techniques to the weapon we had. It wasn't that difficult," the Elder Dwarf says. Yeah, but it's not normal to be able to create something like this in one day. Seeing the stunned looks on Tenko's and my face, the Elder Dwarf wears a smug look on her own face.

"Wow, I can't wait to shoot it...but how are we going to get this to Crimson Cove? It won't fit in the transfer circle. Even if we get it there, it's too big to get into the cave."

"Oops!" blurts out the Elder Dwarf.

"Don't tell me you hadn't thought of that."

"No, I was focusing on making it big and awesome. I'm sorry, Master. I've wasted your time by making something useless." She looks down apologetically.

The Elder Dwarf is really smart, but sometimes she gets so absorbed in new technologies or new developments of modern military equipment that she loses sight of the task at hand.

It's hard not to fault her for it, but that enthusiasm is her greatest strength. I gently pat the Elder Dwarf on her head as she casts her eyes down.

"It's too big to use in a dungeon, true. Just watch out for these things in the future. But the weapons you make are never useless. What say we use this for defense instead of offense? When I build a dungeon someday, this will have a great impact if we set it up to hold the enemy in check on the floor. This solid armor and super firepower...it could repel any invading monsters."

"Master, are you just saying that to console me?"

"No, I'm just saying what's on my mind. You've made something awesome."

"Yeah, you did! We couldn't let it go boom in the dungeon, but we're going to do it now!" Tenko jumps onto the tank. She must be trying to cheer up El, too.

"There's a handle at the top. You can pull it up and climb inside."

"I got in!"

"There's a disc inside. If you place your hand on it and wish for it to move, the tank will go in the direction you desire."

"Yay. ♪ This is fun."

The tank has the ability to make sharp turns and move freely. The tank tread has also been improved so it can travel on any terrain at high speeds. Tenko is getting a bit carried away with the speed, but I think it's going about seventy kilometers per hour. With such enormous weight and speed, it can easily destroy most monsters.

"El, how do I get it to go boom?"

"Think hard about your target, and then wish for it to fire."

"I'll aim at the cliff over there!"

The turret rotates and the mortar moves up and down to set at an angle. This is impressive—it can aim in any direction. Spiky objects shoot out from the tank to secure it to the ground, and the gun lets out a ferocious roar, sending a shock wave through the surrounding area. The ammunition arcs into the sky, blasting the cliff into pieces.

A 160-mm tank gun is super-powerful, in a whole other class from a firearm. In addition to this power, Tenko's stats have been added to it, but that's not all.

"Mm-hm, the new mithril power is a jackpot. So is the magical transfer, which is now available due to this enhancement. I added an explosive that will detonate by charging magic in the ammunition. It's much more powerful than the old one. I went for speed in the magical transfer. It uses magic as well as explosives for thrust to

continue acceleration after discharge. All the power of the Golem Core transfers to the mortar when the tank is idle."

"Is that what happens when you load that stuff into a mortar of that caliber?"

It's incredibly powerful. The tank has been made enormously heavy to withstand this amount of power, but it can also be secured to the ground with spikes. Tenko and the Elder Dwarf, who are S-ranked, wouldn't stand a chance if this hit them, which means it can wipe out almost any monster in an instant.

A Demon Lord would lose everything if a crystal ball in his dungeon were destroyed. A very powerful monster is always assigned as the Guardian of his dungeon to protect his crystal ball, but this may do the trick for me.

"You said this is driven by the Golem Core. Can you make this move at its will like our Golems?"

"Mm-hm, it's possible. But, unlike when Tenko uses it, it's unable to raise its stats and it loses power."

"It's powerful enough as it is. Make this tank...well, a Golem tank, when you have a chance. It's going to be the Guardian of my dungeon. Good job, Elder Dwarf. Now I have the mightiest Guardian."

"Mm-hm, glad to be of service."

The Elder Dwarf grips my shirt in her fist. As I stroke her hair, she leans against me. Unlike Tenko, she has a cool demeanor, and it's unusual for her to allow herself to be coddled like this. She doesn't seem to mind—in fact, she looks quite content. I'll try to be more open with her in the future.

"All right, Tenko, Elder Dwarf. We've tested our new Guardian. Let's go hunting."

"Yay!"

"Mm-hm, okay."

They're much more highly motivated than yesterday. This must have been a nice change of pace. We have achieved our original goal of solving Tenko and Elder Dwarf's boredom, *and* obtained a Guardian for my dungeon. All is well.

We head out to the Crimson Cove together. We'll give it our all. Then we hunt.

THE END

Afterword

Thank you for reading *Dungeon Builder*. I'm Rui Tsukiyo, the author of the original story.

Dungeon Builder is a story about building a city with cute monsters. I hope you enjoy the tale of Procel, the Demon Lord of Creation, as he uses various weapons and tools that he manifests with his Creation power, and advances steadily with his cute but powerful monsters.

If you are interested in the original light novel, check out the *Dungeon Builder* series from GA Novel, too! Just like manga, light novels are entertaining in their own way.

Acknowledgments

To Mr. Hideaki Yoshikawa--
I got excited when I saw Tenko and the other monsters in action. Your manga also gave this story a new charm. I'm very grateful to you for doing this manga!

And thank you to the readers for enjoying this story. I hope you will continue to follow us for a while.

Comment by: Rui Tsukiyo
Art by: Hideaki Yoshikawa

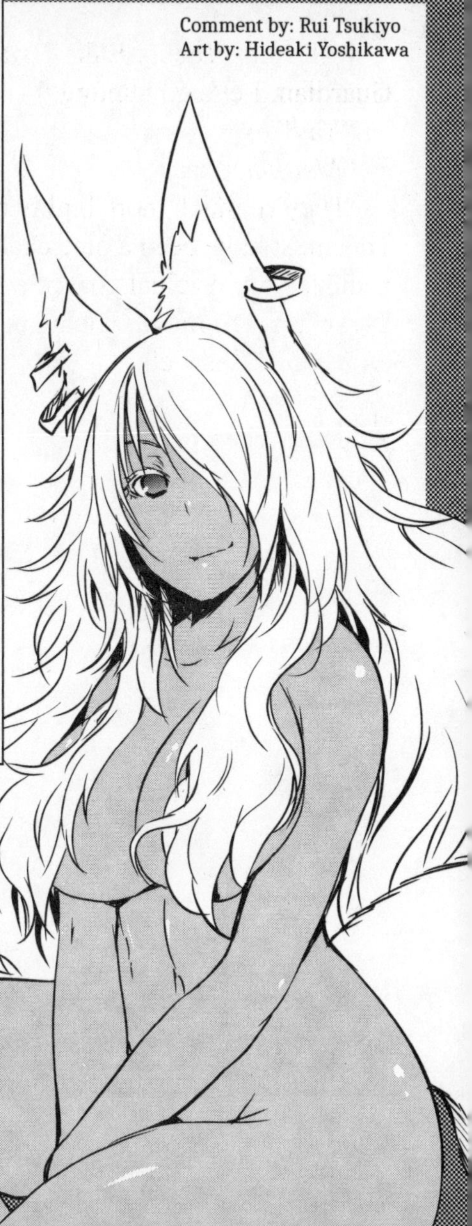
I'LL DO MY BEST TO CREATE A GREAT MANGA. DON'T YOU LOVE A DARK-COMPLEXIONED WOMAN WITH ANIMAL EARS AND BIG BOOBS?
吉川英朗
2018.10
HIDEAKI YOSHIKAWA
WIGHT AGREES.

DUNGEON
BUILDER:

THE DEMON KING'S
LABYRINTH IS A
MODERN CITY!